Government by Pen

MAURICE LEE, JR.

Government by Pen:

Scotland under
James VI and I

UNIVERSITY OF ILLINOIS PRESS

Urbana   Chicago   London

LIBRARY OF CONGRESS CATALOGING IN PUBLICATION DATA

Lee, Maurice.
Government by pen.

Includes index.
1. Scotland—Politics and government—1371–1707.
2. James I, King of Great Britain, 1566–1625. I. Title.
DA803.15.L43   941.1′04   79–16830
ISBN 0–252–00765–4

To the memory of my friend Sir James Fergusson
of Kilkerran, late Keeper of the Scottish Record Office,
who first suggested that I should write about this period.
I hope that he would have liked this book.
I wish that he were here to read it.

Preface

WHEN I BEGAN the research for this book I had two objectives in mind. One was to continue the study of Scottish politics in the reign of James VI, with particular emphasis on the interaction of politics and religion, which I had begun a number of years ago in my book on Maitland of Thirlestane; the other, closely allied to it, was to test the accuracy of that famous remark of King James which for far too many historians has served as a substitute for both thought about, and analysis of, what went on in Scotland after the union of the crowns of England and Scotland in 1603. "This I must say for Scotland, and I may truly vaunt it," said James to the parliament of England in 1607, "here I sit and govern it with my pen, I write and it is done, and by a Clerk of the Council I govern Scotland now, which others could not do by the sword." Both purposes originally led me to a study of the political career of Alexander Seton, earl of Dunfermline, who, like Maitland, became lord chancellor, held the office from 1604 until his death in 1622, and therefore presumably was the principal instrument of government by pen if James's vaunt turned out to be true.

This approach turned out to be unsatisfactory, however. First, Dunfermline's career began well before the union of the crowns; a proper account of it would entail going over a good deal of fairly familiar ground and making the book inordinately long. Second, as I hope the following pages will make clear, Dunfermline during the years of his greatest power was nothing of an innovator and used the methods of consensus and compromise; his lineaments, unlike Maitland's, tended to disappear behind the collective face of the privy council over which he presided. But the decisive consideration was the fact, an astonishing fact, really, that a chronological narrative account of Scottish politics after 1603 simply does not exist. The older treatments, those of Hill Burton, Hume Brown, and Andrew Lang, for instance, concentrate their chronological narrative on religious developments. Some other matters get treated topically—the highlands, the borders, the constitution, etc.—but politics as such is almost completely ignored. Not many historians have worked on particular aspects of the period between the union and the civil war. S. G. E. Lythe on the economy, W. R. Foster on the church, Athol Murray on financial institutions are among the notable exceptions; my indebtedness to them will be apparent in the following pages. Much more of this sort of work, almost impossible to do from this side of the Atlantic, badly needs doing. The best modern account of this period as a whole, that of Gordon Donaldson in his volume in the *Edinburgh History of Scotland* series, is well balanced, judicious, perceptive—and topical. There is no need to repeat here the high opinion I have expressed elsewhere of Professor Donaldson's excellent book; the fact remains that neither he nor anyone else has written a chronological political history of the years after 1603. This book is an attempt to fill part of that gap; I hope some day to follow it with a study of the reign of Charles I prior to the outbreak of the revolution.

The picture of Scottish politics after 1603 which emerged from my research is rather different from the one King James painted for his English legislature, rather different, indeed, from the one which I imagined would emerge when I gave my study of Maitland the subtitle *The Foundation of the Stewart Despotism in Scotland.* Despotism was possible in Scotland after 1603, and the arbitrary regime of the years 1606–11, the years of the hegemony of the lord treasurer, the earl of Dunbar, had many of the characteristics of despotism. This was especially true with respect to Dunbar's handling of those religious questions which have preoccupied so many previous scholars. The period following Dunbar's death in 1611 was anything but despotic, however. These were the years of Dunfermline's pre-eminence and then, after his death, of that of a triumvirate of his colleagues. Government by pen did indeed exist after 1603, but not as King James pictured it. There was, of course, a great deal of correspondence, both official and unofficial, between Edinburgh and Whitehall. But in Dunbar's day the wheels turned because of the frequent appearances in Edinburgh of the great man himself; in Dunfermline's and thereafter it might

Preface

more accurately be said that the governing pen was in Edinburgh, not in Whitehall. This is, in bare outline, the case which will be argued in the following pages.

Authors accumulate a great many obligations in the course of putting together a book, and I am no exception. My thanks go first to Rutgers University and its Research Council, whose generosity with both time and money made possible the research for the book, and its writing and publication, and next to the membership of S.F.A., the staffs of the Rutgers University libraries, the Princeton University library, the New York Public library, the British Library, the Public Record Office, London, the Edinburgh University library, the Scottish Record Office, especially the Keeper, Mr. John Imrie, and Assistant Keeper, Dr. Athol Murray, and the National Library of Scotland, especially its Keeper of Manuscripts, Dr. Ian Rae, who was enormously helpful. Many friends and colleagues have provided counsel, and Professor Richard Schlatter has read the manuscript to its advantage. I owe much to numerous conversations over the years with my friends Professors Gordon Donaldson and Sidney Burrell. Mrs. Shirley Meinkoth has typed and retyped, cheerfully, promptly, and accurately. My copy editor at the University of Illinois Press, Mrs. Bonnie Depp, has efficiently rooted out a lot of inconsistencies and cleaned up my messy punctuation. And my wife has kept me in food and drink, occasionally darned my shirts, and almost never grumbled over my preoccupation with King James's ancient kingdom.

Contents

Abbreviations frequently used in the notes

APS   *The Acts of the Parliament of Scotland,* 12 vols., ed. T. Thomson and C. Innes (Edinburgh, 1814–75)

BM   British Museum, London

CSPD   *Calendar of State Papers, Domestic Series,* 4 vols., for the reign of James I, ed. M. A. E. Green (London, 1857–59)

CSP Scot.   *Calendar of State Papers Relating to Scotland and Mary Queen of Scots, 1547–1603,* 13 vols., ed. J. Bain et al. (Edinburgh, 1898–1969)

CSP Venetian   *Calendar of State Papers . . . Venice,* 9 vols., for the reign of James I, ed. H. F. Brown and A. B. Hinds (London, 1900–1912)

LEA   *Original Letters Relating to the Ecclesiastical Affairs of Scotland . . . 1603–1625,* 2 vols., ed. D. Laing, Bannatyne Club (Edinburgh, 1851)

LSP   *Letters and State Papers during the Reign of King James the Sixth,* ed. J. Maidment, Abbotsford Club (Edinburgh, 1838)

M&K   Historical Manuscripts Commission, *Report on the Manuscripts of the Earl of Mar and Kellie* (London, 1904), *Supplement* (London, 1930), both ed. H. Paton
M&K Supp.

NLS   National Library of Scotland, Edinburgh

PRO   Public Record Office, London

RCRB   *Records of the Convention of the Royal Burghs of Scotland,* 6 vols., ed. Sir J. D. Marwick (Edinburgh, 1866–90)

RMS   *Registrum Magni Sigilli Regum Scotorum,* 11 vols., ed. J. M. Thomson et al. (Edinburgh, 1814–1914)

RPCS   *The Register of the Privy Council of Scotland,* 1st and 2nd series, ed. J. H. Burton, D. Masson, and P. H. Brown (Edinburgh, 1877–1908)

Government by Pen

SHR	*Scottish Historical Review*
SHS	Scottish History Society, Edinburgh
SRO	Scottish Record Office, Edinburgh
Calderwood	David Calderwood, *The History of the Church of Scotland,* 8 vols., ed. T. Thomson, Wodrow Society (Edinburgh, 1842–49)
Laing	Historical Manuscripts Commission, *Report on the Laing Manuscripts,* vol. I, ed. H. Paton (London, 1914)
Melros	*State Papers and Miscellaneous Correspondence of Thomas, Earl of Melros,* 2 vols., ed. J. Maidment, Abbotsford Club (Edinburgh, 1837)
Melvill	*The Autobiography and Diary of Mr. James Melvill,* ed. R. Pitcairn, Wodrow Society (Edinburgh, 1842)
Nichols, *Progresses*	J. Nichols, ed., *The Progresses, Processions, and Magnificent Festivities of King James the First,* 4 vols. (London, 1828)
Salisbury	Historical Manuscripts Commission, *Calendar of the Manuscripts of the Marquis of Salisbury,* 23 vols., ed. M. S. Giuseppi *et al.* (London, 1883–1973)
Scot	William Scot, *An Apologetical Narration of the State and Government of the Kirk of Scotland since the Reformation,* ed. D. Laing, Wodrow Society (Edinburgh, 1846)
Spottiswoode	John Spottiswoode, *The History of the Church of Scotland,* 3 vols., ed. M. Russell and M. Napier, Spottiswoode Society (Edinburgh, 1847–51)

NOTE

Dates are given Old Style, save that the year is taken to begin on 1 January (as it did in Scotland starting in 1600). Money is given in pounds Scots; where pounds sterling are meant, the word *sterling* is used. The ratio of pounds Scots to sterling was 12:1. A merk is two-thirds of a pound. The spelling and punctuation of quotations have normally been modernized.

Government by Pen

1

The Scotland of James VI

SUNDAY, 3 APRIL 1603, was a uniquely memorable day in the lives of the citizens of Edinburgh—a day of rejoicing and at the same time of apprehension about the unknown future. Their king, James VI, ruler of Scotland in name for over thirty years and in fact for almost twenty, had been proclaimed king of England three days before, "with noise of trumpets, playing upon instruments, singing, and great acclamation of the people,"[1] and today he was to bid them farewell and, through them, all their fellow Scots. There was an emotional scene in St. Giles Church; the king asked his hearers for their prayers, and promised to return to visit them at least once every three years.[2] Two days later he was gone, and on Wednesday, 6 April, he crossed over into the land of which he was now King James I, whose crown he had awaited so impatiently for so many years.

There is no reason to doubt the sincerity of James's promise,[3] but, for whatever reasons, he did not keep it; he journeyed to his ancient kingdom but once, and then only after fourteen years had gone by. But even if he had kept to his proposed schedule of triennial visits, it was clear that the Scottish political scene would be greatly altered. The king would be an absentee, with many problems other than those of Scotland to concern him. Precisely how Scotland would be governed in future was not clear to anyone in the spring of 1603, not even to James himself. But of his ability to solve the problem of governing at long distance the king had not the slightest doubt.

The Scotland which James left behind him in 1603 was an orderly and moderately prosperous country, far different from the

quasi-medieval kingdom which he began personally to govern in
1585. For this improvement the king rightly arrogated much of
the credit to himself. In 1585 the powers of the crown were
theoretically considerable, but its resources were not. Scotland
was a poor country with a predominantly agrarian economy. The
towns, and the middle class which dwelt in them, though growing,
were as yet neither particularly large nor particularly wealthy;
trade was not extensive, and there was little manufacturing. The
king's ordinary revenues were small, taxation was rare, and the
tax-collection machinery was antiquated. He had no standing army
and no trained bureaucracy, and many important offices had become hereditary in the families of the aristocracy. Great nobles,
virtually petty kings on their own lands and secure in the loyalty
(unforced or coerced) of their tenants and kinsmen, paid heed to
royal orders only if they saw fit to do so, and frequently caballed
together to seize the person of the king and thus control the
government. Between the formal end of the regency of the earl
of Morton in March 1578 and the overturn of the regime of the
earl of Arran in September 1585 there were at least six such
aristocratic coups which were more or less successful and one
which failed. Some of them the king encouraged and welcomed;
others had the blessing if not the actual support of the English
government and/or of the Scottish kirk. The church which had
emerged since the overthrow of the Catholic ecclesiastical order in
the civil war of 1559–60 was Calvinist in theology, and by the
mid-1580s was dominated by a group of ministers headed by Andrew Melville, who denounced episcopacy as unscriptural and
wanted the creation of a full-blown presbyterian polity. These
men tended to be suspicious of the young king, who did not look
to be developing into their ideal of a godly prince. *Coups d'état* at
the highest level went along with other forms of lawlessness: feuds
and private warfare, brawls in the streets of the towns, cattle raiding in England. These things took place in areas where the crown
had some power; what went on in the highlands and the western
and northern isles the government often did not even know.

It was clear enough to the king and everybody else that the
principal obstacle to the increase of the crown's authority lay in
the great power and lawless behavior of the Scottish aristocracy.

James and his principal adviser, John Maitland of Thirlestane, appointed lord chancellor in 1587 and the dominant figure in Scottish politics for most of the decade after 1585, therefore set themselves to bring these fractious men and their dependents under control.[4] To achieve this, the first necessity was peace and the absence of outside—i.e. English—interference in Scotland's internal affairs; the Anglo-Scottish treaty of 1586 substantially accomplished both these aims. The second step was to mobilize the support of the other important elements in Scottish society for this policy. The townsmen could be counted on, in the interests of law and order and expanding trade, and by and large they steadily supported Maitland's government. The kirk Maitland won over by persuading the king to make concessions, step by step, to the opinions of the Melville group. Most important, Maitland enlisted the support of large numbers of his own class, the lesser gentry, the lairds; they held the key to his success because he needed them to serve in his government. So he brought them into politics, by the statute of 1587 which provided for their representation in parliament and by using a substantial proportion of the church property annexed to the crown in 1587 as rewards to this group, and, often enough, to the younger sons of peers, for loyal government service.

It should be stressed that the object of the king's and Maitland's policy was to bring the aristocracy under control, not to ruin it as a class, weaken its economic and social position, or deprive it of political influence. James was prepared to tolerate, though not to favor, even those families with a long record of ambivalent political conduct, like the Douglases, or whose head he disliked and whose ambitions he distrusted, like the earl of Argyll and the Campbells. The king made his point of view clear in *Basilikon Doron,* his "Instructions to his dearest son," written in 1598. The great vice of the nobility, wrote James, was "a feckless arrogant conceit of their greatness and power, drinking in with their very nourish-milk, that their honor stood in committing three points of inequity: to thrall by oppression the meaner sort that dwelleth near them to their service and following . . . to maintain their servants and dependers in any wrong . . . and for any displeasure that they apprehend to be done unto them by their neighbor, to take up a plain feud against him and (without respect to God, King, or commonweal) to bang it out bravely, he and all his kin, against him and all his." The remedy, said James, was to force the nobility to obey the law, to "root out these barbarous feuds," and to make use of the law-abiding members of the class in government.[5] The king had no intention, however, of attempting to undermine the aristocrats' control of their landed estates, which was the real basis of their power: land was overwhelmingly the principal source of wealth in Scotland, where three-quarters of the population could be classified as rural tenants and laborers.[6] He would have preferred that the office of sheriff cease to be hereditary, and to eliminate heritable grants of regality, which made the recipient virtually a petty king with almost complete control over the lives of those within the boundaries of his grant: these things "in the hands of the great men do wrack the whole country." But James saw the difficulties in the way of such a direct assault on the position of the nobility. There was "no present remedy" but to hold the occupants strictly accountable, and in case of vacancy to make no more hereditary grants.[7]

James was certainly right in regarding hereditary officeholding as a major obstacle to the creation of an efficient governmental system under the crown's control. His unwillingness to move very vigorously against it indicates not only a shrewd appraisal of political realities but also the cautious, rather conservative nature of his and Maitland's approach to the problem of turning into reality that vision of kingship to which James, as a believer in and theoretician of the doctrine of the divine right of kings, wholeheartedly subscribed. In one respect, to be sure, there was very little difficulty. The power of the crown was constitutionally very great indeed; the problem was to exercise it. The king controlled the executive, since he appointed the members of the privy council, the motor of the governmental machine. His grip on parliament was virtually unbreakable because of his control of the committee known as the lords of the articles. By 1594 this committee had become the only channel through which legislation could get to the floor of parliament. This left the legislative initiative entirely in the hands of the government, since the council dominated the membership of the committee. The convention of estates, a less formal version of parliament, with the same categories of membership and much the same legislative powers, was extensively used before 1603 as a means of getting things done quickly and efficiently. Because it had no committee of the articles, however, governmental control was less sure, so after 1603 it was very rarely summoned.[8]

Control over the judiciary was not quite so secure, since the office of justice general had fallen into the hands of the earls of Argyll, where it remained until the reign of Charles I, and members of the court of session, the chief civil court, were appointed for life—*ad vitam aut culpam*—which was also changed by Charles I to appointment during the king's pleasure. With respect to criminal justice Maitland did what he could, by turning the king's advocate into a public prosecutor who could bring any criminal case into court even if the injured party declined to do so, and by attempting to revive the old system of justice ayres. This was not very successful; most cases of importance continued to be tried in or near Edinburgh. As for the court of session, Maitland's chief concerns were that the justices be wealthy enough to minimize the possibility of corruption—a statute of 1592 stipulated a minimum income for judges—that nominees be qualified and demonstrate their qualifications before admission to the bench, and above all that seats on the court should not become hereditary. Following the election of Maitland's second cousin Alexander Seton as president of the court in 1593, it was stipulated that, when a vacancy occurred in future, the king would, after twenty days, present at least three nominees to the members of the court, who would then elect the most qualified, presumably after applying the required procedure for testing the qualifications of candidates. This enactment was aimed at one more aspect of the operation of the system of hereditary tenure of office, namely, a judge's collusive resignation in favor of someone else, usually his son or other close relative. It was a practice difficult to prevent, since the judges' lifetime appointments put them in a position to bargain, and seats on the court were highly desirable, not so much for the emoluments involved but because they carried with them exemption from various obligations, including taxation. The reform was not very effective. The king approved in theory, but he was generous to his courtiers and unwilling to deny them when they importuned him. So resignations *in favorem* continued after 1593, and friends and relatives of powerful politicians continued to obtain seats on the bench, along with some very able lawyers. Maitland's effort to increase the supply of trained lawyers, and thus of potential judges, by establishing a professorship of law at the new college of Edinburgh unfortunately proved abortive; the professorship never did materialize in James's reign.[9]

James's and Maitland's policy with respect to government could hardly be called revolutionary, but it did produce a severe reaction on the part of those aristocrats astute enough to understand the long-range implications of that policy for themselves or snobbish enough to resent the king's dependency on the advice of a "puddock stool of a night," as that quintessential aristocratic ruffian Francis Stewart, earl of Bothwell, called Maitland. The reaction was strong enough to drive Maitland into partial eclipse in the last years of his life, but he lived long enough to see the triumph of his policy. In 1595 both Bothwell and George Gordon, earl of Huntly, the leader of the Catholic party and the murderer of the earl of Moray, with whom he was at feud, were driven into exile, Bothwell never to return. Never again, outside the highlands, would there be armed rebellion against the government of James VI or forcible defiance of the orders of that government by a single great lord. The governmental machine which Maitland constructed had weathered its first and most important crisis.

After Maitland's death late in 1595 James changed his course somewhat. He was acutely aware that his great chancellor had died very opportunely; the resentments Maitland had caused died with him. He was not replaced, either literally or figuratively. The chancellorship itself remained vacant for three years; when James finally did fill it, in December 1598, his choice was the earl of Montrose, an elderly nonentity. More important, no one took Maitland's place as the king's *eminence grise;* from now on James intended to be his own chief minister. There were many who aspired to fill Maitland's shoes. One was Alexander Seton, the new president of the court of session and the head of the committee which managed Queen Anne's property for her. In 1596 he became the head of a committee charged with the reorganization of the royal finances, and thus looked like a possible successor to

Maitland, both as chancellor and as the king's principal adviser. But the committee's reforms caused resentment, and Seton was a Catholic whose presence so near the seat of power helped to bring on the famous religious riot in Edinburgh in December 1596, of which he was the primary target. Other potential successors to Maitland fared equally badly. The king's cousin Walter Stewart, Lord Blantyre, appointed lord treasurer in 1596, looked possible for a time, but his health broke under the strains of office, and he resigned in 1598. James Elphinstone, who became secretary of state in 1598, was personable and adroit, but he too was a Catholic, and his anti-English tack in the conduct of foreign policy led to an embarrassing series of defeats for the king in the convention of estates in 1600 when that body refused to vote a tax to raise an army to make good James's claim to the English throne by force.[10] This fiasco cost Elphinstone his influence, though not his office. In 1603 the likeliest candidate as Maitland's successor was Sir George Home of Spott, appointed lord treasurer in 1601, a polished courtier and skillful politician who turned out to be a vigorous administrator. But the fact was that in 1603 Maitland's only successor was the king himself.

Maitland's death made it easier for James to modify the late chancellor's policy toward the aristocracy. The symbol of the new tack was the earl of Huntly, who, properly contrite, was allowed to return in 1596 and eventually was readmitted to the privy council. The king had made his point: he was prepared to seek the advice of his nobility, but he would make the decisions, and they would obey. Furthermore, he would appoint whom he pleased to office, a point underscored by his reorganization of the privy council in 1598. Hitherto the council had had no fixed membership; it consisted of the officers of state, plus any noble or prelate who happened to be around, plus anyone else the king might name. Now it was to have thirty-two members who were expected to work at the job, and only officers of state were automatically included.[11] Henceforth only those nobles in favor with the king could expect the honor of a seat at the council table.

The kind of nobleman who found favor with the king was one who either was not at feud with anyone or was prepared to make a peaceful settlement under the king's auspices if he was. Aristocratic feuds had preoccupied James from the beginning. In 1587, to celebrate his approaching majority, he feasted his nobles at the Market Cross in Edinburgh and, after they were suitably mellowed by wine, persuaded them to walk down the High Street to Holyroodhouse hand-in-hand.[12] He also took more practical steps, especially as his prospective accession to Elizabeth's throne drew nearer; he was determined to leave a peaceful realm behind him when the great day finally came. Parliament in 1600 created an elaborate mechanism for settling feuds, including hearings by the privy council and the appointment of oversmen and committees of arbitration. The king made full use of the machinery, took a personal hand in many of the settlements, and succeeded in February 1603 in patching up the most serious of all the aristocratic quarrels, that between Huntly and the earls of Argyll and Moray, which had led among other things to Huntly's murder of Moray's father in 1592. There is no reason to believe that any of the parties to these settlements had suddenly been overcome by feelings of Christian charity or forgiveness. But they could see that the king was serious about putting an end to their quarrels and that soon, as Elizabeth's successor, he would be in a position to compel them to desist. It was better to bargain while bargaining was possible. So James made a good deal of progress, and when he went south the great majority of these feuds had been at least superficially patched up.

Noblemen's quarrels were not the only source of disorder, of course. There were also the perennially difficult highlands and borders, where, indeed, feuds compounded the turmoil. Maitland's government had done very little about the situation in the highlands, which seemed far less pressing than a good many other matters. Occasionally an effort was made, not very successfully, to compel highland landlords and clan chiefs (not necessarily the same persons) to find surety that they would produce in court any accused tenant and/or clansman of theirs, in accordance with the so-called general bond,[13] but that was about all. Sooner or later it would be necessary to try to extend royal control in the highlands. Such an effort, if successful, would gravely weaken the power of two great families, the Campbells and the Gordons. For almost one hundred years the government's highland policy had consisted chiefly in strengthening these two clans, the Campbells (earls of Argyll) in the west and the Gordons (earls of Huntly) in the northeast, and in counting on them, in return, to protect the more settled lowlands from the depredations of the other highland clans. In the mid-1590s Huntly's exile, the simultaneous weakening of the clan Campbell by a series of murderous internecine feuds, and a slackening in the rate of increase of highland population owing to famine and disease which reduced the pressures on land supply, offered the best opportunity since the forfeiture of the Lord of the Isles in 1493 to bring the highlands back within the orbit of the central government. It was an opportunity which, in the years after 1597, King James did his best to exploit.

James's view of the highlands was that it was a potentially very rich area inhabited by incorrigible barbarians. The proper solution, therefore, was to drive out or extirpate these ruffians and replace them with lowlanders who would create a civilized and prosperous (and rent- and tax-paying) society there. It was this idea which lay behind the legal maneuvering which led to the forfeiture of Lewis to the crown in 1598 and the creation of a company of gentleman-adventurers to "plant" the island with lowlanders. The company's efforts met with intense resistance, not only from the people of Lewis who were directly threatened but also from other highland chiefs who feared that, if the experiment on Lewis were successful, their turn would come next. The occasional efforts to overawe other sections of the highlands by punitive expeditions were not much more successful, in part because the government found it very difficult to get lowlanders either to turn out when summoned to participate in such expeditions or to pay taxes to hire soldiers for the purpose. The old policy of reliance on Huntly and Argyll was no longer viable either. Politically it ran counter to the whole thrust of James's and Maitland's policy toward the aristocracy; in addition, the king disliked the current earl of Argyll, while Huntly, whom he did like, was not fully employable on account of his religion. Furthermore both these men were quite prepared to encourage lawlessness in the highlands in the interests of their own wealth and power; Argyll in particular, with his ambitious plans for the aggrandizement of the clan Campbell, inspired widespread mistrust.[14] There was, in fact, no coherent highland policy in 1603, a condition symbolized by the king's exasperated decision, just before his departure for England, to sign a decree abolishing the very name of MacGregor after some of the members of that broken and lawless clan committed a bloody and successful assault on their enemies, the Colquhouns of Luss, in what became known as the "Slaughter of the Lennox." A new highland policy was urgently required.

Creating a minimum of order on the borders was far more crucial than in the highlands, since good relations with England hinged on the outcome. For generations before the Reformation the Scottish government had regarded the borders as the first line of defense against England, and had encouraged the lords and lairds of the area to go raiding across the frontier, which of course produced English retaliation. One consequence of this state of affairs was that border landlords frequently used their landholdings not to maximum economic advantage but for the purpose of providing themselves with as many retainers as possible. Like highland clan chiefs and tacksmen, they let the land in small holdings, which encouraged the tendency to lawlessness, and for the same reason: like the highlanders, many borderers needed other people's goods in order to live.[15] And they did not confine themselves to Englishmen's goods; they were just as apt to raid and steal from each other as they were from the auld enemy. After 1560, on account of the changed relationship with England consequent on the Reformation, the government tried to put a stop to the raiding, and strong regimes, like those of the regents Moray and Morton, had been able to do so, chiefly by the use of the judicial raid. This involved the sudden application of overwhelming force in order to round up malefactors and hang them in batches, a method which dealt with symptoms rather than causes.

Maitland's government worked hard on the border problem, and achieved considerable success, by the application of the general bond, and by the appointment of border officials who were either Maitland's relatives or his political allies and who would cooperate with their English opposite numbers to provide for redress of grievances. By the early 1590s the system was functioning well enough to withstand the challenge of the rebellion of Bothwell, whose strength lay chiefly on the borders. To be sure, Maitland did not put an end to lawlessness on the border; that most spectacular of Jacobean deeds of derring-do, Scott of Buccleuch's extrication of Kinmont Willie Armstrong from Carlisle castle after he had been illegally seized by English forces, took place six months after Maitland's death. Yet perhaps the most significant aspect of Buccleuch's exploit was that it led to a protracted negotiation, which wound up with Buccleuch spending five months in ward in England, rather than to a series of retaliatory raids. The important people on both sides of the line, many of whom were young men in the later 1590s, could see that the days of the border as an international frontier were numbered, and so, therefore, was its life style: genuine cooperation now was apt to pay dividends later. After 1597 the chief trouble spot was the Scottish west march, which suffered from the ugly feud of the Maxwells and the Johnstones and which was full of Catholics, thanks in large measure to the patronage of the Maxwells. With this exception the borders were on their way to becoming what King James would call them after 1603, the "Middle Shires."[16]

To say that the Scottish economy was in transition in the 1590s would perhaps not be very illuminating. The economic policy of King James and Maitland was anything but innovative; neither was much interested in the details of economic and commercial questions or, indeed, knew very much about them. James believed that the first duty of the government was to look after the welfare of the consumer rather than that of the producer or the merchant, "to foster abundant home supplies rather than to encourage the export trade."[17] The king was well aware of the economic advantages of peace, and his remaining at peace was perhaps his most significant contribution to Scottish economic growth. He also believed that if the government provided peace, trade should automatically increase; if it did not, the explanation must be political or personal—misgovernment or greed—rather than the state of the market, foreign or domestic.[18] English economic success and prosperity, which he exaggerated, vastly impressed him; he held up the English example as one for Scots to follow in such matters as attracting foreign artisans to build up new industries, and he tended to believe after 1603 that economic measures which his English councillors recommended to him as beneficial for England could and should be applied without change in Scotland as well.[19] The king was contemptuous of merchants as a class; they believed it was "their lawful gain and trade, to enrich themselves upon the loss of all the rest of the people. . . . They buy for us the worst wares, and sell them at the dearest prices." They were also responsible for the debasement of the coinage.[20] One authority sums up the king's views and behavior this way: "In most . . . respects the policy towards both foreign and internal trade remained essentially medieval. By chance rather than by intent there were elements savouring of mercantilism. . . . in most commercial affairs his interference was spasmodic and generally ill informed."[21]

Such an attitude was less harmful in Scotland than it might have been elsewhere, since the Scottish economy was still so overwhelmingly agrarian in character. The principal element in the middle class, the merchants, were chiefly concerned to preserve both their dominance in municipal affairs as against the challenge of the craft guilds and the commercial monopoly of the group of towns, approximately fifty in number, known as the royal burghs, as against all other towns.[22] The royal burghs had a legal monopoly of foreign trade and "possessed the sole right of carrying on crafts, selling and buying commodities, and in . . . [them] fairs and markets alone could be held."[23] With a few exceptions they alone were represented in parliament, and they were responsible for the burghs' share of the taxation when a tax was voted—one-sixth of the national total, which is a good indication of the economic importance of the middle class by comparison with the other elements in Scottish society: the church paid one-half of such a tax and the nobility one-third.[24]

By the later sixteenth century representatives of the royal burghs met annually in a convention in order to promote their common interests. These interests turned out for the most part to be those of traders rather than manufacturers, which was to be expected, given the dominant position of the merchants in burgh governments. The convention was usually critical of the granting of industrial monopolies and suspicious of proposals for the introduction of new industries, especially if they involved the importation of foreign artisans with special privileges, proposals which James periodically made efforts to implement, especially with respect to textiles. The burghs were also quite unwilling to endorse or adopt any policy which would cost them any money: in 1598 they rejected James's request to approve, and pay for, the appointment of a resident conservator in London to settle disputes among Scots merchants there on the ground that such an appointment would be unnecessary and unprofitable. The government regularly consulted the convention with respect to economic policy, but the burghs could not themselves determine policy, as they discovered in 1597 when the government, over their bitter protests, enacted a general levy on imports of 5 percent, the first such levy in Scottish history.[25] Nor could they always decide who was to govern them. From the 1590s on, the crown regularly interfered in the choice of town officials and punished those towns which showed signs of recalcitrance.[26] Their exports were chiefly foodstuffs, wool, hides and skins, and the products of extractive industries, such as coal and salt; cloth and manufactured products came to approximately 20 percent of the total value.[27]

The rural nature of the Scottish economy and the unhelpful attitude of the government were not the only hindrances to economic growth in the later sixteenth century. There were definite symptoms of rural overpopulation, which must have been offset to some degree by periods of very bad harvests in the 1580s and 1590s, notably the period 1594–98, which amounted to "a four-year phase of genuine national shortage," and by periodic visitations of plague.[28] There was a serious inflation, complicated by debasement of the currency. Scottish prices in the last decades of the sixteenth century rose twice as rapidly as in England and France, while the value of the Scottish pound by comparison with the English fell from about 4:1 in 1560 to 12:1 by the death of Elizabeth. In spite of the government's periodic attempts to hold the line on prices and to forbid the export of necessities like coal, real wages for the unskilled fell substantially during this period—which is one indication of population growth, as was the attention given to poor relief, where, predictably, James followed the English model—though the skilled craftsman managed to hold his own.[29]

By the turn of the seventeenth century, however, there were indications that a period of prosperity was at hand. The currency became more stable after 1600, which helped to slow down inflation. Although plague remained a problem until about 1609, the famine years were over after 1598. The amount of grain imported from the Baltic fell by more than 50 percent in the first decade of the seventeenth century as compared to the 1590s, and by almost 50 percent more in the second decade. The last forty years of the sixteenth century was a period of great expansion in the coal industry. Towns began to prosper; their incomes increased, and the first two decades of the seventeenth century saw a great burst of activity in municipal building, particularly in Edinburgh.[30] There was much building in the countryside as well, often enough stressing the amenities of life rather than military defense.

Much of the new building was the work of lairds, whose economic position vis-à-vis that of the great lords was improving in the later sixteenth century. This was in part the result of the spread of the form of landholding known as the feu farm, which was not very widely used prior to the reign of James IV but which developed very rapidly thereafter.[31] By contrast with the traditional wardholding tenure with its feudal obligations, a feu farm was based entirely on the cash nexus: an entry fee plus an annual fixed rent called a feu duty. Like wardholding, a feu farm meant heritable tenure in perpetuity. The motives for the introduction of feus varied. On church lands the purpose of the benefice-holder was usually to feather the nests of his relatives by making these grants for small entry fees and low feu duties, thus effectively dilapidating the benefice. On temporal lands the usual purpose was to increase the income of the grantor of the feu, often the crown; in the words of I. F. Grant, "it was generally the Crown that took the initiative in feuing, not the occupiers who clamored for feus."[32] In the long run, however, it was usually the occupier who profited, with the continuous rise in prices and fall in the value of money, unless the feu duty was owed in the form of victual. It was not only individual landholders but also towns which benefited from this state of affairs; virtually all towns held of the crown in feu farm, and their obligations became progressively less onerous. In 1600 the crown attempted to remedy this situation by demanding payment in pounds sterling, which would have increased the duty twelve times. The towns naturally resisted, but in the end the larger towns were coerced into paying more, and the crown's rents virtually doubled.[33] The vast majority of feu holders were lairds, who thus became more independent of the great lords and more apt to support the efforts of the king and Maitland to reduce them to obedience. A great noble could stem the tide to some degree by feuing only to his own relatives or, like the earls of Huntly, by making extensive use of bonds of manrent, by which the parties agreed to aid each other in times of difficulty. But the real gainers were the lairds and thus, by extension, the crown.

The government's gains from the feuing movement were political, however, rather than economic. If the country was beginning to prosper, the royal exchequer was not. James VI's fecklessness and profusion in financial matters are so well known as to need no recapitulating here, and Maitland, though he had more caution than his master, had no great interest or skill in financial matters and was preoccupied with other questions. The financial administrative structure was cumbersome and responsibility was diffused. The normal revenues of the crown, small enough to begin with, did not notably increase in the Maitland era. The most substantial increment was the pension paid to James by Elizabeth after 1586 in consequence of the Anglo-Scottish league. It averaged £4,000 sterling a year, and when, for whatever reason, it was late in arriving, the Scottish government was immediately pinched. Direct taxation was somewhat heavier, but it was still inefficiently collected, and the revenues from export duties—there was as yet no general import duty—rose very slowly. There was a persistent search throughout the reign for new supplies of gold and silver— James never lost his interest in the possibility of a windfall—partly because of the sixteenth-century belief in the value of specie, partly because of an acute bullion shortage in Scotland which was a major factor in the repeated debasement of the coinage. None of these searches had any substantial results. Not much more success attended the king's granting of industrial monopolies, which James awarded in the hope of income for the crown or to creditors who could not otherwise be paid off.[34] And, of course, with the inflation prices and governmental expenditure were steadily rising.

So, too, in consequence, were the king's debts, as he found it necessary regularly to anticipate revenue.

James's major effort to bring about some sort of financial reform came just after Maitland's death with the appointment of the so-called Octavians in January 1596, an eight-man committee most of whose members had commended themselves to the king by their successful management of his wife's estates. They were given a sweeping grant of authority over financial matters and offices, and the king agreed to do nothing in such questions without their consent. Their task, as they and James saw it, was to husband resources by eliminating mismanagement and waste, and to cut costs by reducing or stopping pensions and weeding out superfluous personnel. They set vigorously to work; within a month they had discharged seventy people from the king's household, and by the end of the year had succeeded in cutting household expenses by about 20 percent.[35] In addition to this sort of economy they improved financial administration by ending much of the diffusion of responsibility which had previously existed, encouraged the sending of a punitive expedition to the highlands to try to induce the chiefs to pay the crown what they owed, and made a number of legislative recommendations, the most important of which was the customs duty on imports previously mentioned. In short, they were very successful—so much so that by the middle of 1596 the standard English device of applying pressure on James by cutting off his pension proved ineffective when Elizabeth tried it in the dispute over Buccleuch and Kinmont Willie.[36] Yet after only little more than a year their authority was diluted, and financial power was concentrated in the hands of one of their number, Lord Treasurer Blantyre, who proved conspicuously unable to handle it.

There were a number of reasons for the brevity of the Octavians' tenure of power. The harvest was bad. Their economies made them a lot of enemies, especially among the holders of crown lands whose tenure was threatened by the antiquarian researches of the clerk register, Sir John Skene, and the courtiers whose pensions were cut. They were badly overworked and they bickered among themselves. They were, in the words of one presbyterian minister and historian, "almost all either Papists known or inclining to Popery or malignancy,"[37] a fact which alarmed the

English government as well as the kirk. The worried ministers attributed to their malign influence the king's willingness to allow the detested Popish Huntly to return from exile, and his unwillingness to be lenient with David Black when that hot-tempered cleric preached an outrageous series of sermons calling Queen Elizabeth an atheist and all monarchs "devil's bairns." The result was the famous presbyterian riot in Edinburgh on 17 December 1596; the principal target of the rioters was the chief of the Octavians, Lord President Seton, "a shaveling and a priest, more meet to say mass in Salamanca nor (than) to bear office in Christian and reformed commonweals."[38] This ugly confrontation, which was encouraged by those courtiers who for their own reasons wished to see the Octavians fall, convinced James that his commission was a greater political liability than it was a fiscal asset. He was not ungrateful for their useful work; he did not deprive them of their offices,[39] and by way of asserting his authority he compelled Edinburgh to accept Seton as its provost in 1598. But most of them were forced into the political background, with the conspicuous exception of the Protestant Blantyre. The king was willing to dispense with their financial services because he believed that his financial difficulties would end with his accession to the English throne.

So after 1597 James made little serious effort to amend the unsatisfactory financial situation of his government. Proposals in late 1599 and early 1600 for new types of taxation met fierce resistance and were dropped, as was the plan to force the burghs to pay their rents to the crown in sterling instead of Scots money. An attempt in 1601 to squeeze more money out of the duties on wine led to protest and eventual modification; the council had to explain that its purpose was moral—to cut down on drunkenness—rather than fiscal, and to deny the rumor that it planned to put a tax on food.[40] A succession of officials wrestled with the intractable fiscal problem; one of them, Comptroller George Home of Wedderburn, virtually absconded because he could not meet the obligations of his office, and at one point had to be threatened with the seizure of his property to compel him to resume his duties.[41] James finally found an efficient financial administrator in Sir George Home of Spott, the leader of the group of courtiers who had caballed against the Octavians; he became lord treasurer in 1601. He attempted no serious innovations or economies, however; he had no wish to court the fate he had meted out to his predecessors. In 1603, then, the financial problems of the Scottish crown were far from solved, and the government lived from hand to mouth. But since England flowed with milk and honey, James did not greatly care.

The affairs of the Scottish church were of far more concern to James than his financial plight, and were in far more satisfactory condition in 1603, though by no means completely so. The king very much disliked the radical presbyterian faction, led by Andrew Melville, which dominated the church when he began to rule in 1585, and made no secret of his feelings. In *Basilikon Doron* he fumed about those "fiery spirited men in the ministry" who fantasized about a democratic form of government in which "they fed themselves with the hope to become *Tribuni plebis:* and so in a popular government, by leading people by the nose, to bear the sway of all the rule." To this end they preached "that all Kings and Princes were naturally enemies to the liberty of the Church, and could never patiently bear the yoke of Christ: with such sound doctrine fed they their flocks." If the more moderate elements in the ministry dared to reprove them, they raised the cry of parity in the church: "parity the mother of confusion and enemy to Unity, which is the mother of order." These ministers, said James, were "very pests in the Church and Commonweal, whom no deserts can oblige, neither oaths nor promises bind, breathing nothing but sedition and calumnies, aspiring without measure, railing without reason, and making their own imaginations (without any warrant of the word) the square of their conscience."[42]

James meant every word of this diatribe. He nevertheless grudgingly accepted Maitland's view that compromise with the dominant faction in the church was essential if he was ever to gain control over his fractious aristocracy. So the crown recognized the legality of the recently established system of presbyteries and the pre-eminence within the church of the General Assembly, the national convention of the church which took place once or twice a year. In return the ministers acknowledged the existence of the office of bishop and accepted a definition of the church's jurisdiction which excluded politics: sedition, either in or out of the pulpit, was the king's affair. Many of the clerical extremists disliked this compromise, but in fact their position in the church was to be strengthened by it and that of the bishops weakened. The annexation of the temporalities of benefices to the crown in 1587 fell more heavily on the bishops than on anyone else, and within half a dozen years virtually all presentations to benefices were made to the presbytery rather than the bishop.[43] Finally, in 1592, came the climax, the so-called Golden Act, which legalized the presbyterian system of church polity, although it did not abolish the office of bishop.

After Maitland's death the king's course began to change. The chancellor's advice had been sound: the ministers had for the most part supported James's government and, as the exile of Huntly and Bothwell indicated, the aristocracy had been brought under control. The alliance with the kirk had served its purpose; James could now afford to jettison it and to try to bring the church, in its turn, under his control. The Edinburgh riot of December 1596 gave the king his opportunity, but that fiasco was the occasion, not the cause, of the king's shift of policy; the evidence indicates that James's preparations were in train before the riot occurred. James's first plan was to get control of the church by controlling the General Assembly: determining the time and place of its meeting, facilitating and encouraging the attendance of the large, hitherto unorganized group of moderates among the clergy and throwing obstacles in the way of that of the Melvilleans, manipulating clerical salaries (which were admittedly too low), above all, promoting the election in each assembly of a group of commissioners friendly to him who would have authority over church matters when the assembly was not in session and who, James hoped, could be employed as a sort of committee of the articles, preparing the agenda for the next assembly meeting and thus turning the assembly into a rubber stamp for the decisions of its own commissioners. James had some success with this policy, but in 1600 it broke down decisively over the question of clerical representation in parliament. The General Assembly which met at Montrose in March of that year rejected the king's proposals and accepted instead a series of restrictions which would have meant the subordination of the church's representatives in parliament to the assembly itself. The king's own commissioners of assembly, friendly to him though they were, regarded the Montrose meeting's decisions as binding on them.

So James turned to the alternative means of royal control over the church, which he certainly personally preferred but which was fraught with far greater political risks: the revival of diocesan episcopacy. Bishops were anathema to many people in Scotland besides the followers of Andrew Melville. Outside the clergy the groups most immediately concerned were those who had acquired clerical property as a result of the act of annexation of 1587, mostly nobles and lairds and a number of town governments as well. "The nobility having their livings will never be brought to return them," commented the English agent in Scotland. "I can no way see how the king will effect his aimed at intent."[44] James was well aware of the difficulties created for him by what he now called "that vile act of Annexation."[45] The restoration of episcopacy might even revive that coalition of aristocrats and preachers which had been fatal to his mother and which Maitland's efforts had so recently broken up. But he had no alternative. So he proceeded, very gradually, to fill the vacant bishoprics. By 1603, however, only six of the thirteen Scottish sees were held by working ministers, and three, including St. Andrews, had no incumbent of any sort. The bishops could vote in parliament, the General Assembly had authorized some of them as individuals to conduct visitations, but not always in their own dioceses, and James had named two of his new appointees to the privy council. But of *ex officio* authority over the ministers of their dioceses they as yet had none. In 1603 the king's grip on the church was still rather tenuous, exercised through his partially filled bench of bishops and his occasionally unreliable commissioners of assembly, four of whom were bishops. There was still a long way to go before James's twin goals, of control of the kirk through bishops and of uniformity with the Anglican church, could be attained. Even so, he had come a long way from that day in the summer of 1596 when Andrew Melville had contemptuously called him "God's sillie vassal."[46]

All in all, James had every reason to feel satisfied with what he called his kingcraft as he prepared for his journey to London in that exhilarating spring of 1603. Through a combination of skill and good luck in his conduct of foreign policy and his relations with the various English factions he had succeeded to the throne of the Tudors without bloodshed and without opposition. Scotland was far more peaceful and prosperous than it had been for generations, the aristocracy under control and the church on the way to being so. He and Maitland between them had brought into being a group of loyal and diligent government servants who had been vital to his success. To be sure, not all of Scotland's problems had been solved—the treasury was as empty as ever, and no satisfactory approach to the intractable highland problem had yet been devised. But these and all other difficulties would be resolved by the union between England and Scotland which James contemplated. It was to be not merely a union of the crowns but, rather, a genuine union of government and people, the merging of the two ancient kingdoms into what the Scottish historian John Major had called Greater Britain. Furthermore, it was to be a union in which, where institutions and practices differed, the English version was to be preferred. "St George surely rides upon a towardly riding horse," James had written to Robert Cecil, "where I am daily 'burstin' in daunting a wild, unruly colt."[47] Greater Britain—this was the vision which danced before the king's eyes as he made his way south with the welcoming shouts of his new subjects ringing in his ears. "What God hath conjoined then, let no man separate," he was to say to his first English parliament and on the first issue of the combined coinage of the two kingdoms.[48] Whether it would be possible to bring about this political marriage remained to be seen.

NOTES

1. *Calderwood* VI, 210.

2. *Ibid.*, pp. 215–16.

3. In Aug. 1603 James wrote to the archbishop of York to arrange an exchange of property which would give him possession of two of the archbishop's manors, which he planned to use as stopping places en route to Scotland; see *CSPD 1603–1610*, p. 33.

4. For Maitland see M. Lee, Jr., *John Maitland of Thirlestane and the Foundation of the Stewart Despotism in Scotland* (Princeton, N.J., 1959).

5. C. H. McIlwain, ed., *The Political Works of James I* (Cambridge, Mass., 1918), pp. 24–25.

6. This is the estimate of T. C. Smout, *A History of the Scottish People 1560–1830* (London, 1972), p. 135.

7. McIlwain, *Works,* p. 26.

8. For parliament see R. S. Rait, *The Parliaments of Scotland* (Glasgow, 1924), esp. pp. 336–38, 367–73. The method of choosing the committee of the articles varied throughout the reign; the crown occasionally had difficulty in getting all of its nominees chosen, but it never lost control. Rait argues, p. 163, that the king could control the business undertaken at a convention of estates, but he himself points out, p. 154, that three conventions between Dec. 1599 and June 1600 refused to vote the king the money he wanted. These bodies were not always as tractable as Rait's account suggests.

9. The standard account of the court of session is R. K. Hannay, *The College of Justice* (Edinburgh, 1933); see esp. pp. 99–100, 109–20, 126–27, 150. Sir Alexander Grant, *The Story of the University of Edinburgh during Its First Three Hundred Years* (London, 1884) I, 184–90. Smout, *Scottish People,* pp. 100–101. For Maitland's role see Lee, *Maitland,* pp. 126–27, 219–21.

10. 29 June 1600, George Nicolson to Sir Robert Cecil, *CSP Scot.* XIII, 661–64.

11. *RPCS* V, 499–501. The penalty for prolonged nonattendance was dismissal, but it was never invoked.

12. *Calderwood* IV, 613–14.

13. The general bond was feudal in origin; it was based on the idea that a feudal superior was responsible for the conduct of his vassals; see Lee, *Maitland,* pp. 125–30.

14. 28 Nov. 1602, Nicolson to Cecil, *CSP Scot.* XIII, 1085.

15. H. M. Conacher, "Land Tenure in Scotland in the 17th Century," *Juridical Review* L (1938), 34. A. J. Youngson, *After the Forty-five* (Edinburgh, 1973), p. 13.

16. The standard account of the borders is T. I. Rae, *The Administration of the Scottish Frontier, 1513–1603* (Edinburgh, 1966).

17. I. F. Grant, *The Social and Economic Development of Scotland before 1603* (Edinburgh, 1930), p. 355.

18. See, for instance, his letter to the privy council on 11 Aug. 1616, *RPCS* X, 602.

19. McIlwain, *Works,* p. 27. S. G. E. Lythe, *The Economy of Scotland in Its European Setting 1550–1625* (Edinburgh, 1960), pp. 87–88.

20. McIlwain, *Works,* p. 26.

21. Lythe, *Economy of Scotland,* pp. 87–88.

22. In 1619 the convention of royal burghs was expressing concern at the growth in numbers of the burghs of regality and barony, which provided local markets. In 1620 it fined Stirling for electing a craftsman as a bailie; only merchants were to serve as burgh officials. See *RCRB* III, 97, 110–11.

23. Grant, *Social and Economic Development,* p. 367.

24. The distribution of taxation among the burghs is a good indication of their relative importance and of the dominant position of Edinburgh. The tax stent roll which was adopted in 1597 and continued without change throughout the reign stated that of each £100 of taxation Edinburgh would pay £28 15 shillings, Dundee £10 15 sh., Aberdeen £8, Perth £6 3 sh. 4 d., Glasgow £4 10 sh., and so on down to Whitthorn, which paid 5 sh. There are a total of fifty burghs on the roll. See *RCRB* II, 10.

25. *Ibid.* I, 497–98, II, 19–21. *APS* IV, 118. In 1612, after James had been in London for almost a decade, the burghs decided to keep a paid agent in London, after a dispute over customs rates. In 1616 they concluded that such an agent was not a good investment. See *RCRB* II, 340, 353, 357–58, III, 49–53. For the convention of royal burghs see Theodora Pagan, *The Convention of the Royal Burghs of Scotland* (Glasgow, 1926), and her article, Theodora Keith, "The Influence of the Convention of the Royal Burghs of Scotland on the Economic Development of Scotland before 1707," *SHR* X (1912–13), 250–71, esp. pp. 252–62.

26. On this point see, e.g., *RPCS* VI, 34, and Rait, *Parliaments,* p. 302.

27. This according to a much-quoted set of figures for 1614, *M&K,* pp. 70–74. The figures are approximately £578,000 for raw materials and £130,000 for manufactured goods.

28. Lythe, *Economy of Scotland,* pp. 20, 28. Smout, *Scottish People,* p. 143.

29. Lythe, *Economy of Scotland,* pp. 30, 101–2, 107, 110–11. R. Mitchison, "The Making of the Old Scottish Poor Law," *Past and Present* 63 (1974), 59–63. *RPCS* VI, 98–99.

30. Lythe, *Economy of Scotland,* pp. 32, 46, 64, 119–20. See also T. M. Devine and S. G. E. Lythe, "The Economy of Scotland under James VI," *SHR* L (1971), 95. J. U. Nef, *The Rise of the British Coal Industry* (London, 1932) I, 43–46.

31. What follows is based principally on Grant, *Social and Economic Development,* pp. 265–85, and Smout, *Scottish People,* pp. 126–34.

32. Grant, *Social and Economic Development,* p. 276.

33. G. S. Pryde, ed., *Ayr Burgh Accounts 1534–1624, SHS* (Edinburgh, 1937), p. xviii. Pryde points out, pp. xxxvi–xxxviii, that Ayr itself profited from the feuing of its own lands because the feu duty was paid in victual.

34. Lythe, *Economy of Scotland,* pp. 92–93. There was also, of course, the standard mercantilist motivation behind the grant of some of the monopolies; see *ibid.,* pp. 40–42.

35. 29 Jan. 1596, Nicolson to Robert Bowes, *CSP Scot.* XII, 136. G. P. MacNeill, ed., *The Exchequer Rolls of Scotland* XXIII (Edinburgh, 1908), 151–52, 206, 276–77.

36. 14 July 1596, James Hudson to Cecil, *CSP Scot.* XII, 278–79. See also 3 July, Bowes to Lord Burghley, *ibid.,* p. 264.

37. John Row, *The History of the Kirk of Scotland,* ed. D. Laing, Wodrow Society (Edinburgh, 1842), p. 165.

38. *Calderwood* V, 548.

39. This fact, and the fact that Blantyre attempted to follow their policies, has led Dr. Athol Murray, in his informative and useful article, "Sir John Skene and the Exchequer, 1594–1612," *Miscellany One,* The Stair Society (Edinburgh, 1971), to conclude, pp. 129–31, that the Octavians remained a cohesive and effective group until 1598. The political eclipse of most of the members in 1597 is apparent, however.

40. *RPCS* VI, 200–201, 205–6, 291.

41. *Ibid.* V, lxxxvii–lxxxviii, 525–26, 530–31, 550–51, 553–54.

42. McIlwain, *Works,* pp. 23–24.

43. G. Donaldson, "The Polity of the Scottish Church 1560–1600," *Records of the Scottish Church History Society* XI (1955), 224–25.

44. *CSP Scot.* XIII, 629–30.

45. McIlwain, *Works,* p. 24.

46. *Calderwood* V, 439–40. These two paragraphs are based on M. Lee, Jr., "James VI and the Revival of Episcopacy in Scotland, 1596–1600," *Church History* 43 (1974), 50–64, which see for a full discussion of this question.

47. John Bruce, ed., *Correspondence of King James VI of Scotland with Sir Robert Cecil and Others in England during the Reign of Queen Elizabeth,* Camden Society (London, 1861), pp. 31–32.

48. McIlwain, *Works,* p. 272.

2

Scotland without James: The Abortive Union

Q UEEN ELIZABETH'S death was hardly unexpected in Edinburgh; nevertheless the king and his officials behaved as if they had been caught by surprise. James was not even proclaimed until 31 March 1603, five days after the news arrived, and money had to be borrowed for the journey south.[1] A spate of enactments followed which made temporary arrangements for the government of the country under the new circumstances. A signature stamp was entrusted to Sir Patrick Murray, the comptroller's brother and the king's chief ecclesiastical trouble-shooter. The privy council was given the power to take actions which normally required specific royal approval, such as the granting of passports and commissions of lieutenancy and the auditing of exchequer accounts. The king renewed the powers of the committee which managed the queen's properties. Finally, on 7 April, when he arrived at Berwick, James entrusted the charge of both the English and Scottish borders to the Scottish privy council, on the ground that it was closer geographically to the area than the English council in London, an act which illustrated the extent of his ignorance of the English administrative structure.[2]

A large number of Scots accompanied the king on his journey south, great lords like his close cousin Ludovic Stuart, duke of Lennox, and his trusted friend with whom he had been raised and educated, John Erskine, earl of Mar; ministers like his highly useful chaplain Patrick Galloway, Bishop Lindsay of Ross, and Lindsay's son-in-law John Spottiswoode, minister of Calder, a man rapidly rising in the king's favor; important officials such as Lord Treasurer Home, Secretary Elphinstone, and Comptroller Murray; and the gentlemen of his bedchamber, among many others. It was obvious that the king intended to keep some Scots permanently with him in London, for both political and personal reasons, but who they would be was not at all apparent as yet, perhaps not even to James himself.[3] It was equally obvious that not all of those who went south with James would remain; he had virtually denuded the Edinburgh administration of its officials. The most important political figure left behind was Lord President Seton, not because he was out of favor but because he was in charge of little Prince Charles, who was adjudged to be too frail to travel.[4]

The king's hasty departure left a good many loose ends for the councillors who remained behind to cope with. One of the most urgent was communication, and the council acted promptly. On 5 May it appointed postmasters at Edinburgh, Haddington, Cockburnspath, and Berwick and spelled out their duties. Postmasters were to move the royal mails on within fifteen minutes of their receipt, and to guarantee an average traveling time of six miles per hour in summer, five in winter. Their financial rewards were substantial and promptly paid, and for the most part they did their jobs well enough. The system's principal weaknesses, according to reports made in 1619 and 1620, were that the postmasters, because of their own financial mismanagement, often had an insufficient number of horses, and kept their records sloppily. A letter normally took a week to pass between London and Edinburgh, often less, in winter occasionally longer. There were remarkably few complaints about slow service—though Seton once grumbled to Cecil that an important letter took five days to reach him. In urgent matters, he said, letters should take no more than three days in summer and four in winter. This was expecting a lot: Robert Carey, on his breakneck ride from London to Edinburgh to announce Queen Elizabeth's death to James, took two and a half days. Significantly enough, however, there is no record of any dissatisfaction with the service on the part of the king.[5]

A second step taken in the summer of 1603 was the creation of a police force, which the government had long believed to be necessary but was unable to afford: here was the first tangible benefit for Scotland from her new connection with her wealthier neighbor.[6] In July James authorized Comptroller Murray to raise a guard of forty men; its function was to enforce the ordinances of the council and pursue those at the horn—outlawed—beginning, the council decided, in the west march.[7] This guard was to do a good deal of useful service in the next few years.

The existence of the new gendarmerie, though welcome to the council, did nothing to solve the immediate problem of governmental organization. Furthermore, it became clear that for the time being, until his vision of unity became a reality, the king intended to govern as he had since Maitland's death. In September he scolded the council for assigning pensions and annuities without his specific authorization, and he issued full instructions regarding compensation for a number of servants he had taken south with him expecting to place them in court posts in England. He discovered that he could not remove the incumbents, he explained, and so he was sending the servants back; they were to receive a total of £10,000. In October he ordered the more extensive use of fines as punishment for various breaches of the peace, a device which, at the council's suggestion, he extended to aristocratic feuds. There followed in the next months instructions regarding the wardship of the earl of Athol, a dispute between Edinburgh and Leith, the repayment of the ex-comptroller Home of Wedderburn for expenses incurred while in office, the conditions under which the presbytery of Aberdeen could excommunicate the marquis of Huntly and under which the earl of Cassillis could be released from ward, into which he had gone for what the council termed his unmannerly insolence to his wife in its presence.[8] It was clear enough that James fully intended to govern Scotland with his pen.

Seton and his colleagues obviously could not complain of the king's behavior, although they were aware that in time it would cause difficulties, as James's familiarity with the Scottish situation on a day-to-day basis lessened, as inevitably it must. What they did complain of was that James had made their task very difficult by taking so many officials with him to England. In his capacity as president of the court of session Seton asked James in May to follow the rules laid down for the filling of vacancies and not permit resignations *in favorem* if, as many people supposed, "your majesty is to retain there some of our number."[9] This letter having produced no results, Seton in July sent a letter of warning to Sir Robert Cecil. The Scots who had gone south with the king were being neglectful, said Seton, and so many important people had gone to England that those remaining behind simply did not have the authority to crack down on troublemakers. The government's willingness to act was being tested, and if the few unimportant breaches of the law which had occurred up to now went unpunished, much worse would happen in future. The vacuum was due to the king's absence, and it had to be filled.[10]

This letter apparently made an impression. Seton had been something of an unknown quantity to Cecil, himself a very able and efficient administrator; he recognized a kindred spirit, and it seems likely that he urged the king to act. At any rate Comptroller Murray was promptly sent home to organize his police, and in February 1604 the council, with the king's authorization, issued an order prohibiting Scottish officials and noblemen from going to court without special license, on the ground that the absence of so many of them in England was impairing the efficiency of the Scottish government.[11] In that same month another of Seton's suggestions began to be implemented: the lawyer Edward Bruce, Lord Kinloss, who had been appointed to the English office of master of the rolls, resigned from the court of session. His replacement, Sir Alexander Hay of Fosterseat, later in the year received an appointment to the council and had a long and useful career on both bodies.

James's response to Seton's requests for the regularization of the Scottish administrative structure had been rather minimal because he believed that reconstitution of the machinery of government in Edinburgh would be impractical until the results of the forthcoming union negotiations were known. The king had already taken some anticipatory steps by arranging for the general circulation of the coinage of the two countries at the existing 12:1 ratio and for a new common issue. He also planned for a common flag combining the crosses of St. George and St. Andrew, the first Union Jack, as it were, which was adopted in 1606 and which Scottish shipowners later complained of because St. George's cross obscured St. Andrew's. In May 1603 there was a proclamation against either country's harboring of fugitives from the other. In the following month the Scottish council decreed, at the suit of an English merchant, that as King James's subject he did not have to pay the export duties imposed on foreigners; by the end of 1604 there was reciprocation in that the 25 percent surcharge levied in English ports on merchandise imported by aliens was dropped for Scottish-owned goods.[12] On 12 January 1604 the king sent his instructions regarding the union to the Scottish council. Parliament was to meet on 10 April. Its only business was to be the union. It was to accept the idea in principle—to which, said the king optimistically, there should be no opposition—and name a commission to negotiate terms with a group of English commissioners; whatever agreement they reached would be subject to parliamentary ratification. Seton was instructed to look into the precedents for the holding of a parliament in the monarch's absence, draw up the necessary documents, and send them to London in time for the king to sign and return them before parliament met.[13] These orders, and Seton's appointment as vice-chancellor in February, made it clear that James intended Seton to be the leader of the Scottish delegation at the forthcoming union negotiations; as the most highly placed lawyer in the king's inner circle he was the obvious choice.

When the news of the king's plan for union became public, the anti-episcopal elements in the church became alarmed. Their greatest fear was that the negotiations would deal with religion and would lead to a unified church which would certainly be episcopal in polity and very probably Anglican in doctrine. The government's policy since James's departure had done nothing to reassure them—the appointment of the Catholic Lord Home as lieutenant of the marches, for instance, and the frustrating of the presbytery of Aberdeen's attempts to deal with the backsliding Huntly. They did not like what they heard about the Hampton Court conference, "very favorable for the bishops and grievous to all that looked for reformation."[14] They also had not liked the elevation of John Spottiswoode to the archbishopric of Glasgow in July 1603. The supporters of Andrew Melville regarded Spottiswoode as a Judas. He had been one of them in 1596, gathering signatures on a petition supporting the embattled Black and loudly demanding the dismissal of the king's Popish councillors; by 1600, they thought out of greed and ambition, he had gone over to the king's side on the question of bishops—and perhaps he had been an *agent provocateur* in 1596.[15] Spottiswoode's clerical opponents certainly did him a great deal less than justice. There is no reason to doubt the sincerity of his conversion to the view that episcopacy represented the most viable system of church government, given the king's opinions and his power to impose his will, which was enormously increased, of course, after 1603. Furthermore, the archbishop came genuinely to admire the king and to be eager to follow the royal wishes. The king in turn came more and more to depend upon Spottiswoode for advice and information in ecclesiastical affairs. But neither Spottiswoode nor anyone else was able to make policy in this area; James's decisions on all major religious questions were his own.

When parliament met in April 1604, it became apparent that a good many people besides the ministers were worried about the union: a delegation of aristocrats requested a conference with the lords of the articles about it. Before anything much could be done, however, the king ordered a prorogation until July because of delays in the English parliament.[16] The prorogation meant further friction with the kirk because it entailed the postponement of the General Assembly, originally scheduled for July 1604, now postponed until the first Tuesday of July 1605: it was apparent that the king would not permit a meeting until after the completion of the union negotiations. The presbytery of St. Andrews decided on a gesture of defiance. Their representatives, led by James Melville, Andrew's nephew, appeared on the appointed date and protested against what they called the violation of the law involved in the postponement of the assembly, an action which prompted a royal proclamation prohibiting unauthorized assemblies of clergy.[17]

It was apparent that James's tactics had reopened the whole question of the right to determine the time and place of meetings of the General Assembly, which had been a major bone of contention in 1596 and thereafter but which, James thought, had been settled in his favor. The king's clerical opponents were not mollified by the actions of the July session of parliament, which ratified all previous legislation in favor of the kirk and against Papists, and which guaranteed that the forthcoming negotiations would not prejudice the present state of the kirk. At its meeting in September 1604 the synod of Fife, under James Melville's leadership, threw down the gauntlet: it declared that the General Assembly could legally meet without the king's permission. James's commissioner, Sir Alexander Straiton of Lauriston, decided to temporize. Perhaps Melville was right, he said, but it was better to hold a meeting with royal permission, which he was sure would be forthcoming. He promised to hold a meeting the following month at Perth with the commissioners of assembly and representatives of all the synods to discuss the question. Calderwood says that George Gledstanes, a minister in St. Andrews since 1597 and bishop of Caithness since 1600, misrepresented the synod to the king, who ordered the Melvilles and some others into ward, but that the council refused, "thinking it a dangerous preparative to ward men unheard and uncondemned."[18] If so, it was the first occasion—the first of many—on which the council, on the basis of its superior knowledge of the situation, decided not to carry out the king's instructions. Gledstanes received his reward, however. In October 1604 the king appointed him to the archbishopric of St. Andrews, which had been vacant for twelve years.

The meeting at Perth did not go well for the government. The Melvilleans upbraided the commissioners of assembly for their pusillanimity at the recent parliament and charged that their authority had lapsed, since their commission lasted only until the next General Assembly, the time for which had passed. The commissioners could not accept this argument and thus admit that the king could not postpone an assembly meeting. They professed weariness in their task, but, they said, in church matters the king would deal only with them. The other major issue was the question of the bishops' having voted at the recent parliament without warrant from an assembly, which, according to the stipulations adopted at the Montrose assembly of 1600, they were not entitled to do. The commissioners took the line that the bishops could be dealt with at the next General Assembly, and were met with the reply that such a meeting would no doubt be put off "till custom had corroborated corruption." The meeting voted to present a number of petitions to the king, including one that "the godly and faithful brethren in England persecuted by the bishops might find favor with his Majesty," which "the court clawbacks opposed profanely and ridiculously," and, more important, it petitioned to hold a General Assembly. Lauriston promised to act as advocate for them as best he could.[19]

By the end of 1604 the Melvilleans' fear that the supporters of episcopacy planned to turn the union negotiations to their advantage led some of them to preach against union, if one can believe their enemy Huntly, and they seem to have had some cause for alarm. The elevation of Richard Bancroft, the kirk's severest critic in the English hierarchy, to the archbishopric of Canterbury in October 1604 was anything but reassuring. The Venetian ambassador wrote in 1606 of the king's desire to introduce the Anglican religion into Scotland as a necessary preliminary to union.[20] Archbishop Spottiswoode, writing to the king in January 1605 of some attacks on him from pulpits in Edinburgh, remarked, "I write this to hold your Highness in mind of the general business, which, being perfected, shall give a conclusion to this and suchlike broils."[21] Whatever the truth of the suspicions of the opponents of episcopacy, it seemed very likely that another postponement of the meeting of the General Assembly would lead to serious trouble.

ii

As is well known, the union of England and Scotland was an idea whose time had not yet come. "He [James] hasteneth to a mixture of both kingdoms and nations, faster perhaps than policy will conveniently bear," wrote Sir Francis Bacon, the most eloquent English supporter of union, before the start of the negotiations.[22] There were, to be sure, a number of factors working in favor of union: common Protestantism and the sense of standing together against the onslaught of the forces of militant Catholicism, the anglicization of the Scottish language, the steadily increasing trade, the beginning of a flow of Scottish students to English universities and of Scottish ministers to English benefices.[23] In each country union had a handful of genuine supporters as well as those who merely followed the king's lead. But in neither country was there very much enthusiasm, and there was a great deal of genuine hostility, owing to the belief that union would somehow mean the taking over of that country by the other. For the majority of Scots the feeling was deep-rooted and understandable. They had been fending off English assaults on their independence for three hundred years, and what the Southron had not been able to win by the sword he would now achieve by the imposition of English men, methods, and institutions. The Scots were very keenly aware of the example of the Netherlanders, a people which had given a king to a more powerful state and in the next generation had risen in rebellion in defense of their liberties against that king's son, a person completely alien to them, both as a ruler and as a man. Secretary Elphinstone, now raised to the peerage as Lord Balmerino, put the view of Scottish officialdom well when he wrote to Robert Cecil, "Most of us all could be rather content to continue in our wonted condition nor (than) to match with so unequal a party, strengthened by the continual presence of our Prince, to whom time and subsequent ages will make us strangers." Despite his lack of enthusiasm, Balmerino pledged that he would do his best to "impede all course of contrary opinion." The king himself acknowledged the lukewarmness of his Scottish subjects when he told the English parliament in 1607 that they had not asked for union, "nor even once did any of that nation press me forward or wish me to accelerate that business."[24]

For the most part the opponents of union in Scotland expressed themselves very indirectly. On the surface there was a willingness to accede to the king's wishes, perhaps because they realized that the English did not want union either. English opposition was much more outspoken and direct, and was expressed vividly in parliament. Englishmen disliked and despised the Scots as a race, and at the same time they feared them. The gang that had come south with the king was bad enough; union would simply open the floodgates. Not only would they take over the government completely, they would also wreak economic havoc because of the built-in competitive advantage their lower standard of living gave them.[25] In an age given to thinking in biblical imagery, it is not surprising that the Scots were continually compared to Pharoah's lean kine.

Just how many Scots followed King James to London is not clear, but it seems likely that there were nowhere near as many as Englishmen believed there were. In some ways James behaved with considerable restraint. He retained in office virtually all of Elizabeth's major officials, not merely the indispensable Secretary Cecil but also the treasurer, the lord keeper, the lord admiral, etc. He did appoint half a dozen Scotsmen to the English privy council, but only two of them got major official positions: Sir George Home became chancellor of the exchequer and Lord Kinloss master of the rolls. This kind of appointment caused special resentment in England; that of Kinloss was especially disliked, since as master of the rolls he had a lot of legal work to do. James saw his error and did not repeat it. He certainly did not attempt to govern England by means of Scots.

On the other hand, the Scots who were at court were extremely conspicuous. They filled the bedchamber and household offices. Lennox became steward of the household, John Murray keeper of the privy purse, Sir George Home master of the wardrobe, and Mar's cousin Sir Thomas Erskine captain of the guard. Erskine's tested and unswerving loyalty made this a perfectly reasonable appointment, but the displaced Sir Walter Raleigh nursed a grievance, with ultimately tragic results for himself. The Scots also partook lavishly of the king's bounty; virtually all the gifts of money James made during the first year of his rule in England were to Scots. In some cases they were payments of royal obligations, but within five years pensions to Scots were costing the English treasury more than £12,000 sterling annually.[26] Scots were favored in other ways too. There were Garters for Lennox and Mar. "No Englishman, be his rank what it may, can enter the Presence Chamber without being summoned," wrote the Venetian agent in May 1603, "whereas the Scottish lords have free entrée of the privy chamber, and more especially at the toilette." In July the future conspirator Guy Fawkes, in a memorandum written for the Spanish government, dwelt upon the increasing unpopularity of the Scots and the quarrels they were causing at court.[27]

James came gradually to see that his generosity and permissiveness to his fellow countrymen were causing trouble, and he apologized, after his fashion. "My first three years were to me as a Christmas," he told the English parliament in March 1607. "I could not then be miserable: should I have been over-sparing to them? They might have thought Joseph had forgotten his brethren." But he did not put an end to his open-handedness.[28] Even if he had, the damage was done as far as English public opinion was concerned. The union would mean more Scots, quarrelsome, beggarly, covetous, and proud, in England's green and pleasant land. The English wanted none of it.

The storm signals in both countries were perfectly visible by the spring of 1604. Seton wrote a fairly cheerful letter to Cecil in March, saying that most people accepted the idea of union in principle, but "some suspect the particular conditions may engender greater difficulties." Balmerino, Mar, and Cecil himself were much more pessimistic, especially as reports began to circulate in Scotland of hostile speeches being made in England. Balmerino urged that the English make a gesture by repealing those statutes which were "disgraceful and prejudicial to this country," and agreed with Cecil (and the English judges) that James's plan to merge the ancient names of *England* and *Scotland* into *Great Britain* was premature.[29] The Scottish parliament, when it met in July to appoint the commission, was unusually balky, approving a list of commissioners differing from the one James had forwarded, carefully stipulating that the fundamental laws of Scotland, its liberties and privileges, should suffer no infringement, and refusing to vote a tax for the commissioners' expenses.[30] The convention of royal burghs was somewhat more generous with expense money for its representatives on the commission, but its instructions to them make it clear that the convention hoped to take advantage of the negotiations to improve the competitive position of its members, all of whose rights and privileges were to be maintained. The tone of these instructions, and the details of the suggestions and requests, indicate no particular enthusiasm for union among the leadership of the Scottish trading community, and no willingness to make any concessions to obtain it. Their English opposite numbers felt exactly the same way. There was not enough positive economic attraction for either party, and as one authority has put it, "neither nation seriously desired close economic integration." Only if there had been immediate, discernible economic advantage would the prospect of union have been acceptable to the trading community on either side of the Tweed.[31]

The commissioners met in late October 1604 and completed the treaty in little more than a month. This remarkable speed was due to a good deal of preliminary spadework, to the decision to postpone dealing with a number of tricky questions of detail, and to the skill with which the chief delegates, Seton and Cecil, conducted the negotiations. The commissioners worked well enough together in spite of the chilly political atmosphere in England, which at the end of the negotiations prompted the Scottish commissioners to urge James to prevent any of the other English commissioners from following the example of Lord Admiral Nottingham and entertaining them at supper: such festivities exacerbated English public opinion, which did not like to see any honor paid to Scots.[32] James was pleased with the treaty, anticipated its successful implementation by adopting the title of *King of Great Britain* against his ministers' wishes, and rewarded the principal negotiators with earldoms. Early in 1605 Cecil became earl of Salisbury, and Seton, earl of Dunfermline.[33]

The king was optimistic that the parliaments of the two kingdoms would ratify the treaty in due course; regardless of its fate in the legislatures, however, it would not bring about any sort of amalgamation of the machinery of the two governments.[34] There would be separate administrations in London and Edinburgh for the foreseeable future, with that of Scotland being divided between the king in London attempting to govern by his pen with the aid of his advisers there, and the privy council in Edinburgh, obligated to execute the royal orders without question but in fact not always doing so. These circumstances also meant that James would no longer be his own chief minister, as he had been for the past decade. The king had no intention of relaxing his control over policy, but day-to-day administrative decisions would devolve upon someone else, and, of course, administrative power meant political power, as all those involved knew very well. One of the unexplored problems of Scottish history, unexplored because historians have too readily accepted King James's boast about governing with his pen, is that of the real locus of power after 1603.

Of the Scots around the king the most obvious candidate for the position of James's *eminence grise* in Scottish affairs was Lord Treasurer Home, now earl of Dunbar. For one thing, he was the one great Scottish officer of state who remained at court. For another thing, Dunbar, the quintessential courtier, a fat *faux bonhomme* who knew the virtues of patience, stood high in James's favor, was very ambitious, and had demonstrated undoubted administrative skill in his handling of the treasury since his appointment. Of the many other Scots in London there were five who were politically important, potentially at least. The duke of Lennox involved himself comparatively little in Scottish politics. His great position— he was the only duke in either kingdom until 1623—and his personal closeness to the king made it possible for him to intervene effectively when he wished, however, and sometimes he did, usually when his personal interests were at stake. The earl of Mar, who at this point in his career spent a great deal of his time in England, was rather more politically minded than Lennox and also had the king's confidence and trust. But Mar was lazy and often had to be pushed into taking political action. One of those who did the pushing was his cousin Sir Thomas Erskine, captain of the guard, who, like Mar, had been brought up and educated with James. He was one of those who had fought for James on that memorable day in Gowrie House in August 1600; the king trusted him completely. Erskine was ambitious and maintained a considerable correspondence in Scotland; he was a channel through whom to reach the king and through whom the king kept himself informed. So was John Murray of Lochmaben, the keeper of the privy purse, whose importance grew with the years; both Erskine and Murray wound up with earldoms. Finally there was Alexander Hay of Whitburgh, a clerk of the council, who was the London secretary for Scottish affairs and whose position was recognized in 1608 when he was promoted to joint secretary of state with Balmerino.

All the men in London had the king's ear; for the members of the Edinburgh administration, and others in Scotland with political ambitions, the problem was one of getting through to James with their views. The king's correspondence with his officials in Edinburgh was largely formal—an average of about sixty letters of instruction a year are recorded in the council's register of missive letters.[35] More important were the letters written privately, to James himself, to other Scots at court, and to English officials. There was a lot of such correspondence, which meant that James was, on the whole, very well informed about what went on in his ancient kingdom.

Of all the Scots in Edinburgh the new earl of Dunfermline was unquestionably the most important. He had gained far more than anyone else from the negotiation of the treaty of union; in addition to his earldom he had at long last obtained the office of chancellor, which he had coveted since Maitland's death and which made him the official head of the Scottish administration. Dunfermline had much to recommend him to James as a principal adviser for Scottish affairs. He was diligent, clever, and loyal, and came from a family which had been loyal to the end to James's mother—and James set much store by that.[36] He was learned and deferential, and made a fine art of writing letters to the king which combined in suitable proportions classical allusions, Latin tags, and fulsome flattery. He had large numbers of useful family connections, and made more by the marriages he arranged for his large brood of daughters and nieces, and for himself—he had three wives, all from noble families. After the lesson he learned as to the dangers of the politics of confrontation in 1596, he had turned into a conciliator and compromiser whose object was to have as few political enemies as possible, a stance which, he now realized, was vital for church Papists like himself. He cultivated the Scots around the king, like Erskine and Lochmaben, but his principal pipelines to James were Salisbury, with whom he became very friendly during the union negotiations, and Queen Anne, whose financial affairs he still managed and whose favorite lady-in-waiting, Lady Jean Drummond, was his sister-in-law.

There were three other important people in the Edinburgh administration who might have posed a threat to Dunfermline's pre-eminence, but they all suffered from handicaps of one sort or another which inhibited their doing so. Secretary Balmerino was still expiating his blunders in the conduct of foreign policy in 1600–1601. He was clever, but James did not altogether trust him. His office was now far less important anyway, since there was no longer such a thing as an independent Scottish foreign policy; the foreign interests of the nation, and of individual Scots abroad, mostly merchants, were now in the hands of the English diplomatic service, which frequently neglected them, causing frustration and irritation in Edinburgh.[37] David Murray, Lord Scone, the comptroller, was greedy and rather erratic, and temperamentally unsuited to the arts of persuasion—a useful hatchet-man, but not much more. Lord Advocate Thomas Hamilton, a former Octavian, the best brain of the three, suffered from his comparatively humble origins—he was "Tam o' the Cowgate," after all—and from the fact that, as a lawyer, he was a member of the profession of which Dunfermline was the head.[38] Other important officials, like John Arnot, the treasurer-depute, and later George Hay and Gideon Murray of Elibank, could not effectively mount a challenge to the chancellor by themselves, seldom contemplated it, and, indeed, found it to their advantage not to do so. All these men, save Balmerino, who lost much of what he had, got rich from their government service, and normally thought it foolish to risk what they had in what would probably be a futile undertaking.[39]

Bishops did not get rich from government service, or from their dioceses either, and Archbishop Spottiswoode, who became a privy councillor in May 1605, was hostile to Dunfermline, whom he regarded as a dangerous concealed Papist, constantly intriguing on behalf of his co-religionists. He would cheerfully have seen Dunfermline out of office, but he too suffered from various handicaps which in the end rendered his efforts nugatory. For one thing, George Gledstanes turned out to be a poor choice as archbishop of St. Andrews, fussy, politically naive, and afflicted with nepotism; by the time he died and Spottiswoode became primate in 1615, Dunfermline's position was unassailable. Second, very few of Spottiswoode's episcopal colleagues turned out to have much political ability or drive. The two who did, Andrew Knox of the Isles and James Law of Orkney, were both preoccupied with problems peculiar to their dioceses. So Spottiswoode could count on very little help within his own organization. Finally there was the matter of an issue. Spottiswoode's best chance was to persuade the king that Dunfermline opposed the restoration of diocesan episcopacy. There was some truth in this. But once the chancellor gave way on this point, there was very little the archbishop could do.

The great lords were potentially another source of opposition to Dunfermline, but for one reason or another none of those remaining in Scotland was either willing or able to challenge the existing regime. Some became the chancellor's friends; others were not politically minded. Argyll the king disliked, and his preoccupation first with the western highlands and then, late in life, with Catholicism effectively neutralized him. Only the king's old friend Huntly represented a potential threat, and Huntly suddenly discovered that he, too, had to abide by the rules. The marquis and the presbytery of Aberdeen were at loggerheads, as usual, over his religious opinions. Late in 1604 James blocked one attempt to excommunicate him, but the dispute soon began again, and in March 1605 Huntly decided to go directly to court and make a personal appeal to the king. According to the recent decree of the privy council he needed a license to do this, and he did not have one. The chancellor and his colleagues wrote to James urging that the king refuse to see him, the king followed their advice, and Huntly had to return to Scotland, humiliated and rather crestfallen. The chancellor pointed the moral to Huntly at a meeting of the privy council: happily the king was now so powerful that he could deal with any of his subjects, or all of them together, according to the law and their just deserts, not according to their power. Dunfermline expressed to Salisbury his satisfaction at this result: "It will make the courses of all our great hidalgos the more temperate."[40]

The great hidalgos were, indeed, more temperate during the last two decades of James's reign, not only from necessity but also because they discovered that obedience paid dividends. The men in charge of the Scottish government in both Edinburgh and London were prepared to reward loyal and obedient aristocrats, the more so as the king, now that he had reached his promised land, believed that it was no longer necessary to exercise frugality. Scottish crown land was no longer required to support the royal household or as a counterweight to the landed possessions of the great nobles. So it was extensively feued, and various courtiers and officials received gifts out of the royal rents in victual, which declined in consequence between 15 and 25 percent from 1602 to 1605.[41] As a class the nobility received favored treatment in other ways as well. As a result of the contretemps over Huntly, for example, the council declared that presbyteries and synods were not to start the process of excommunication against any aristocrat without prior notification to the commissioners of assembly, who in turn were required to notify the king.[42]

The fact of the matter was that the Scottish nobility had effectively ceased to be even potentially a political threat to the power of its absentee king. Dunfermline and Dunbar, nobles themselves and scions of noble houses, were not the objects of the sort of class jealousy which had prompted the earl of Bothwell to compare Chancellor Maitland to a toadstool, and they had no desire to weaken the aristocracy any further: it was not necessary. The nobility was now to be cosseted into acceptance of the existing regime and cooperation with it. But the measures to compel obedience to the law were not relaxed in their favor, and the council successfully remonstrated with the king when he suggested that a noble ordered into ward for an offense other than rebellion could be warded in his own house; such a plan would end all justice in Scotland. James, who never directly admitted to being wrong if he could help it, indirectly accepted the council's position by ordering it not to use Edinburgh castle for debtors other than nobles, on the ground that it was getting too crowded.[43]

Another problem which concerned the position of the nobility in the state was that of the heritability of public office. At this stage it arose in connection with the court of session. The procedures established in 1594 to provide qualified replacements for vacancies there and prevent resignations *in favorem* had not worked very well. There had been two cases of close relatives succeeding one another, and with the king now far away and therefore less able to judge the qualifications of men who might have great talent but little influence, Dunfermline in 1605 was prompted to raise the question of the qualifications of future nominees with the king. James agreed that they should be mature, and with ten years' experience at least—but, he added, these limitations would not apply to nobles, their eldest sons, and knights with an income of £2,000 a year. James ordered that a panel of six senior advocates be drawn up, from which he might select future nominees. Having made these rules, the king proceeded to pay almost no attention to them. Only two of the men on the panel received appointments during Dunfermline's lifetime.[44]

Resignations *in favorem,* and the passing of public office from father to son, were to remain features of Scottish life throughout the reign of James VI, even in those offices, such as sheriff, where the king and everyone else recognized the pernicious effects of the system. The impulse for reform of this system had originally arisen from the crown's desire to increase its own power at the expense of its numerous overmighty subjects; now that the crown had at its disposal all the resources of England, there was much less need to alter the old system. The king's will could and would be done with the instruments currently available; as long as law and order, peace and prosperity, prevailed, it was easier to leave the present system alone. So the drive for fundamental change in governmental machinery, which had been a feature of the Maitland regime, gradually slackened. Much more typical of the new era was the kind of tidying-up reflected in the council's decree of 1606 setting out a list of prices to be charged for the issuance of various writs and seals and its resistance to James's frequent proposals, prompted by his own generosity or a suitor's importunity, that an exception be made for someone's private profit.[45]

Orderly administration depended on obedience to the law, of course, and law and order were less than adequate in some areas, notably the highlands and borders. As for the highlands, the king still held to the view that, once they were pacified, their economy would flourish; his favored policy to that end was still that of the extirpation or expulsion of the inhabitants and their replacement with colonies of lowlanders. It was a policy which the councillors regarded dubiously because of the expense involved; they were prepared to countenance it only in Lewis, where in 1605 the gentlemen-adventurers, armed with a new commission, made another effort to get control of the island. They were no more successful than before, and in September 1606 appeared the first hint of what was to be the ultimate solution there, in a commission of fire and sword to the chancellor's friend Kenneth MacKenzie of Kintail against the Clanranald and other lawbreakers in Lewis.[46] The problem in the southern highlands was more complicated, owing in part to internecine feuds in the MacDonald family, in part to the devious behavior of Argyll, who had his eye on the MacDonald patrimony in Kintyre. The earl's preoccupation with Kintyre led him to neglect his obligation to pursue the clan Gregor; not until he had obtained and consolidated a legal grip on the peninsula did he turn his full attention to that nameless race.[47]

There was some discussion in 1603 of using Argyll to collect the king's rents in the isles, but the council had to prod him to get him to do anything at all in 1604 and 1605, and this may explain the decision in 1605 to continue the unsuccessful policy of the last few years, of summoning the lieges and putting on a show of force in order to collect the rents. Lord Scone, who was both comptroller and captain of the new police force, was the obvious choice to lead the expedition. The commission issued to Scone in August 1605 indicated what the council really wanted in the highlands: that more money be got out of the area by agreement with the local chiefs. The expedition was no more successful than its predecessors, however. There were the usual delays, and more than the usual grumbling on the part of the lieges. Scone did get to Kintyre in September, but his summons to the chiefs was honored largely in the breach, and his survey of the crown lands in the peninsula showed a considerable increase in waste land since the last survey, made in 1596. There was one important result, however: the confiscation of the holdings of Angus MacDonald of Dunyveg, which in the following year were leased to the earl of Argyll for 10,000 merks annual rental, a step which foreshadowed the next phase of highland policy, which was to develop in 1607.[48]

On the borders the council pursued a much more vigorous policy, chiefly because it was now possible to crack down on lawlessness with real hope of success. On his return from England in March 1605 Dunfermline found the Edinburgh tolbooth full of

Maxwells and Johnstones, which he regarded as "a very great and good novelty."[49] In the same month the king appointed a commission of justiciary for what were now called the "middle shires," five Englishmen and five Scots who were to meet together frequently to preserve order, deliver fugitives, disarm the lawless, end feuds, and see to the swift administration of justice; they were to report to both privy councils every two months. To help them do their job, a local police force was established; on the Scottish side it consisted of a twenty-five-man troop of horse under the command of Sir William Cranston, the deputy lieutenant on the borders. The council agreed to supply the commissioners with a clerk and urged them to act both swiftly and severely. Speed was important because border jails were notoriously porous, and the burghs there complained about having to support the impecunious ruffians lodged in them to await trial.[50]

The commissioners set to work, and in the first year or so of their appointment they, by their own report, executed 32 malefactors, banished 15, and outlawed 140, not counting 27 executed on three different occasions at special assizes held by the earl of Dunbar. The English figures for approximately the same time period were 52 executed and 45 outlawed.[51] Despite this exemplary show of severity—on the Scottish side a man was executed for the theft of a single sheep—there was considerable dissatisfaction in both countries with the way the system worked. The English commissioners complained repeatedly about Cranston, who, they charged, was allowing English fugitives to go about openly in Edinburgh and elsewhere; Cranston in his turn complained of overwork and of the unreasonable English demand that he be everywhere at once. Cranston also suffered from the handicap of most Jacobean officials: his pay, and that of his men, was normally far in arrears.[52] So much friction developed between Cranston and the English commissioners that finally, in May 1606, Cranston challenged the chief of the English commission, Sir Wilfred Lawson, to make a formal charge against him if he thought he could make it stick.[53] No charge was made, but not even the intervention of Dunbar, who arrived on the borders in May, could smooth things over for long. Clearly something had to be done.

On 4 March 1606 the Scottish council gave the king its considered judgment on the question. The present system worked badly because there were too many commissioners, which made getting a quorum difficult, and because there was no one person in charge. The council proposed, therefore, that there should be only two commissioners on each side, plus a chief who should be someone with interests on both sides of the border; Dunbar was the logical man. The councillors were careful not to blame Cranston, and the king agreed. He publicly approved Cranston's work and gave him a general pardon for any illegalities he might have committed in the pursuit of order, and in December 1606 he appointed Dunbar as chief of a revamped border commission with virtually full power to reorganize border administration.[54]

iii

The establishment of Dunbar's hegemony over border administration at the end of 1606 was no surprise. It was, in fact, a consequence of his new hegemony in Scottish politics. At the beginning of 1605, after the conclusion of the union negotiations, Dunbar and Dunfermline appeared to be on about an equal footing with James, with the chancellor having perhaps a slight advantage. By the middle of 1606 the scales had tipped decisively the other way; Dunbar was firmly in control, and remained so for the rest of his life.

The crisis which undermined Dunfermline's position had to do with the church, and was not altogether of his own making. Rather surprisingly, it had nothing to do with his personal beliefs. The issue was whether he had improperly authorized the clerical opponents of the bishops to hold a General Assembly in the summer of 1605. It might seem surprising that the Catholic chancellor could be charged, and with some justice, with favoring the antiepiscopal party in the Scottish church: these, after all, were the people who had nearly ruined him in 1596 and who were most vehement in their hatred of Popery. The surface explanation is that Dunfermline disliked Archbishop Spottiswoode and feared his political ambitions. This is true enough; in addition to his personal animosity, Dunfermline shared the traditional hostility of his class to clergymen who meddled in politics. But there was also a good deal of political calculation in his attitude. By showing himself to be sympathetic to the bishops' opponents in the church, he could simultaneously lessen their hostility to him as an individual and perhaps hedge round the powers of the restored episcopate with some restrictions. Dunfermline's political strategy was sound enough, but his tactical errors and miscalculations in the delicate situation which developed in 1605 gave his enemies a handle against him which almost ruined him.

The crisis began with the publication on 7 June 1605 of James's decision to postpone the meeting of the General Assembly scheduled for Aberdeen in July. The king had no intention of allowing the assembly to meet again until the position of the episcopate was far more secure than it currently was, but of course the letter to the presbyteries announcing the postponement did not say this; it merely stated that the king did not want the assembly to meet until after the next meeting of parliament, which was scheduled for November. The postponement, while not unexpected, was galling enough to the anti-episcopalian faction in the church; what made it still worse was that, contrary to previous practice, it set no future date to which the meeting was postponed. One of these ministers, a respected moderate, John Forbes, whose account of the affair is the fullest we have, thereupon sought out Dunfermline and made clear his distress, and that of his like-minded colleagues, at the king's decision.[55]

Dunfermline was alarmed. The ferment of the previous year had convinced him that this postponement would cause real trouble from the anti-episcopal faction in the church. So he did what he could to meet objections which seemed not unreasonable. According to Forbes, the chancellor promised that the council would request rather than order the ministers to disperse, and Forbes in his turn promised that the assembly would do no more than put off its business to some future time. The council's letter, dated 20 June, was studiously polite. It stated that the king had not consented to the meeting; therefore, to avoid his majesty's wrath, the ministers should dissolve themselves and go home, and ask the king's permission before appointing a new meeting date. The letter was addressed "To our truest friends, the brethren of the ministry, convened at their Assembly at Aberdeen"; because of this, the ministers assembled there—a very small number, since most presbyteries had heeded the letter of postponement and sent no delegates—argued that the letter could not be received until the meeting was formally constituted. Lauriston, the royal commissioner, accepted this and nominated Forbes himself as moderator. Once organized, the assembly formally received the council's letter and agreed to dissolve—but not *sine die*. The assembly would meet again at Aberdeen on the last Tuesday of September, and the presbyteries were to be so notified.[56]

At this point Lauriston suddenly woke up to what he had done. The king had specifically ordered that the assembly was not to convene, and Lauriston had allowed it to do so. Worse still, Lauriston's action had called in question the authority of the present commissioners of assembly, whose mandate ran from one assembly to the next, and therefore technically expired with the present convening. Lauriston desperately tried to recover by declaring that he did not recognize the present gathering as a lawful assembly, and, producing the king's proclamation forbidding the holding of an assembly, ordered the ministers to disperse on pain of horning.[57] After they had done so, he went still further and declared that, on the day before the assembly was due to convene, he had publicly forbidden it to meet, by open proclamation at the Market Cross in Aberdeen. "He was not able," says Calderwood, "to produce one man in all Aberdeen to verify this lie," but the council chose to believe him and on 18 July denounced the ministers for disobedience to the king's commands.[58] Whatever they may have felt about Lauriston's veracity, the councillors really had no choice; for the sake of the commissioners' authority they had to accept his story.

This action put Dunfermline into a very awkward position. Before Lauriston invented his story, the chancellor had talked to three ministers who had been present—though not Forbes—and, on being assured that no act against either the bishops or the commissioners had been moved, had, according to Forbes, expressed his satisfaction with their proceedings.[59] As evidences of the king's anger multiplied, however, it behooved the chancellor to walk very warily. On 25 July Forbes was brought before the council and asked if he thought the recent gathering in Aberdeen was a lawful assembly. He attempted to sidestep, saying that it was up to the next General Assembly to make that determination, a line which the accused ministers were steadfastly to take for the next year and a half. The council pressed him, and he said that his private judgment was that it was lawful. That was enough for the council. Forbes and some of the other ministers were ordered to ward in Blackness; it was, said Dunfermline, the king's will. Forbes, he said, had broken a promise—no doubt he was thinking of the setting of a precise date for the reconvening of the assembly. Forbes denied that he had broken any promises, and Dunfermline, seeing the abyss at his feet, dropped the matter, but not quickly enough: Archbishop Spottiswoode remembered the exchange. It showed that Dunfermline and Forbes had been in touch with each other before the Aberdeen meeting; there might be something here "to procure the Chancellor his disgrace, as suspected to be an enemy to the estate of Bishops."[60]

The news of the goings-on at Aberdeen enraged King James. He had hoped that a convention of estates planned for early August could make some progress in restoring the powers and estate of the bishops, but both Spottiswoode and Dunbar agreed that to try to do anything for the bishops except in parliament would be too risky, and the planned meeting of the estates was cancelled.[61] Now, instead of progress in the direction of greater control of the church, it looked as if many of the old questions about meetings of the General Assembly were about to be reopened.

James was determined to punish the people responsible for the recent meeting at Aberdeen and those ministers who refused to admit its illegality, and the temporizing attitude displayed by the most radical of Scottish synods, that of Fife, at its meeting in September, encouraged him to believe that a policy of severity would be successful.[62] So the wheels began to turn. On 24 October 1605 Dunfermline presided over the decisive meeting of the privy council. Fourteen ministers, led by Forbes, declared that the question of the lawfulness of any General Assembly could only be determined by the kirk, i.e., by another General Assembly, and that therefore the council did not have jurisdiction in this case. They were careful to point out that they were declining jurisdiction in this case only, and that they were declining the council's jurisdiction, not the king's. They were willing to present their arguments as to the legality of the meeting, without withdrawing their declinature. The council found their conclusions unacceptable and returned them to prison until the king's further pleasure was known.[63]

This was a serious setback for the chancellor. He and Hamilton had tried very hard to persuade the ministers to give way on the jurisdictional question, even if they were unwilling to admit the illegality of the Aberdeen meeting. Dunfermline wanted them to throw themselves on the king's mercy; if they did so, they would probably be released, or at worst warded for a time in their own parishes, and the possibility of a real confrontation would be averted.[64] Dunfermline knew how James would react to their declinature of jurisdiction, however narrow and technical the ground, and there were indications already that the king's anticipated severity would produce an ugly backlash. James Melville's long *Apology for the Prisoners of the Lord Jesus Presently in the Castle of Blackness* was being circulated to some effect. The fact that the warded ministers had to pay their own expenses, while the Catholic ex-abbot of Newabbey, a perennial troublemaker, got a merk a day from the government while in prison, caused resentment.[65] Spottiswoode himself urged the king not to make an issue of the jurisdictional question, which could lead to a treason trial, and simply exile all those who held that the Aberdeen meeting was lawful. The continued imprisonment of the ministers was very unpopular, said Spottiswoode, and the bishops were being blamed for it. In making this plea for leniency Spottiswoode suggested that the council's hard line was deliberately designed to produce an anti-episcopal reaction: "This, and many other things, Sir, are done of mere policy, to disappoint your Majesty's affairs in the Parliament, specially that concern our Estate."[66] The king was not moved.

The sudden appearance of Dunbar in the middle of winter indicated that the king had decided on his course of action. The ministers were given one more opportunity to abandon their declinature; they refused,[67] and their trial for treason went for-

ward—one of the most celebrated trials in the reign of James VI.
It was arranged very quickly, to minimize the accuseds' opportunity for preparation, and was held on 10 January 1606 in Linlithgow rather than Edinburgh; the six ministers, including Forbes,
who were warded in Blackness, a few miles from Linlithgow, were
those put on trial. Dunbar carefully packed the assize: six of the
fifteen jurors were Homes. Two of the ministers' counsel refused
to appear; young Thomas Hope, who bore the brunt of the defense, did a remarkably skillful job and made his reputation as an
advocate, but he could not save his clients. They were found guilty
by a vote of nine to six, with five of Dunbar's relatives voting to
convict.[68]

To obtain even this slim majority, Lord Advocate Hamilton had
to threaten the jurors with a charge of willful error—an indication
of the political weakness of the government's case. Whatever the
technical legal merits of the charge, to try these men for treason
for what they had done was excessive, and everyone in Scotland
knew it. After the trial Balmerino sent an account of the proceedings to the king. It had all been very difficult, said the secretary,
and if Dunbar had not managed it with his combination of secrecy,
adroitness, threats, and jury-packing, they might not have gotten a
conviction. He urged the king to deal with the other eight ministers who were awaiting trial on the same charge by a simple process of banishment if they refused to withdraw their declinatures.
Lord Advocate Hamilton said much the same thing and shuddered
at how near they had come to failure; there should be as few such
trials as possible, he said, since it was so difficult to get an honest
jury![69] As for the chancellor, he wrote Salisbury that the value of
the trial was that it showed that even ministers could be convicted
of treason if they violated the law. Even so, the amount of resentment generated outweighed the value of the moral lesson. "I desire not his sacred Majesty to put us oft to such proofs, for I assure
your Lordship in truth in this kingdom the puritanism is very far
predominant, and albeit this be done to his Majesty's will and
wish, it is not without a greater grudge and malcontentment nor
(than) the consequence of it can be of avail."[70]

James, however, was in no mood to be conciliatory, and saw no
necessity for it. On 22 January he ordered the trial of the other

eight ministers. The conviction of the first batch, more careful jury selection, and the publication of a declaration in defense of the government's proceedings, which Balmerino was instructed to write, would make it easier to get another conviction, James explained. After the second trial he would reveal his decision on the ministers' punishment. The councillors were horrified, and sent back a reply which, for all its polite language, amounted to a refusal to comply. A further trial was unnecessary, they said, since the legal point respecting jurisdiction had been made. Given the state of public opinion, a second jury might not convict. There was a veiled but unmistakable threat that there would be resignations if the king insisted on the second trial. The king was sufficiently impressed to agree to wait for a while, until he had a chance to talk to Dunbar and others, and until there was an opportunity to see if his severity would have any useful effect. He quickly learned that it had not. In February the various provincial synods refused to accept a series of articles which, in one version at least, would have amounted to an acknowledgment of royal supremacy over the church. It was evident that the ministers were not cowed.[71]

James was clearly discontented with the way matters were going in his ancient kingdom, and he was on the watch for saboteurs. The chancellor's enemies decided to take advantage of the king's mood to launch a campaign against him and, to a lesser degree, against Secretary Balmerino. The origins of this intrigue are obscure. Dunbar may have begun it, out of ambition and irritation at the chancellor and the secretary for saddling him with the odium of the Linlithgow trial,[72] but the man who took the lead was Archbishop Spottiswoode. In his *History* the archbishop maintained that Dunfermline, and Balmerino too, were violating the king's command to them to promote the position of bishops in the church. This allegation did them something less than justice, but many people believed it.[73] The line Spottiswoode took with the king, according to Forbes, was that the ancient nobility, who were the chief obstacles to the revival of episcopacy, regarded Dunfermline and Balmerino as upstarts, and would more readily acquiesce in the king's ecclesiastical policy, which many of them did not like,[74] if the two were dismissed. There were also, said Forbes, less disinterested motives. Spottiswoode was "puffed up with hope to be chancellor," and Dunfermline's alleged hostility to episcopacy was based in part on fear for his position. By the end of February 1606, owing in part to a letter from Forbes himself, in part to the persuasions of Spottiswoode, Dunbar, and Lord Fleming, Montrose's nephew, who resented Dunfermline's having displaced his uncle as chancellor, James had reached the point of willingness to oust Dunfermline and Balmerino if they could be convicted of "undutifulness."[75]

The attack focused on Dunfermline; if he could be brought down, it would be an easy matter either to oust Balmerino or to cow him. The ground chosen was the chancellor's "intelligence, foreknowledge, and approbation of the Assembly at Aberdeen"; Forbes was to be his principal accuser. This was fortunate for Dunfermline. There were more witnesses to his subsequent approval of the way the ministers had behaved at Aberdeen, but Forbes was not one of them, and what Spottiswoode knew about was the connection between Dunfermline and Forbes. He was also fortunate in that his enemies overreached themselves. They attempted to intimidate Forbes, the only witness they had, by telling him that if he could not make his charges against the chancellor stick, his accusations would be turned against him. Forbes promptly shut up, either because he felt that his story would be insufficient or because "they did intend rather to disgrace him than to harm the Chancellor." So in his hearing on 24 May before eight councillors, including Dunbar, who had recently returned to Scotland to take a hand in the game, Forbes was extremely cautious. He would not, he said, accuse the chancellor of anything, but merely answer any accusations the councillors might have to make against himself. When pressed, he asked that Dunfermline be summoned to face him. The councillors refused on the ground that the chancellor had denied having any conversation with Forbes about the assembly. Forbes thereupon replied that he would not undertake to prove anything about his own conversation with Dunfermline prior to the assembly, since it was obvious that the chancellor had the only witness, his close friend Alexander Burnet of Leys, in his pocket. He would simply undertake to show, by witnesses other than himself, that Dunfermline had afterward approved what they had done, and would write to the king to that effect. The day set for the hearing was 13 June; in the meantime Forbes was imprisoned in Edinburgh castle.[76]

The chancellor soon heard all about Forbes's interrogation from someone who was present, probably the lord advocate, who was hostile to Forbes,[77] and he quickly decided on his defense. On 25 May he wrote to James, and with the proper classical allusions put the matter very simply. Forbes, a condemned traitor, accuses the king's chancellor, who denies the charge. Forbes upholds the lawfulness of the Aberdeen meeting; the chancellor has condemned it as seditious and unlawful. "Your Sacred Majesty has to judge, which of the two is most worthy of credit."[78] Dunfermline's argument was put with great skill and was extremely effective, especially as Forbes was apparently shifting ground, no longer seeking to prove prior approbation of the assembly, and relying on others to make his charges stick. Dunbar and Fleming attempted to keep James in a hostile frame of mind, but by this time the chancellor had mobilized his allies, both in Scotland and at court, especially the queen and the earl of Salisbury. So the king made up his mind. The June hearing was to be held, but the chancellor was not to be adjudged guilty on the basis of anything said by a convicted felon like Forbes; "neither would he have him put from his office albeit that matter were proven."[79]

"And so," wrote William Scot, "Mr. John Spotswood, Bishop of Glasgow, the delator, was disappointed at that time": the chancellor would survive. Dunbar therefore made sure that the hearing on 13 June was meaningless.[80] Dunfermline himself wrote again, once more protesting his innocence and saying that "I was never so careful to have your Majesty served to all contentment in any other thing, as I was in that particular in staying of the Assembly at Aberdeen, because it was so highly recommended unto me by your Sacred Majesty"[81]—and in his defense he could point to the council's proclamation of 20 June 1605. The disgruntled Spottiswoode alleged that James was convinced that both parties were lying, and that Dunfermline would betray the interests of the crown to satisfy his hatred of bishops.[82] This is certainly not true; if James had believed this of Dunfermline, he would have dismissed him without question.

So the chancellor escaped disaster, but at the cost of losing all chance of becoming the king's principal adviser in Scottish affairs. His skillful conduct of the union negotiations had given him an opportunity, but his recent miscalculations had convinced James that Dunbar was the man to carry out the royal program, especially in the church. Dunfermline had overestimated the size of the backlash which another postponement of the General Assembly would produce, as the small size of the gathering at Aberdeen demonstrated. Where Dunfermline had temporized with Forbes and his associates, Dunbar had been ruthless with them—and ruthlessness, in James's view, might well be necessary to restore the bishops to their ancient authority. The lord treasurer had triumphed and was now supreme in the king's councils. The most active period of James's absentee kingship was about to begin.

NOTES

1. *RPCS* VI, 554–55.

2. For these acts see *ibid.*, pp. 556–61.

3. Two indications of this are that the only official formally empowered before James's departure to appoint deputies for the exercise of his office was Lord Advocate Hamilton and that one of the six Scots immediately appointed to the English privy council was Secretary Elphinstone. These two, as it turned out, were among those who did not remain permanently in England.

4. James in fact went south without his family, but Queen Anne and the two older children were expected to follow shortly, which they did.

5. This paragraph is taken largely from W. Taylor, "The King's Mails, 1603–1625," *SHR* XLII (1963), 143–47. See also *RPCS* VI, 566–68, 570–71, VII, 63, X, 832–39, XII, 82–83, 365; PRO, SP 14/64, no. 40.

6. Previous efforts, in 1597 and 1600, to establish such a force had foundered for lack of funds. T. I. Rae, *The Administration of the Scottish Frontier, 1513–1603* (Edinburgh, 1966), p. 219. 11 Aug. 1600, Nicolson to Cecil, 19 Oct., Hudson to Cecil, *CSP Scot.* XIII, 682, 713.

7. *RPCS* VI, 581–82, 584–85, 590–92.

8. *Ibid.*, 407–9, 589–90, 594–96, 598, VII, 464, 577, XIV, 410–12, 417–18, 2nd ser., VIII, 258–59. *Melros* I, 4–5. *LEA* I, 353–54.

9. *LSP*, p. 56.

10. PRO, SP 14/2, no. 57.

11. *RPCS* VI, 602.

12. *Calderwood* VI, 229. *RPCS* VI, 577, VII, xxxi, 488–89. S. G. E. Lythe, *The Economy of Scotland in Its European Setting 1550–1625* (Edinburgh, 1960), pp. 201–2. For the coinage see also 1 Apr. 1603, Secretary Elphinstone (now Lord Balmerino) to Cecil, *Salisbury* XV, 26–28.

13. *RPCS* VI, 596–97.

14. *Calderwood* VI, 248. Calderwood prints the official version of the decisions of the conference and the covering letter from Patrick Galloway, *ibid.*, pp. 241–46.

15. William Scot thought so; see *Scot,* p. 72.

16. 30 Apr. 1604, Balmerino to James, 4 May, Balmerino to Cecil, Sir William Fraser, *The Elphinstone Family Book of the Lords Elphinstone, Balmerino, and Coupar* (Edinburgh, 1897) II, 168–71. *APS* IV, 261–62.

17. *Calderwood* VI, 264–67. *Melvill,* pp. 560–64. John Forbes, *Certaine Records Touching the Estate of the Church of Scotland,* ed. D. Laing, Wodrow Society (Edinburgh, 1846), pp. 376–77. *RPCS* VII, 13–14.

18. *Calderwood* VI, 263, 270–71. *Melvill,* pp. 560, 565–66. *APS* IV, 264.

19. There are accounts of the meeting in *Calderwood* VI, 271–73, *Melvill,* pp. 566–69, and *Scot,* pp. 129–31. The quotation is from Calderwood's account.

20. 10 Dec. 1604, Huntly to James, *LSP,* pp. 60–62. 3/13 Sept. 1606, Giustinian to the doge and senate, *CSP Venetian 1603–1607,* p. 401. For Bancroft see G. Donaldson, "The Attitude of Whitgift and Bancroft to the Scottish Church," *Transactions of the Royal Historical Society,* 4th ser., XXIV (1942), 95–115.

21. *LEA* I, 12–13. The phrase "general business" is Delphic; the letter was written within two months of the conclusion of the union negotiations, however, which suggests that that is the reference.

22. Quoted in Lythe, *Economy of Scotland,* p. 200.

23. On this question see G. Donaldson, "Foundations of Anglo-Scottish Union," in S. T. Bindoff, J. Hurstfield, and C. H. Williams, eds., *Elizabethan Government and Society* (London, 1961), pp. 282–314.

24. 14 May 1604, Balmerino to Cecil, *Salisbury* XVI, 98–99. C. H. McIlwain, ed., *The Political Works of James I* (Cambridge, Mass., 1918), p. 301. For the parallel with the Netherlands see C. V. Wedgwood, "Anglo-Scottish Relations, 1603–40," *Transactions of the Royal Historical Society,* 4th ser., XXXII (1950), 34–35.

25. For a summary of the English arguments on this point see Lythe, *Economy of Scotland,* pp. 207–9.

26. *Salisbury* XX, 305–6. Nichols, *Progresses* I, 269–71. For James's gifts during his first year see *ibid.,* pp. 426–27. It ought to be mentioned, by way of balance, that of the sixty knights of the Bath created at James's coronation only seven were Scots.

27. Nichols, *Progresses* I, 169, 190. *CSP Venetian 1603–1607,* p. 33. A. J. Loomie, *Guy Fawkes in Spain,* special supplement, *Bulletin of the Institute of Historical Research* (London, 1971), pp. 61–63.

28. McIlwain, *Works,* p. 295. In Jan. 1608, for instance, he gave a two-year authorization to the courtier-poet Sir William Alexander to collect arrears of taxes owing to the English government from the years 1547–88. There is no evidence that Alexander made much money out of this, but the feelings toward Scots of any Englishman he dunned can well be imagined. See T. H. McGrail, *Sir William Alexander* (Edinburgh, 1940), p. 62.

29. 14 Mar. 1604, Seton to Cecil, 4 May, 14 May, Balmerino to Cecil, *Salisbury* XVI, 39–40, 86–87, 98–99. 28 Apr., Cecil to Balmerino, PRO, SP 14/7, no. 85. 4 May, Mar to Cecil, PRO, SP 14/8, no. 10.

30. *APS* IV, 263–64. *Calderwood* VI, 262–64. James's letters of instructions in May and June 1604 are in *RPCS* VII, 457–61.

31. *RCRB* II, 182–83, 189–91. For the economic problems involved see S. G. E. Lythe, "The Union of the Crowns in 1603 and the Debate on Economic Integration," *Scottish Journal of Political Economy* V (1958), 219–28, and his *Economy of Scotland,* pp. 199–215. The quoted phrase is on p. 209.

32. NLS, Denmilne Mss. I, no. 21.

33. Seton rejoiced in a good many different titles during his career: prior of Pluscardine, Lord Urquhart, and most recently Lord Fyvie. For convenience's sake I have referred to him thus far only as *Seton;* henceforth he will be called *Dunfermline.*

34. The text of the treaty is in John Bruce, *Report on the Events and Circumstances Which Produced the Union of the Kingdoms of England and Scotland* (London, 1799) II, lxxv–xciii. There is a convenient summary in *RPCS* VII, xxxii–xxxiv. BM, Add. Mss. 26,635, contains an account of the meetings of the commissioners. See also *Spottiswoode* III, 145–56, and D. H. Willson, "James I and Anglo-Scottish Unity," in W. A. Aiken and B. D. Henning, eds., *Conflict in Stuart England* (London, 1960), pp. 43–55.

35. SRO, PC 9/1.

36. As Sir William Bowes wrote in 1599, "He is resolved to take none for faithful to him, which were not faithful to his mother"; see *CSP Scot.* XIII, 466.

37. On this point see, e.g., 27 Mar. 1606, Dunfermline to Salisbury, PRO, SP 14/19, no. 88, and 16 May 1609, the council to James, *RPCS* VIII, 579–80. In 1609 the convention of royal burghs was driven to appoint a consul in Lisbon because the English consul, while collecting a ducat from each Scottish ship that put in there, was doing nothing about the Scots' needs and complaints; see *RCRB* II, 279–80.

38. Hamilton was connected with the great noble family, but for three generations his forebears had been either lawyers or merchants in Edinburgh.

39. The rewards these men and other privy councillors received are detailed in William Taylor, "The Scottish Privy Council 1603–25" (Ph.D. thesis, Edinburgh University, 1950), App. D.

40. 20 Apr. 1605, Dunfermline to Salisbury, *Salisbury* XVII, 149–50. See also *RPCS* VII, 19–21, 34; 10 Dec. 1604, Huntly to James, *LSP,* pp. 60–62; 9 Mar. 1605, Dunfermline, Scone, and Balmerino to James, and to Alexander Hay, NLS, Denmilne Mss. I, nos. 32, 33; n.d., Huntly to Dunfermline, *ibid.* II, no. 36; 20 Apr., Dunfermline to James, *LSP,* pp. 71–72.

41. H. M. Conacher, "Land Tenure in Scotland in the 17th Century," *Juridical Review* L (1938), 18–19. For the figures on the rents in victual see BM, Add. Ms. 24,277, ff. 3–4b. P. Hume Brown, *History of Scotland* (Cambridge, 1912) II, 241, points out that for the most part Scotsmen received their rewards in gifts out of Scottish rather than English revenues.

42. *RPCS* VII, 19–20.

43. *Ibid.*, pp. 59, 530–31, 533, 415. *Spottiswoode* III, 164–65.

44. R. K. Hannay, *The College of Justice* (Edinburgh, 1933), pp. 118–25.

45. *RPCS* VII, 164–77, 490–91. NLS, Denmilne Mss. I, no. 45.

46. *RPCS* VII, 255. See also *ibid.*, pp. 84–90, 204–5, 229–30. For the king's views see his letter of 11 Feb. 1605 to the council, *ibid.*, pp. 465–66.

47. On this point see A. Cunningham, *The Loyal Clans* (Cambridge, 1932), p. 157.

48. 28 Oct. 1603, Balmerino to Cecil, *Salisbury* XV, 273–74. *RPCS* VII, 59–60, 91–92, 115–17, 528, 589–90. D. Gregory, *The History of the Western Highlands and Isles of Scotland,* 2nd ed. (London, 1881), p. 308.

49. 3 Mar. 1605, Dunfermline to James, *LSP,* pp. 67–68. *RPCS* VII, 58.

50. *RPCS* VII, 701–7, 709–12.

51. *Ibid.*, pp. 717–20. *Salisbury* XVIII, 212–13.

52. NLS, Mss. 5723, pp. 175–76, 286–88, 290–91, Mss. 5724, pp. 553–56. *RPCS* VII, 714–17.

53. NLS, Mss. 5274, pp. 636–37, 646–48.

54. *RPCS* VII, 286–87, 486–87, 504–5, 506. NLS, Mss. 5275, pp. 989–93.

55. Forbes, *Certaine Records,* p. 384. 9 June 1605, Balmerino to James, *LSP,* pp. 65–66. See also 2 May, Lauriston to James, *LEA* I, 17–18.

56. Forbes, *Certaine Records,* pp. 385, 388–90.

57. *RPCS* VII, 62. *Calderwood* VI, 283–84. The council had issued this proclamation on 20 June, the same date as its letter to the assembly.

58. *Calderwood* VI, 286. *RPCS* VII, 82–83.

59. Forbes, *Certaine Records,* pp. 401–2.

60. *Ibid.*, pp. 403–6. The quotation is on p. 406. Forbes claims, *ibid.*, pp. 389–90, that Dunfermline had in fact agreed in their conversation that it would be all right to continue the assembly to another date, and had reneged on this promise in the council's letter.

61. Fraser, *Elphinstone* II, 149, 150.

62. For this meeting see *Calderwood* VI, 296–97, and *Scot,* p. 138.

63. Forbes, *Certaine Records,* pp. 429–34, 438. *Calderwood* VI, 345–54. *Spottiswoode* III, 161–63. *RPCS* VII, 134–37.

64. Forbes, *Certaine Records,* pp. 433–34, 451–52.

65. *Calderwood* VI, 367–68. *Melvill,* pp. 599–612, gives his text.

66. 26 Dec. 1605, Spottiswoode to James, *LEA* I, 24–25.

67. Forbes, *Certaine Records,* pp. 453–61. *Melvill,* pp. 618–19. *Calderwood* VI, 374–75.

68. There are accounts of the trial in *Scot,* pp. 149–55, *Calderwood* VI, 377–91, *Melvill,* pp. 620–26, and Forbes, *Certaine Records,* pp. 363–96. See also R. Pitcairn, ed., *Ancient Criminal Trials in Scotland* II, pt. 2 (Edinburgh, 1833), 494–502.

69. *RPCS* VII, 478–80. *Melros* I, 10–12.

70. PRO, SP 14/18, no. 31.

71. *RPCS* VII, 480–86. Forbes, *Certaine Records,* p. 498. *Calderwood* VI, 392,

396. *Melvill,* pp. 627–31. 1 Jan. 1606, Patrick Galloway to James, *LEA* I, 27–28.

72. Forbes, *Certaine Records,* pp. 498–99.

73. *Spottiswoode* III, 157, 174. *Calderwood* VI, 477.

74. See, e.g., 13 Jan. 1606, Fleming to James, *LEA* I, 34.

75. Forbes, *Certaine Records,* pp. 501–3, 513.

76. *Ibid.,* pp. 513, 537–38, 541–45.

77. *Ibid.,* p. 545.

78. *LEA* I, 50–51.

79. Forbes, *Certaine Records,* p. 547. See also *Calderwood* VI, 477.

80. Forbes, *Certaine Records,* pp. 547–50. *RPCS* VII, 492–93.

81. *LEA* I, 52–53.

82. *Spottiswoode* III, 174–75. The archbishop's account of the events of May and June is very inaccurate. He telescopes the two hearings into one and claims that Dunfermline was present, got into an argument with Forbes, and admitted that the ministers thought him Popish.

3

Dunbar in Power:
The Triumph of the Bishops

DUNBAR'S SUPREMACY in Scottish politics was to last for four and a half years, from the middle of 1606 until his death in January 1611. In these years and thereafter King James made no further attempt to act as his own chief minister in his ancient kingdom. Dunbar as his agent carried out his wishes, and they expected the council in Edinburgh to do as it was told. Dunbar was a courtier still, as he had always been. There is no evidence that he had any substantive ideas of his own about policy; his function was to translate the royal wishes into accomplished facts. This meant that he concerned himself primarily with matters which preoccupied the king—the "middle shires," for instance, and especially the church and the union. In other areas, such as the highlands and economic policy, where James's attention was intermittent, the council in Edinburgh had more scope for independent action.

Dunbar's fundamental concern, then, was procedural: how to implement the king's commands and thus maintain his supremacy. His problem was not simple. Keeping his influence with James hinged on remaining at court; at the same time he was well aware of all the pitfalls, all the potential foot-dragging, obfuscation, and intrigue, involved in trying to govern at long distance. So he did what he had to do: he traveled. He went back and forth between London and Edinburgh at least once a year, usually more often, frequently in very bad weather, a considerable expenditure of time and energy which may well have shortened his life. His appearances in Scotland had something of the impact of a royal visit.

Even before his final triumph over the chancellor no one doubted that Dunbar was the bearer and interpreter of the king's wishes, and the council treated him accordingly.[1] His occasional employment of the tactics of surprise, of not revealing the king's orders until he judged that the psychological moment had arrived, added to his effectiveness.[2] So did his skill at isolating those he had marked down for destruction, and his obvious willingness to be as ruthless and intimidating as necessary. For Dunfermline and his colleagues in Edinburgh these methods posed certain problems, apart from the obvious one of remaining on good terms with the occasionally unpredictable Dunbar. There had to be constant reference to the court for decisions on a great many questions, which was often a handicap where speed would have been helpful or where only local knowledge and investigation would serve. It also meant absenteeism with its resulting inefficiency—in September 1608, for instance, the council had to ask James to allow Justice-depute Hart to return to Scotland from court, since his absence was causing serious delays in the administration of justice.[3] But there is no doubt that Dunbar's system worked. Scotland was indeed governed from London during these years, the years of King James's celebrated boast, but it was less government by pen than it was government by visitation.

The years of Dunbar's predominance saw a good many important developments in Scottish public life, the most controversial of which was the reimposition of diocesan episcopacy. The first major step in this direction after Dunbar's triumph over the chancellor was taken at the parliament held in Perth in July 1606. The decision to meet in Perth rather than Edinburgh was taken at the last minute. The official reason for the transfer was that there was plague in Edinburgh, which was true enough, but the real reason, according to Calderwood and the other presbyterian historians, was that the atmosphere of the capital was too hostile to episcopacy and that the chancellor was too popular there.[4] The king and Dunbar had carefully prepared the way for this parliament, known as the red parliament because of the dazzling display at the opening procession. There were negotiations with individual nobles who held the temporalities of some of the bishoprics.[5] In addition, James provided Dunbar with a letter expressing his desire for "the

dissolving of that discommendable act of Annexation and reestab-
lishing . . . the estate of bishops." Dunbar showed this letter to
various members of the aristocracy, who undertook to write to
James promising their support in parliament.[6] The commissioners
of assembly had of course been told, and all the "well-affected"
among them were pleased, though some, like Gledstanes, were
worried that they might be "made rather notional than real
bishops." The choosing of the committee of the articles was carefully managed and the king's slate unanimously accepted. William
Cowper, the minister at Perth, was allowed to preach just before
the opening of parliament, which he did "to the contentment of
the godly," but the government was careful to stipulate who
should preach while parliament was sitting.[7]

For all the king's precautions it was not easy to get his program
through. The repeal of the act of annexation caused serious
qualms to all the many members of the landowning classes who
had profited materially from the religious vicissitudes of the last
seventy years or so; there was a struggle in the articles, which the
government won thanks chiefly to the chancellor—or so the
council reported to James. The government's task was made no
easier by a tactical slip on the part of Patrick Galloway, one of the
king's designated preachers, which gave the opponents of episcopacy the chance to raise the issue of the bishops' violation of the
restrictions voted at the Montrose assembly; Dunfermline had to
rebuff an attempt to have the committee of the articles write these
restrictions into law.[8] The act of repeal was carefully drawn in
order to cause as little controversy as possible; among other things
it contained a general statement ratifying all previously granted
erections out of the temporalities of nonepiscopal benefices. This
was not nearly enough to reassure the landed classes and guarantee its passage, however. And so there were rewards, very large
numbers of rewards and payoffs of all sorts, varying enormously in
size and importance. The great—Lennox, Mar, and the rest—had
their abbey lands turned into temporal lordships. The marquis of
Hamilton got Arbroath, in spite of the archbishop of Canterbury's
rather plaintively expressed suggestion to the king that it might go
to one of the poorer bishoprics instead;[9] James knew better than
to try anything as politically dangerous as that. The king's officials

also received their reward; the ratification of the earldom of Dunbar occupies five pages of print in the official record. London Scots like John Murray and Sir Thomas Erskine shared in the largesse. About 75 percent of the acts of this parliament consisted of these rewards, which went to various burghs as well as individuals. Nor did the bounty stop there. Four earldoms were handed out, and various lesser titles too, the last such large-scale distribution of peerages for thirteen years. Contrary to the opinion of some historians, James was well aware of the dangers inherent in the inflation of honors, especially Scottish honors: too many Scots peers would have a bad effect on English opinion and make further trouble for the union.[10]

Thus "the lords," wrote Calderwood bitterly in the palmy days of Archbishop Laud, "sold the liberties of the kirk, or purchased these temporal lordships with the thralldom of the kirk." And now they repent their partiality to the bishops, "for none are so earnest to stir up the king to revoke these erections, seeing they have gotten their own turn done. . . . But it is no wonder that traitors to God be traitors to men."[11]

The repeal of the act of annexation did not mean instant riches for the church. Many of the bishoprics were in very bad financial condition—just how bad the government tried to discover, but it proved difficult to get the necessary financial data. The king was anxious to do what he could without alienating the landed classes; one thing he could, and did, do was to give the bishoprics monastic properties still in the hands of the crown. Four of the poorer sees, Ross, Dunblane, Galloway, and the Isles, eventually profited in this way.[12] Other clergymen were worse off than the bishops, and the government knew that many of them might suffer on account of the wholesale erections of abbatial lands into temporal lordships. So parliament appointed a mixed clerical-lay commission to decide on the stipends of the ministers of those kirks contained on the erected lands. No beneficiary of these erections could get his charters officially confirmed until he had guaranteed the stipend the committee determined. One hundred thirty-three parishes at least had stipends assigned in this way. Many stipends were increased, some substantially; almost half obtained the 500 merks or more which the parliament of 1617 considered a satisfactory income.[13] The committee's work constituted the first real step toward the achievement of the "constant platt," the dream of an adequate stipend for every Scottish minister, which by fits and starts was gradually to be realized. King James believed thoroughly in this objective, although his occasional erratic generosity to his favorites was one of the obstacles standing in the way of its achievement. In this case he would have liked to extend the committee's charge to include kirks affected by all the confirmatory acts passed in this parliament, not just those involving abbey lands, and to give the committee greater coercive power than it ultimately received, but the council vetoed these suggestions on the ground that they would "breed . . . miscontentment" and thus jeopardize the whole legislative program.[14]

The other major action of this parliament was the voting of the very substantial tax of twenty shillings for each poundland of old extent. This was the largest tax the Scottish parliament had ever voted; the council calculated that it would bring in a total of 400,000 merks, a figure which, for tactical reasons, it did not make public while parliament was in session. The money was badly needed. The king's largesse had cut into the revenues from crown lands, and the implementation of the free-trade provisions of the union treaty entailed an immediate loss of customs revenue without any compensating gain. Officials still went personally into debt and were pursued at law by the government's creditors, who still found it difficult to collect what was owing to them. The departure of the court saved the treasury some money, of course, but there were new expenses like Scone's police force and Cranston's border guard. And many long-neglected projects now demanded attention, such as, for example, the provision of money to prevent further erosion of the town of Dumbarton by the sea and the Leven, and to repair the damage already done. In most such matters the king's attitude was unhelpful. There was no thought of providing Scotland with any financial aid from the English treasury, and James evinced considerable reluctance to spend Scottish money in this way either. On the contrary, one of his letters suggested that he planned to appropriate some of the proceeds of the tax of 1606 to his own use, possibly in connection with a visit to Scotland planned for 1608 which never materialized.[15]

The Scottish council in its reports to the king gave the lion's share of the credit for the success of the parliament to the chancellor, but not everyone agreed. Archbishop Spottiswoode, as might be expected, gave the credit to Dunbar, and so, indeed, did Dunfermline himself: "The Earl of Dunbar, by his industry, travail, diligence . . . has marvelously advanced the good success of all has been done . . . both in the Borders . . . and also in the parliament, where his behavior with the diversity of humours of our noblemen and others, show well he had narrowly remarked many lessons . . . of your sacred majesty's proceedings in such affairs."[16] From this time on the chancellor coupled praise for Dunbar with his praise for James in his letters to the king; he wanted no repetition of the events of the previous spring.

After the dissolution of the parliament James, Spottiswoode, and Dunbar moved rapidly to consolidate the gains they had made there with respect to the church by eliminating the remaining major clerical opponents of episcopacy, those who had not been entangled in the affair of the Aberdeen assembly. On 22 May 1606, before parliament met, James had written to eight of these, including the two Melvilles, inviting them to come to court in September to discuss the points of disagreement between him and them. The timing of the invitation was designed to further the episcopal cause at the parliament by showing the king in a conciliatory light; it had the incidental advantage of providing one more reason for postponing the General Assembly. The king's letter was studiously polite. Even so, the ministers were suspicious and reluctant to go, but they concluded that they really had no choice. As Dunbar pointed out to them, they could go willingly or under compulsion, but go they would.[17] So they went. The discussions were predictably inconclusive; eventually six of the eight were permitted to return to their parishes. But the two Melvilles were never to see Scotland again. Exile was also the fate of John Forbes and the five others convicted for their part in the Aberdeen assembly; they left Scotland in November 1606 after an emotional farewell from a large crowd, a scene described by Dunbar, who was not there, as "a thousand people railing against his Majesty's proceedings."[18] The eight ministers charged with Forbes's offense but not yet tried were ordered into ward in remote places like

Caithness and Kintyre. This order meant that James had accepted his councillors' advice; the eight would not be tried. In the course of time most of them returned to their parishes.[19] But for Forbes and his friends, as for the Melvilles, exile was to be permanent.

With the removal of these men the heart went out of the clerical resistance. The way was now clear to complete the job of imposing diocesan episcopacy, thus bringing nearer that union of the churches which, Archbishop Bancroft told James Melville, was now the object of the king's policy.[20] The first step was a conference at Linlithgow which James summoned in December 1606. The ostensible purpose of this meeting was to deal with the problem of Papists "and removing of jars in the kirk." The king's letters to the presbyteries indicated whom they should send, a large number of laymen and councillors were present, and Dunbar, amply provided with cash, went north to manage things. A moderator was chosen from a slate named by the king, but the gathering was told that this was not a General Assembly; it was simply a meeting called by the king. The crucial point was James's remedy for the "jars." Each presbytery was to have a permanent presiding officer, a constant moderator named by the king, who provided a list of his choices. The implication was that this was a temporary measure; as soon as there was unity within the church, the old system of election of moderators would presumably be restored. The doubters were assured that no attack upon the authority or independence of the General Assembly was intended, and that the designated constant moderator had to be accepted by the presbytery and was removable for cause. The bishops, who were to be moderators of their own presbyteries, protested that they wanted no additional jurisdiction, and if the next General Assembly, now set for July 1607, found them wanting, they would resign their bishoprics. So the conference agreed to accept the king's plan.[21]

The meeting went smoothly enough; Dunbar received his usual meed of praise for his adroit handling of its proceedings, and afterward he and Dunfermline kept Christmas in Edinburgh with great pomp, to the scandal of those Calderwood called the godly.[22] But there was one faintly ominous note. "Two noblemen, out of simplicity, desired a copy of such things as were concluded. It was answered, that could not be instantly done," and in fact no text was available for half a year, "after . . . it was returned back again from court."[23] The reason soon became clear: the record was to be altered, in three significant ways. The meeting was to be called a General Assembly. The bishops' renunciation of additional jurisdiction was qualified to cover only "tyrannous and unlawful" jurisdiction. And, above all, constant moderators were to be imposed on synods as well as presbyteries. This last decision may have been the king's—Calderwood alleges that he was annoyed at the paucity of results at Linlithgow, and blamed the bishops for their pusillanimity in not getting more—but its haste and callousness suggest the hand of Dunbar. It surfaced in April 1607, when Lord Scone, as the king's commissioner, vainly tried to impose a constant moderator on the synod of Perth and lost his temper in the process.[24] For the next year and a half the great issue in the church was whether or not the presbyteries, and particularly the synods, could be forced to accept these permanent moderators. Gradually, one by one, they did, succumbing to unrelenting governmental pressure, manipulation of stipends, and threats.[25] The bishops, as moderators of their synods and of the presbyteries of their cathedral cities, acquired their first *ex officio* ecclesiastical function, and thus took a major step toward the restoration of their ancient authority.

The privy council was unenthusiastic about the Linlithgow conference, perhaps because Dunfermline had reportedly been slandered there, and showed it in December 1606 by refusing Gledstanes's request that it order the presbytery of St. Andrews to accept him as moderator; it "will not mell with matters of the General Assembly without the King's express direction."[26] Dunfermline himself, after his recent brush with disaster, wanted to involve himself as little as possible in the affairs of the church, an attitude he maintained for the rest of his career, and he and his colleagues were by no means disposed to do favors for the bishops or incur any responsibility for their unpopular acts. In fact, there were already indications of concern on the part of some councillors about the potential power of the restored bishops. In January 1607 the lord advocate urged James to quash such ancient episcopal temporal rights as the archbishop of St. Andrews's grant of regality. The king ignored this; instead, in June 1607 he restored the long-disused power of the archbishop of Glasgow to nominate the provost and bailies of his burgh.[27]

James did not often permit his council the luxury of inaction in church matters, however. In his view it was the council's task to help to implement his ecclesiastical vision, and it could hardly ignore his specific instructions on such matters as the pursuit of noble Papists, the requirement of a new, anti-Papal oath of allegiance, or the imposition of constant moderators. On the other hand, Dunfermline and his colleagues were quite prepared to intervene to prevent what they regarded as unfair or tyrannical action on the part of the church. They would not allow presbyteries to abuse the power of excommunication by using it to force people accused of crimes in civil courts, such as adultery, to take oaths and in effect testify against themselves. They were very reluctant to allow clergymen to try witchcraft cases, preferring to issue special commissions to laymen. They would not allow the newly restored bishops and the holders of erected benefices to dump an unfair proportion of the tax voted in 1606 on their feuars and tenants, and ordered the prelates and holders to produce a tax roll to justify their exactions. There was one exception to the council's faintly anticlerical attitude, however: ministers' salaries. It was quite willing to compel lay holders of church benefices to pay the ministerial stipends they owed out of the thirds.[28]

A case which caused something of a stir in the first months of 1608 illustrates pretty well the tensions that existed between the bishops and the lay majority in the council. John Moray, the minister of Leith, was an opponent of episcopacy; he also happened to be the husband of the chancellor's late wife's sister. Through the initiative of his friends one of his sermons got into print. The king ordered Balmerino to examine him. The secretary reported favorably, and Moray himself wrote to the king, expressing his chagrin that the sermon had been published and pointing out that two bishops who had been present when it was delivered had not complained at the time. But Spottiswoode and his friends were not willing to let the matter drop. According to Calderwood, they culled some passages out of the sermon which apparently constituted an attack on the king's civil authority. So, on 25 February 1608, Moray was haled before the council to answer this charge.

He asked time to consider and on the next council day replied that the passages had been taken out of context and asked that his punishment be left to his presbytery or synod. Gledstanes charged that this amounted to a declinature of jurisdiction. Dunfermline, says Calderwood, replied "tauntingly, 'Albeit ye be Lord of St. Andrews, yet it seemeth ye have never been in St. Andrews. He giveth in a supplication and ye call it a declinature: that is no good logic.'" The council nevertheless rejected Moray's request, and the sermon was read. Its language was ambiguous; the council decided to release him. James, who had already made up his mind that Moray's sermon was seditious, was very angry. The council was quick enough to act in matters involving the private interests of its members, wrote James, "but in the punishing of any puritan preacher . . . our pleasure in that matter must be at least some half dozen several times sought, and the same signified to you, before we can have any of our directions in these matters executed." Moray spent a year in ward in Edinburgh castle in consequence. When he was released, he was not permitted to return to Leith. At the bishops' suggestion James ordered him to be sent to a Popish area in the southwest, where he would "find some other subject to work upon than the estate of bishops." The bishops carried out this order without providing any stipend for him and his family, an action Dunfermline called barbarous, partly because of "the gentlewoman his wife's quality." The king accompanied his order with a letter scolding the council for its failure ever to ward recalcitrant ministers on its own initiative and for releasing them without orders from him, a practice which, he said, it was to cease forthwith.[29]

The council had much to keep it busy besides disgruntled ministers. Dunbar found additional, sometimes unnecessary, work for his colleagues as a way of retaining his power. One of his devices was to complain to James of laxity in the Edinburgh administration, which usually responded with assurances, often from the chancellor's pen, that everything was quiet and going well. Dunbar told the king that there was widespread grumbling on account of the recent taxation; the council denied it. If Papists were flourishing, as the king had heard, the kirk had not complained to the council about it. The earldom of Athol was concededly in a mess, on account of what Dunfermline called the earl's "imbecility and weakness"; the council warded him for his failure to preserve order in his domains or pay his debts. The king ordered him to be sent to court, but the order came unsealed and in an irregular form, so the council delayed executing it. James flew into a rage and described its behavior as intolerable disobedience; the council replied with a dignified explanation which concluded with a request that the king send his instructions in the usual way henceforth, and James calmed down. On the whole, however, Dunbar's tactics were successful in maintaining his political control. James notified his councillors in January 1607 that Dunbar on his return from Scotland would report on their performance. And Dunbar undoubtedly inspired the king's order of May 1608 that the council's votes on important issues be recorded and sent to him.[30]

In the exchange over Athol James complained that the council dragged comparatively minor offenders like the earl off to Edinburgh castle while known murderers like the master of Crawford walked freely in the High Street. The council rejoined that any malefactor could slip into Edinburgh at night, and that it was looking for Crawford. The noble lawbreaker and participant in feuds was still a problem, though less so now because of unrelenting pressure and what Balmerino described to the king as terrorist tactics on the part of Dunbar. One difficulty was that Scone's police force was idle and, the council pointed out, expensive. A letter to James from the "Inhabitants of the Late Borders of Scotland" accused Scone of foot-dragging and giving his friends advance notice of orders to move against them. He was ordered to get on the job and to come to council meetings more often.[31] The council also passed its usual string of generalized enactments, such as the requirement that when the parties to a dispute met to arrange a settlement they be prohibited from bringing long trains of followers, who were apt to exacerbate matters by quarreling with each other, but the really effective work was done in individual cases, sometimes producing genuine settlements, sometimes, when that was not possible, preventing violence from breeding more violence.[32] Peace was slowly coming to the Scottish aristocracy.

Violent behavior was not an aristocratic monopoly, of course. There were occasional riots in the towns, and in January 1608 the council felt impelled to order the magistrates of Edinburgh to do something about crime in the streets. Huntly was instructed to act against a gang calling itself the "Society and Company of Boys" which was operating in his territory, on pain of being reported to the king for laxity. Horse races at Peebles were banned, on the ground that they would attract crowds and create disturbances. And finally, to cut down on vagabondage and the crime which accompanied it, a separate judicial office was created to administer the legislation applying to the poor. William Ogle of Popplehill was given this job and was authorized to appoint deputies in every parish. If the report of the justices of the peace of Selkirkshire to the council in 1611 is typical, the system did not work very well, owing to lack of funds and the uncooperativeness of burgh officials and sturdy beggars alike. The justices suggested that the council allow them to spend the money collected in fines for rioting on various sorts of public improvements like road repair, to put the poor to work; the council did not respond. The local kirk sessions also bore a share of responsibility for the poor, and this meant friction, especially over questions involving the handling of money. Ogle received jurisdiction over a number of other local matters as well: Sabbath-breaking, profanity, fornication, the harboring of vagabonds, and the punishment of people who refused to accept parish offices. This looks like an attempt both to relieve the central courts of the burden of hearing a lot of petty cases and to prevent the kirk session from acting as both accuser and judge in some matters over which it claimed jurisdiction.[33]

"Advertisement is come to me," wrote Dunbar to Mar in November 1606, "that all is done that can be to shake the country loose, both in the Highlands and the Borders. . . . When slaughters are committed the Council takes no care, and the deed doers go peaceably, no way troubled."[34] This remark, a good example of Dunbar's technique of keeping potential rivals on the defensive, did much less than justice to Dunfermline and his colleagues, though the situation in both areas was far from ideal. Dunbar himself was about to take the borders in hand; as soon as his appointment as chief of the revamped border commission was announced in December 1606, he set promptly to work. He personally spent a good deal of time in the area in the early months of 1607, and in spite of a breakdown in his health serious enough to cause King James to send a doctor to him, he managed to hang a number of malefactors on both sides of the border "such as durst not beforetime be meddled."[35] He also arranged that Cranston's border guard would be regularly paid. All the evidence suggests that Dunbar's presence at the head of the border commission invigorated border administration and made it more efficient. When he returned to England, there was a falling-off serious enough to prompt a letter of complaint from the residents of the border to the king.[36] The falling-off was brief, however, thanks to the government's reaction to Lord Maxwell's escape from Edinburgh castle at the end of 1607. His escape enraged James, who wanted him tried for treason when he was caught, which would have been a stretching of the law. A really savage crackdown at the hands of Dunbar and Cranston followed, the violence of which is indicated by the fact that Cranston, who at one point was almost lynched in Dumfries, felt it necessary to get two royal remissions exonerating him and his relatives from legal liability for their actions.[37] Their work, if one believes the chancellor, was effective. Dunbar, he wrote to King James on 12 August 1609, "has purged the Borders of all the chiefest malefactors, robbers, and brigands as were wont to reign there, as clean, and by as great wisdom and policy, as Hercules sometimes is written to have purged Augeas the king of Elide his escuries, and . . . has rendered all these ways and passages betwixt your majesty's kingdoms of Scotland and England as free and peaceable, as is recorded Phoebus in old times made free and open the ways to his own oracle in Delphos. . . . These parts are now, I may assure your majesty, as lawful, as peaceable, and as quiet as any part in any civil kingdom of Christianity."[38] The situation was hardly as ideal as all that, but it is true that the consistent pressure which the government had applied, the unrelenting use of force, had pretty well done the job by this time, to the point where lawlessness was no longer a way of life. The king thought so, and in November 1609 rewarded Cranston with a peerage. Maxwell was to evade the officers of the law for a time, there were to be numerous examples of violence and retrogression, and the pressure on the lawless elements there could not be relaxed. But Maxwell's inability to mount even a pretense of defiance of the government was a clear indication that the days when the border constituted a separate, almost independent element in the Scottish state had finally passed. Henceforth it was to be simply one more area of the country where the king's writ ran—a particularly difficult and lawless area to administer, to be sure, but one which now differed from the lowlands in degree rather than in kind.

One of the obvious solutions to the problem of lawlessness on the border, which was an overpopulated area anyway, was to move the lawbreakers out, to other parts of Scotland or, preferably, out of the kingdom altogether. England clearly was no use as a dumping ground, and as the European continent moved in the direction of a general peace, prompted by both exhaustion and the pacific policy of King James, service in foreign armies became a steadily less feasible alternative. There was one other possibility, however, which all at once in 1608 loomed very large, an area which not only might absorb the surplus population of the borders but which the Scots might also exploit in other ways: Ireland.

There were a good many Scots already in Ireland by 1608, but the prospect of really large-scale Scottish settlement there emerged only in that year, after the flight and forfeiture of the earls of Tyrone and Tyrconnel late in 1607. The initiative for such settlement came from the king, who regarded the Irish as another species of highlander, barbarians to be dispossessed if their soil was ever to be made to flourish; Sir Arthur Chichester, the lord deputy in Dublin, had a rather low opinion of Scots and was not particularly eager to have them there. But come the Scots did, once the terms of settlement were made attractive enough, including some important people like Dunfermline's nephew James Hamilton, earl of Abercorn, who eventually became the most important Scottish proprietor in Ireland. All of the administrative decisions affecting the Ulster plantation were made in London. The council in Edinburgh had no formal responsibility, except for that of receiving applications for allotments and sending them on to London in the summer of 1609, although Dunfermline and Dunbar kept in touch with developments through their friends and relatives who were involved there. Occasionally the Scottish settlers in Ireland made a request of the government in Edinburgh; occasionally the council concerned itself with such matters as stolen goods, smuggling, and the travels and extradition of criminals.[39] But for the most part the settlement of Ireland went on without any direct involvement on the part of the Scottish government. In one respect at least this lack of involvement was not displeasing to the council. Many of the undertenants in Ulster came from the southwest and the west march; many of these wound up in areas physically as far removed from Scotland as possible, which suggests that they were possibly fugitives from justice. The council was happy enough that they were where they were, and left them strictly alone.[40]

Dunfermline and his colleagues paid much more attention in these years to the highlands than to Ireland, and here they were finally able to persuade King James to abandon his colonization-cum-extirpation fantasies and adopt the council's preferred solution, that of direct dealing and cooperation with the highland chiefs themselves, a solution first hinted at in 1602, when Dunfermline's friend MacKenzie of Kintail was admitted to the reconstituted privy council. But it took some little time to win James over to this idea. When Dunbar came north in the winter of 1606 to take charge of the borders, he brought with him a plan from the king which was a variation of the old highland policies. Use would be made once again of Huntly and Argyll; furthermore, as the king made clear in his instructions to the council in May 1607, the same policy was to be followed as lay behind the grant to the gentleman-adventurers in Lewis: the natives were to be wiped out or driven out, and replaced "with civil people and noway either with Badenoch and Lochaber men."[41]

This policy had almost nothing to recommend it to the council. It would be expensive and time-consuming. Past experience suggested that it would not work; if it did, it would enormously increase the power of two already overmighty subjects, neither of whom was trustworthy. It would not produce anything for the treasury for a long time. The councillors dragged their feet until a stinging letter from the king constrained them to open negotiations. With Argyll, who was eager to consolidate his grip in Kintyre, it was possible to come to terms, but the earl, concerned as always only to forward the private interests of the Campbells, made no great effort to accomplish anything outside of Kintyre itself. In the context of the government's broader aims he turned out once more to be a broken reed. With Huntly the council haggled for the better part of four months over the terms of his responsibility, which was to include all the northern isles save Skye and Lewis. The major points in dispute were the size of the annual rent (Huntly offered £400, the council wanted £10,000), the length of time the job should take (the council thought one year, Huntly thought nine), and whether or not the marquis should have a commission of lieutenancy. Huntly gave way on the last two points, but no agreement could be reached on the rent. So, on 23 June 1607, in spite of the king's specific instructions to the contrary, the council broke off the negotiations by renewing the ongoing recusancy charge against Huntly and confining him to the town of Elgin and its neighborhood. The king, who had become increasingly annoyed at the scope of Huntly's demands, signified his acquiescence in this maneuver by transferring Huntly's place of confinement from Elgin to Aberdeen, on the ground that the ministers of Aberdeen were more learned and so more likely to bring about the marquis's conversion.[42]

This fiasco indicated the bankruptcy of the old highland policies. The chancellor's effort to present the king with his ready-made alternative was slightly premature, however. In March 1607, as the negotiations with Huntly were getting under way, Dunfermline arranged a grant to MacKenzie of Kintail of a free barony which included the island of Lewis, and on the day the council ordered Huntly into ward it authorized Kintail to deal with the inhabitants of the northern isles in the king's name. James was not yet ready to accept the necessity of working through the highland chiefs themselves, however. He opined to Balmerino that the adventurers' failure in Lewis was due to their own slackness. The secretary took the hint, organized another group, and in October 1607 received another grant from the king; Kintail's charter was annulled as far as Lewis was concerned.[43] This group of adventurers accomplished no more than its predecessor.

What James deduced from all this was that no individual or group of individuals could bring law, order, and prosperity to the highlands, and income to his treasury, out of their own resources. If his policy was to succeed, the government itself would have to act. James therefore authorized a massive punitive expedition for the summer of 1608, a combined operation using English troops and ships based in Ireland, the purpose of which was to bring about the final subjugation of the western isles. All of the lieges of the kingdom were ordered to muster in Islay and Inverness in July, and a convention of estates was summoned for 20 May to decide how best to accomplish the king's aims. The king's project made the council very uneasy; on 14 April, two days after the summons to the lieges, it commissioned Bishop Knox of the Isles, Lord Ochiltree, and the new comptroller, Sir James Hay of Fingask, to consult with MacDonald of Dunyveg and MacLean of Duart, the two most important chiefs in the southern isles, and report back by 20 May. What they were to try to get from the chiefs were caution for payment of the king's rents, delivery of their fortresses, a guarantee that their followers would obey the law, renunciation of their jurisdiction over their followers and acceptance of the king's wishes respecting their property, virtual disarmament, and education of their children at schools the council designated—a large order which, unsurprisingly, remained unfilled. The king, meanwhile, was writing to members of the forthcoming convention, urging them to act to end the disgrace to Scotland "in having some part thereof still possessed with (*sic*) such barbarous cannibals." So the convention did as the king wished, though not all that he wished. There was "a long and fashious dispute" which ended in a reluctant agreement to "serve according to the laws of the country." But there was to be no tax money. So great was the opposition to taxation for this purpose that Dunfermline and his colleagues made no serious effort even to raise the question. It is quite possible that they acted by design, and that the outcome pleased them well enough; Dunfermline was always opposed to the voting of taxes for purposes he regarded as foolish or unattainable.[44]

Four days after the convention the council sent Bishop Knox to the king recommending the appointment of a single lieutenant for the expedition and asking for various decisions as to his powers and policies while there. The king named Ochiltree as lieutenant and Knox as head of his advisory council, and gave Ochiltree a fair amount of discretion in his handling of the expedition. The most significant aspect of the king's instructions was a subtle shift in their tone. References to barbarism, extirpation, and colonization were conspicuously absent. Instead, Ochiltree was to encourage the islesmen to submit and come in to the council, to hear the terms on which James would be willing to extend them his favor.[45]

Ochiltree carried out his instructions in a literal and rather astonishing way, in spite of the fact that the force at his disposal was by no means as overwhelming as had been planned; he had only about 900 men in all. Nevertheless he obtained rapid surrenders of the castles of Dunyveg and Duart and seriously diminished the warmaking powers of the island chiefs, and of some of their western highland counterparts, by destroying a large number of their ships. Above all, by his celebrated *coup de main* in luring a number of chiefs aboard his ship to hear a sermon and then sailing for Ayr, thus in effect kidnapping them, he managed to bring virtually every important chief in the southern isles into the government's hands; they were promptly warded in Stirling, Blackness, and Dumbarton. There was no fighting; Ochiltree met with no resistance. He also spent a great deal of money — just how much is not clear because he made a hash of the accounts and got into serious financial trouble in consequence.[46] These problems lay in the future, however; for now Ochiltree was something of a hero. He triumphantly reported his achievements to the council and set off for London to tell his story to the king.[47]

The question now was what James and his councillors would do with their success. The main lines of what the council wanted are apparent in Bishop Knox's persuasive letter to the king, written in September 1609, after Ochiltree had seized the chiefs but before his return. Knox told James that he had kept a record of the expedition so that the king would be correctly informed and "also understand how easy it is to your Majesty . . . to establish and induce them all, without hostility or opening of your highness' coffers, to accept of such a solid order as may reduce them to a hasty reformation, in no age hereafter to alter."[48] James was not altogether convinced, but in December 1608 he agreed to appoint a committee to draw up recommendations for him. His instructions for the committee indicate a further shift in his attitude. There was still an insistence that with peace and order the highlands could be made to flourish economically, and still a desire to plant towns, presumably with lowlanders, though he did not say so. But the emphasis now was on civilizing and christianizing the barbarous inhabitants, collecting the king's rents, and reducing the power and lands of the chiefs rather than eliminating them. He was loath, he said, to uproot any of the population there unless absolutely necessary, and he was unwilling to burden his subjects any further "with taxes, subsidies, or obeying of proclamations made for reducing these Isles to obedience."[49]

These guidelines amounted to a virtual abandonment of the colonization policy which James had intermittently pursued for the past decade, partly on account of its demonstrated costliness, for which, it was very obvious, his Scottish subjects were utterly unwilling to pay, and partly because, as he said in his instructions, a much more fertile field for colonization had opened in Ireland for those who wished to make their fortunes. The committee did its work slowly. There were more urgent matters to occupy the council in the first months of 1609, and a certain amount of delay was helpful in bringing the warded chiefs into a properly apprehensive frame of mind. The chiefs made placatory offers to the council but could not obtain their release. To make them still more malleable, Sir James MacDonald, the eldest son of Angus MacDonald of Dunyveg, was put on trial in May 1609 for treasonable fire-raising and for attempting to escape from Edinburgh castle. He was found guilty by a jury headed by none other than Lord Ochiltree and was condemned to death. The sentence was not carried out, however; he was returned to his prison, where he had already spent six years, and would spend six more before he finally succeeded in escaping.[50]

In the spring of 1609 the council sent Bishop Knox to court with its suggestions; he returned in June with the king's authorization to go to the isles with the comptroller after parliament ended, in company with MacLean of Duart, who was to be released for the purpose. The king's letter of instruction was very vague and gave the council considerable discretion, which it now proceeded to use in order to give the policy of pacification through cooperation a thorough trial. On receiving their promise to cooperate, it released all the chiefs, not just MacLean of Duart. It gave Knox very little money, to underline the peaceful character of his mission, and it did not send the comptroller, whose presence would imply that Knox's purposes were chiefly fiscal and punitive. The result was the well-known statutes of Icolmkill, agreed to on Iona in August 1609 by the bishop and the great majority of the important highland chiefs. The main thrust of the statutes was the recognition of the chief's authority. He was responsible for his kinsmen and for the observation of the specific provisions of these statutes, and of all other laws, within his bounds. There was no mention of pains and penalties for violation, no attempt to reduce the chiefs' property holdings, and arrangements were made to improve communication between them and the administration in Edinburgh.

After some delay the king accepted the statutes, a decision which represented a triumph for the council's point of view, the final abandonment of the ten-year-old colonization scheme and in most areas of the still older attempt to govern by means of half-feudal, half-patriarchal magnates like Huntly and Argyll.[51] It was a policy which had the backing of the church, which looked forward to recovering its material and spiritual position there, and of the burghs, which saw possible profit in it.[52] The strength of the government helped to make the chiefs more willing to cooperate, and thus made it possible for the king to live with the clan system and try to amend it rather than wipe it out. At the same time the government's financial weakness led the council in Edinburgh to advocate, and James finally to accept, a policy which promised to produce some income for the government. The statutes worked reasonably well because, as one authority has put it, for the chiefs "for the first time submission had become less dangerous than resistance." In fact, it became positively profitable to cooperate with the government in the interest of peace and order. Rory MacLeod of Dunvegan, for instance, who was chief of his branch of the clan from 1596 to 1626, managed to avoid clan warfare after

1601. Within a few years a flourishing trade in live cattle to the south was under way, and the value of the MacLeod estates in Skye and Glenelg rose substantially.[53]

A great deal of the credit for this success belongs to Bishop Knox. He was the ideal choice as the government's emissary to both the king and the chiefs, a talented man with no self-interested motives who got on well with his colleagues in both church and state. The most likely explanation of the king's gradual acceptance of the council's views is Knox's persuasiveness in personal conversation while at court in 1608 and 1609. The statutes he devised were a very artful diplomatic compromise, reassuring the chiefs, providing for the extension of civilization and religion in the form of the established church, and providing the council with the material benefits it hoped for, in the shape of the requirement that the chiefs appear when summoned and, by implication, meet their obligations to the crown. Knox received his rewards. James made him steward of the isles, gave him a new commission of justiciary there, and made him keeper of the castle of Dunyveg. James also made him bishop of Raphoe, in Ireland, so that he could exercise his energy and talents on civilizing the wild Irish.[54] For all the bishop's skill, he nevertheless might not have succeeded if he had not had the solid backing of the council. On this issue there was no division of opinion between Dunfermline and Spottiswoode, and Dunbar seems to have concerned himself very little, if at all, with highland questions.

The adoption of the statutes of Icolmkill did not mean that peace automatically prevailed everywhere in the highlands, however. The MacDonald country in the southwest was still unsettled owing to the feuds within the family, carefully watched and occasionally stirred by the earl of Argyll in the hope and expectation of profit. In Lewis the final collapse of the last attempt at colonization by lowlanders finally induced the king to accept what had long been Dunfermline's preferred solution there: to turn the island over to his ally MacKenzie of Kintail. In July 1610 Kintail, whose recently granted peerage was a sign of his growing favor at court, received his long-awaited commission of fire and sword; within three years the power of the last of the once-dominant MacLeods had been smashed, and the MacKenzies ruled supreme in Lewis.[55]

Kintail's behavior during his decade of manipulation and intrigue in Lewis ranged from unprincipled to treacherous—egging on the MacLeods to resist the lowland colonizers, for example, and then using the MacLeods' violence as an inducement to the government to authorize him to extirpate them. But he produced the results the council wanted: pacification of the island and payment of rents without cost to the government. Almost alone among the highland chiefs Kintail had foreseen what James's accession to the English throne would mean for the highlands, had thrown in his lot with the government early, and had made the right friends, including the chancellor. He was one of those unscrupulous double-dealers who, like Machiavelli's prince, create law and order because it paid them to do so.

Still another pattern was developing in Orkney. There had been a growing chorus of complaint about the rule of the king's cousin Earl Patrick Stewart, whom the plaintiffs characterized as lawless and tyrannical. "Having undone his estate by riot and prodigality," wrote Spottiswoode, Earl Patrick "did seek by unlawful shifts to repair the same, making acts in his courts, and exacting penalties for the breach thereof." He was certainly heavily in debt, but the evidence of the court books suggests that his rule, "while undoubtedly burdensome, was not oppressive in an arbitrary way."[56] The councillors nevertheless viewed it as both oppressive and arbitrary, and the earl's behavior was not calculated to make them change their minds. Since he was the king's cousin, however, they were unwilling to move against him without specific authorization from James, which they got in December 1608. Six months later Orkney answered their summons and was warded in Edinburgh; his absence brought about no improvement in the inhabitants' condition, since those who governed in his name were just as violent as he. In January 1610 the king, thoroughly exasperated by his cousin's behavior, adopted the same tactics which had worked so well in the western isles. Bishop Law of Orkney received a commission to "take order for a good rule in the church there as for the quietness of the country itself."[57] It was the right move. Putting an end to Earl Patrick's regime took time, but eventually the bishop, a patient and clever man, accomplished it, with the support of the council and the aid of the earl's own stupid behavior. In general Dunfermline and his allies opposed clerical involvement in politics, but the highlands were an exception; there, bishops could be very useful in bringing lawless grandees of various sorts to heel.

The contemplated use in 1608 of English armed forces based in Ireland in Ochiltree's expedition to the western isles is an illustration of what King James conceived to be the advantages of Anglo-Scottish union. By that time, however, the union, in the formal sense of adoption of the union commissioners' report, was effectively dead. The crucial debates were those in the English parliament at the beginning of 1607. They were followed with keen interest in Scotland, and with considerable annoyance at the aspersions cast on the Scots by many of the participants, an annoyance which was not diminished by the fact that the council found it necessary repeatedly to intervene to prevent English courts from exercising improper jurisdiction in cases involving Scotsmen.[58] The Scottish parliament's response was, therefore, correct but most perfunctory. It agreed to repeal all statutes directed against England and to accept the report of the commissioners, provided England reciprocated, which of course she had not. In reporting its action, parliament was careful to stress that its refusal to allow the fundamental law of the kingdom, or its status as an equal partner with England, to be tampered with argued no hostility to the idea of union. A more accurate indication of Scottish opinion than this polite and obedient report is the fact that two years later, on Dunbar's advice, James had parliament pass an act prohibiting all anti-English speeches, rhymes, plays, and other writings as harmful to the union.[59]

The Scots knew that they were safe in accepting the commissioners' draft; it was clear that for the foreseeable future their English counterparts would go no further than they had already gone. The king hated to admit defeat and, indeed, continued to behave as if he had suffered no more than a temporary setback. He continued his campaign to bring the polity of both church and state in his ancient kingdom into greater conformity with that of England. He won his Pyrrhic victory in the English courts in the case of the *post-nati,* and in Scotland he used the style of *King of Great Britain,* though in deference to the outspoken opinions of the common lawyers he did not do so in England.[60] He continued his effort to civilize his northern subjects so that they would be more acceptable to the sophisticated Southron. The towns were to provide enough inns to accommodate travelers and keep their streets clean, so as not to cause offense to the Englishmen who would accompany him on his next visit, James informed the convention of royal burghs in 1608. Furthermore, female dress must be altered: "the wearing of cloaks and plaids is altogether scoffed at by all strangers." He applied pressure on the reluctant English universities to admit more Scottish students and revoke their anti-Scottish statutes.[61] But the dream of the more perfect union, one of James's most statesmanlike visions, had for all practical purposes evaporated.

ii

If the king's projects for union had taken effect, Scottish economic life would have been profoundly affected. The commissioners for union at their meeting in 1604 had spent more time on economic questions than on anything else, and the parliament of 1607 had passed some general legislation equalizing the position of English and Scots traders and goods (on condition that England reciprocated), while repeating the prohibition of the export of wool, sheepskins and fells, cattle, leather, hides, and linen yarn and preserving for Scotsmen their monopoly of fishing their own lochs and seas.[62] The king had already ordered the end of the collection of duty on goods passing between England and Scotland, for reasons more political than economic, and in spite of the violent English opposition to free trade revealed in the debates on union in the English parliament, the policy was continued.

The policy of free trade did not commend itself in Scotland either. The royal burghs were assured by parliamentary act that their special privileges, notably their cherished monopoly of foreign trade, would not be affected; nevertheless the merchants were disgruntled because they were prohibited from exporting the now duty-free English goods from Scotland, or from selling them to foreigners who might export them, and because they could no longer export English cloth from England, which they alleged had been permitted before the union.[63] The council was unhappy about the loss of customs revenues, both from the removal of the duties and from increased smuggling.[64] Furthermore, there was the specter of financial drain. Scotsmen developed a taste for duty-free English beer, for instance. This impelled the council to intervene to lower the price of Scots brew, in order to discourage the importation of English beer without having to take the political risk of limiting or prohibiting it. This evidently did not work well enough, and in 1610 the council fixed the price of English beer at a level higher than that of Scottish beer but lower than the English brewers' costs, if the latter's anguished protest is to be believed. The eventual result was a lively black market in English beer; buyers and sellers cooperated to lie to officialdom and sell the beer at the English brewers' prices. The council made an effort to put a stop to this black market by prohibiting the landing of any beer without guarantees that it would be sold at the legal price, but James gave way to the protests of the English shippers and countermanded the council's order.[65]

Because of the adoption of free trade the Scottish customs farmers claimed a defalcation of £13,000 a year, though they settled, in Professor Lythe's phrase, "with somewhat suspicious readiness" for £10,000. That the farmers exaggerated their losses is suggested by the fact that in July 1609 the customs contract was renegotiated with another syndicate which was willing to pay 115,000 merks a year, 35,000 more than its predecessor.[66] The council nevertheless felt that it could get a great deal more, and not merely by ending the free trade with England; for customs purposes goods were currently seriously undervalued. By the end of 1610 Dunfermline and Dunbar, aided by the failure of the Great Contract and the generally gloomy financial situation of the Scottish government, persuaded James of the truth of their point of view. In November James authorized the drawing up of a new book of rates, and in December he ordered the reimposition of Anglo-Scottish customs duties as of 1 January 1611. Free trade had not benefited the people, he said, since the merchants had simply pocketed their savings instead of reducing prices—James never lost his suspicion of and contempt for traders—and anyway he needed the money. The book of rates was overhauled and reissued, and all the previous regulations respecting Anglo-Scottish commercial dealings reimposed, save that which forced Scotsmen to pay duties at the rate imposed on aliens when importing goods into England, an exemption which the Scots had continually to ask James to compel English customs officials to observe. Finally, in October 1611, a new tack of the customs was set to a syndicate full of councillors' relatives for a whopping 180,000 merks a year, an increase over the 1609 contract of 65,000 merks. The king when he authorized the setting of the new tack urged the council not to demand too high a rental, lest the farmers attempt to recoup at the merchants' expense and trade suffer as a result. The extent to which the council heeded this advice is not altogether clear, but trade did not decline. Five years later, when the tack expired, the existing syndicate retained possession, after an auction, by paying 30,000 merks more for their new lease.[67]

James's acceptance of his councillors' advice as to the ending of free trade is one of many indications of a significant development in the latter part of the first decade of James's English residence. Even before the death of the domineering Dunbar, who in this matter as in so much else had no discernible policy of his own, James began to relinquish decision-making in economic questions affecting Scotland to the council in Edinburgh. The crucial period in this respect began late in 1608, when James started issuing a series of orders prohibiting the export of various goods, notably leather, coal (except to England), and timber. The council had attempted to anticipate the first by appointing a commission in May 1608 to investigate and fix shoe prices, which were admittedly too high. The council had concluded that the problem was not scarcity but overcharging on the part of the tanners; it hoped that the commission, which was supposed to review prices twice a year, would solve the problem. The king nevertheless ordered the prohibition of the export of leather in January 1609, and he was obeyed, the more readily because of England's unwillingness to export treated hides to Scotland.[68] With coal it was a different story. The burghs had petitioned against the export of coal in the interest of a full domestic supply, a petition which the council passed on to James. His reply was the predictable one: ban its export, except to England, with security that it not be re-exported from there. Many of the councillors, however, were personally interested in the coal business, the chancellor among them. So the council was naturally very sympathetic to the petition of the owners of the mines along the Forth that the ban be lifted, on the grounds that there was no current shortage of coal above ground and that foreign sales were vital to full production, which in turn was vital to the welfare of their properties; without full production the mines would flood and future attempts at searching out new sources of supply be discouraged. Coal mining required large initial capital outlays, which would not be forthcoming if the present restrictions were enforced. Furthermore, the sale of coal abroad brought money into the country. The king was unsympathetic. There was a large English market for Scottish coal, he pointed out, and more uses could be found for coal at home; the council's attitude betrayed either weakness or a willingness to seek private advantage. The ban would remain.[69] So it did, formally, but the already existing system of special licenses for export continued to develop, and so did the export trade. The same was true of wool, the export of which was also forbidden, and which continued to flow out of the country at the rate of £50,000 worth a year. The government ended the prohibition of the export of linen yarn in May 1612, on the ground that Scottish linen weavers, through knavery or incompetence, made cloth which was unsalable, with the proviso that the export duty was subject to semiannual adjustment in the interest of preventing scarcity of yarn in the home market—a decision contrary to all the so-called mercantilist canons which should make historians cautious about generalizing too broadly on economic policy. On the other hand, the ban on the export of tallow, the price of which doubled between 1580 and 1600, seems to have been pretty well enforced.[70] The logical conclusion is that the council made no effort to enforce regulations which it believed to be unsound.[71]

The king's most spectacular revelation of his economic ignorance came in the case of timber. In December 1608 he drew up a proclamation prohibiting the export of timber, recently found in great quantities in the highlands, and also prohibiting the erection of any new iron mills in these timbered areas, to prevent consumption of wood that way. The council decided not to issue the

proclamation, and wrote their "simple and weak opinion there-
anent, which we always submit to your Majesty's more rare and
excellent judgment." There was no timber in Scotland, they said,
and none had been exported within the memory of man; in fact,
Scotland had to import timber. There were no iron mills either;
such iron as was made was smelted with branches, boughs, etc.,
good for nothing else. Prohibiting the export of timber might
induce foreign princes to reply in kind; if they did so, the country
would be in serious trouble. They suggested that the king might
prohibit the cutting of certain woods, for the sake of the country's
shipping. The king rather shamefacedly accepted this latter suggestion, though he persisted in the unnecessary prohibition of the
building of iron mills in the highland forests.[72]

After this exchange over timber the tone of relations between
king and council on economic questions began to change. Far
more often than before the king either referred matters to the
council or asked its advice before he acted, even in matters affecting relations with foreign states, like the question of the loca-
tion of the staple in the Netherlands.[73] The king's ways did not
change completely, of course. He continued to issue orders. But
now, sometimes, the council refused to implement them, usually
by a process of delay, and this usually worked.[74] The council used
its greater independence in economic matters to give freer rein to
a series of tendencies which it had been trying to indulge since the
king's departure. It would be an overstatement to assert that the
councillors had a comprehensive economic policy. What they did
have were private interests and pressures which combined together to encourage policies which would maximize the income of
the crown, satisfy the dominant element in the burghs, and further
the economic well-being of the landed classes, many members of
which were making money out of enterprises other than agricul-
ture. Employers were given a good deal of authority over their
employees, including, occasionally, some of the powers of the
state.[75] The most favored beneficiaries were the owners of mines,
especially coal mines. In 1606 in the interest of the mineowners
parliament passed what amounted to a slave-labor statute, which
bound coal workers permanently to their mines. Henceforth no

one was to employ a coal miner or a salt worker who did not have a certificate of discharge from his last employer. Fugitive miners could be pursued for a year and a day, forced back to work, and punished as thieves; those who employed such fugitives could be fined £100 for refusal to surrender them on demand. Vagabonds and beggars could be put forcibly to work. In 1607 the council extended the law to other sorts of miners. The rationale for this brutal legislation was the need to maximize production and minimize labor costs; from the employers' point of view it worked well enough, partly because there was so little alternative for the workers: the owner of the mine was also the owner of the land on which the workers lived. The council in 1612 further protected the landowners' rights by declaring that the recent practice of granting leases of mineral rights to strangers had worked badly. It therefore revived the enactment of 1592 which provided that henceforth each proprietor would work his own mineral deposits and pay the customary 10 percent duty to the crown. Only if the proprietor refused to do so would the government set a tack to an outsider, in the interest of the crown's revenue.[76]

With respect to the burghs the council was concerned to protect the dominant position of the royal burghs, and disliked placing restrictions on their conduct of foreign trade or putting pressure on them to engage in mercantilist experiments whose prospects were uncertain—the repeated suggestion by the king, for instance, that a crash program to improve clothmaking be undertaken by importing a lot of foreign clothworkers. The council was also usually responsive to requests from individual burghs to levy local tolls for particular purposes such as the repair of bridges. On the other hand, the council endorsed monopolies it thought would be industrially useful or, occasionally, which profited one of its members, in spite of protest from the burghs. It was also not disposed to alter customs duties at their behest, especially if the royal revenue and the income of the tacksmen, many of whom were councillors' kinsmen, would suffer. It also, in its own interest as a group of consumers, intervened repeatedly in Edinburgh, sometimes to fix prices (normally the province of the burghal authorities), sometimes to keep markets open and balk the capital's craft guilds' attempts to prevent other guilds-men, notably those of the Canongate, from doing business in Edinburgh.[77]

The general impression left by a study of the council's actions in economic questions during the first decade of James's English residence is that there was a slow but perceptible shift in attitude away from the traditional outlook represented by the king to one which favored the trader, the producer, and the industrial monop-olist. It was a much more business-minded council now, with its two chief members in Edinburgh being the chancellor with his family coal mines and his thorough acquaintance and sympathy with the Edinburgh business community from his decade as pro-vost,[78] and Lord Advocate Hamilton, master of the metals after 1607 and with a brother in the syndicate which held the customs farm and hence with a direct interest in the expansion of trade. The other two principal officeholders, Balmerino and the absentee Dunbar, had no such obvious economic interests, but by early 1611 both of them were gone, and the next decade was to see the tendencies of the period 1603–11 flourish still more extensively. The general prosperity of Scotland in these years was due to many factors, some of which, such as peace and good harvests, were beyond the control of the councillors in Edinburgh. But they de-serve more credit than they have hitherto received for creating an economic climate in which prosperity could flourish, both by their positive actions and by occasional judicious inaction which pre-vented the mischief which some of the proposals emanating from London would have caused.

iii

In the middle of 1608 the king decided that it would be safe to allow the General Assembly to meet. The question of the constant moderators had been settled, and a conference held at Falkland in June 1608 had turned out well. Spottiswoode and his friends per-suaded the ministers there to agree to suspend all public discus-sion or preaching on controverted questions until the assembly, and at the assembly to have such issues dealt with in committee instead of on the floor, a committee which came to be called the privy conference. This was an important gain for the king; the right moderator could see to the choice of the right members of the privy conference, on the analogy of the lords of the articles, and thus help to reduce the assembly to impotence.[79]

It was important that there should be no repetition of the methods employed for the meeting at Linlithgow in 1606: the members must be chosen in the customary way. And so they were; but the bishops exerted pressure, including the traditional juggling of stipends, and with considerable success. The king prepared the ground by making a great show of activity against Papists. He complained to the convention of royal burghs that it was not sufficiently concerned about the growth of Popery in Scotland. He ordered the warding of Huntly, Angus, and Errol, accompanying his instructions with another scolding of the council for its laxity in pursuing nobles who were suspect in religion. Popery was, in fact, the main item on the government's agenda for the assembly: a good, noncontroversial topic guaranteed to produce a minimum of disagreement.[80]

At the end of June Dunbar arrived in Scotland, accompanied by his chaplain, George Abbot, the future archbishop, and another English cleric "to persuade the Scots that there was no substantial difference in religion betwixt the two realms";[81] English ecclesiastics were now a regular part of the lord treasurer's retinue. In his capacity as royal commissioner Dunbar also carried instructions from James to deal with "the suppression of the common enemy [i.e., Popery] and removing of . . . intestine discord." To the latter end the king ordered "a restraint . . . of all impertinent and insolent discourses, too frequent heretofore amongst you."[82] The absence of Andrew Melville and his friends would go a long way to that end; to make assurance doubly sure, some forty laymen were to be present, Bishop Law, the king's choice as moderator, was armed with over £3,000 to be distributed where it would do the most good, and Dunbar and Law together restrained the king's impulse to let his old friend Huntly out of ward, at least until after the assembly was over.[83]

The assembly met on 26 July at Linlithgow, and from Dunbar's point of view went very well. As James wished, the meeting focused on Popery; Dunbar promised suitable action in his master's name. The assembly also asked for freedom for synods and future assemblies, but in very general terms, and it approved the renewal of the appointment of the commissioners of assembly. Virtually the only thing the king did not get was approval of the bishops as visitors in their own dioceses; so no visitors were appointed, save in the far north and the west march, to see to the planting of kirks in those areas. Most important, perhaps, was what did not happen. There was no discussion of the constant moderators, which meant tacit acceptance not only of the genuineness of the meeting of 1606 but also of the king's version of what it had done. Spottiswoode and his colleagues wrote a glowing letter to the king about the meeting, full of praise for the "wisdom and dexterity" of Dunbar and of Doctor Abbot's "excellent sermon."[84]

Lord Chancellor Dunfermline, by his own account, took a good deal of abuse at this meeting—he rightly supposed, commented the archbishop, that he was the target the assembly principally aimed at. "I be even at this present in as great a passion as ever I have been in, for the most manifest and great wrongs of (*sic*) calumnies I have sustained in this General Assembly," wrote Dunfermline to the king on 3 August. The main purpose of this letter was to defend himself against the allegation that he had corresponded with Queen Anne about Scottish affairs behind the king's back, a story which, to Anne's annoyance, Dunbar was apparently spreading at court.[85] The chancellor vehemently denied that he had engaged in any such hole-and-corner behavior, but the harassment continued. He finally wrote in a despairing tone to the king on 14 October, appealing to James's sense of fairness and his insight into human nature, better than "any other we have record of." It was simply not possible, he said, for him to conduct the government of the country effectively under such conditions.[86]

What Dunfermline did not know was that the attacks on him had a purpose quite different from what he supposed. They were the brainchild of Alexander Hay, the Scottish secretary at court, who in the summer of 1608 was knighted, admitted to the privy council, and made joint secretary of state with Balmerino, who was the real target: Hay, a sharp-tongued and ambitious man, wanted to be sole secretary. It was a complicated and Byzantine business which, fortunately for the historian, the king undertook to explain to Salisbury. "Hay is returned with open mouth against the examinate [Balmerino]. He told me of his being at Hampton Court . . . he assured me that she [Queen Anne] spake as far against that man, and condemned him as far of dishonest dealing, as I could have wished. He assured me that she would never open her mouth for him, if it were not by Mistress Drummond's persuasion . . . and therefore he advised me to seem angry at the Chancellor for another cause, for which they already feared my wrath; and he said it would move Drummond, who loved the Chancellor much better than the other, to be so careful in appeasing me towards him, as she would gladly let the other run his destiny."[87]

The story of the fall of Balmerino is well known—how he was induced to confess that, ten years earlier, he had contrived surreptitiously to obtain James's signature on a letter to the pope, an offense for which he was eventually convicted of treason. Cardinal Bellarmine had made the existence of the letter public, and James, to safeguard his reputation for truthfulness and as the Protestant champion—matters of great importance to him at any time and especially at this juncture, in the last delicate stages of the negotiation of the Dutch-Spanish truce[88]—made Balmerino the scapegoat. Indeed, it is quite likely that Balmerino was guilty of the offense with which he was charged, of fraudulently obtaining James's signature to a letter addressing Clement VIII as *Beatissime Pater,* though the fact that the king was in communication with the pope at all was James's doing and not his. After the event he claimed that he had been ill used for having to take full responsibility for what was at worst no more than an overzealous carrying out of his master's wishes. He blamed his disgrace on Hay, whom he accused of "vile and detestable ingratitude,"[89] Spottiswoode, and the bishops. He was aggrieved that his attempt to bribe Dunbar with the offer of the marriage of his eldest son and various pieces of property had failed, though, knowing Dunbar's power, he was careful not to criticize the earl directly. Balmerino may, indeed, have been doing less than justice to the bishops.[90] Since Balmerino was a Catholic, they found him distasteful, but by the time of his fall he was a virtual cipher politically, hardly worth their attention. Spottiswoode dismissed him in his *History* as a weak and corrupt man, though not without ability.[91] His fall caused no important change in Scottish politics; there was no purge of his friends and relatives, or of Catholics in government, as the elevation of his crypto-Catholic cousin Sir Alexander Drummond to the court of session demonstrated.[92] The harassment of the chancellor stopped once Balmerino had confessed, and Dunbar, when he went north to watch over Balmerino's trial, brought with him James's warrant appointing Dunfermline to the English privy council, a clear indication of James's continuing confidence in him.[93]

Dunbar also brought north an authorization to preside jointly with Dunfermline over a convention of estates summoned to hear the king's decisions on various issues which had been accumulating for the last year or so, including those raised at the recent General Assembly. The meeting, in January 1609, was exceptionally well attended and followed the royal directions very closely, under Dunbar's rather terrifying eye. Among other things it took the retrograde step of abolishing the register of sasines established in 1599 as being oppressive to the subject and useful only to the clerks who collected fees from it.[94] The convention's chief purpose was to adopt a series of measures directed against Catholics, the enforcement of which was to be entrusted chiefly to the bishops; on only one matter was the question even raised of whether enforcement by presbyteries would be more appropriate. James got virtually everything he wanted. Only one of his proposals, which would have required a certificate of conformity from the bishop of the diocese before any heir could take over his property, met with serious objection, ostensibly on the ground that it would introduce intolerable confusion into the land law, really because of the power it would give the bishops over the landed classes. So the convention enacted that the bishops would provide an annual list of the excommunicated to the government; no one on the list would be able to inherit, or, indeed, deal in property in any way, until the bishop certified that the person was no longer excommunicate.[95]

Spottiswoode and his colleagues were pleased at the results of the meeting, but they wanted still more, and sent the bishop of Galloway to the king with a memorandum regarding the next steps to be taken. They got most of what they asked for. The severe attitude toward Catholics continued unabated. Huntly and Errol remained in ward, and the council ordered the seizure of their liferents, in accordance with James's current policy of prodding them along the path to conformity without driving them to despair; they were not released until November 1610, after the powers of the bishops had been completely restored.[96] The one major request of the bishops which James did not grant was the appointment of genuine churchmen to the clerical seats on the court of session. The bishops wanted this because they felt sure that the court would oppose what they contemplated as their next major gain: the restoration of their control over the commissary courts, control which the court of session had been exercising for a quarter-century.[97]

The political repercussions of filling the court of session with bishops were more than James and Dunbar were prepared to risk, but they decided that the bishops would get their commissary jurisdiction back.[98] In April 1609 Dunbar arranged a conference between some of the bishops and some of the members of the court of session, who predictably were very critical of the bishops' plan. Dunbar and Spottiswoode realized that some concessions would have to be made to the judges' point of view if their proposal was to be acceptable to parliament, and Dunbar sent the king the draft of a compromise which he thought would cause the least controversy. Normally Dunbar would have discussed this sort of problem with the king in person; he had been away from court since January, a long time for him. His health was beginning to break down in earnest now; he was too ill to go to London and return in time for the parliament, now planned for June. James therefore sent Mar, who was then at court, back north with the assurance that he and Dunbar were the two men James trusted most, and with firm instructions to get the bishops' jurisdiction restored.[99]

Parliament followed the royal wishes and restored the bishops' jurisdiction—the first major accretion to their power which they obtained without even a pretense of consulting the kirk as a whole.[100] The commissary courts did not become independent of the secular government, however. The court of session served as a final court for appeals, which went in the first instance to a four-

man commissary court in Edinburgh appointed by the two archbishops; it also had the power to remove other sorts of cases from
the commissary courts and decide them itself, provided it could
justify its action. As was the case in 1606, concessions to individual aristocrats balanced gains for the bishops, with the erection
of more monastic property into temporal lordships.[101]

Eight months later, in February 1610, James added still further
to the bishops' judicial authority by creating two courts of high
commission, one more step in the process of bringing Scottish
institutions into conformity with those of England. According to
William Scot, James had been contemplating doing this for two
years.[102] Once again he acted without formal consultation with any
Scottish clerical body. As in England, there was one court for each
province. In England the court in London was by far the more
important; in Scotland, by contrast, they were of equal weight.
The reason for this was that James had completely lost confidence
in his primate. Spottiswoode had been the king's principal ecclesiastical adviser for a long time, but until 1609 there was no obvious
evidence of any falling-off in James's opinion of Gledstanes. Then
the indications began to appear. Gledstanes wanted an act of parliament strengthening his position as visitor of the university of St.
Andrews; what he got was a statute which created a large commission of visitors and did not permit the archbishop to act without
the concurrence of the chancellor or his deputy. Gledstanes got
into arguments with the lord advocate over his claims respecting
the collection of customs duties at St. Andrews and with the collector and clerk register over his rentals, and took positions which
were bound to annoy the king in both cases. And he proved not
even to know what was going on in his own diocese. John Fairfoul,
a minister in Dunfermline, prayed for the exiled ministers, and
Gledstanes ingenuously admitted to James that until the king himself informed him, he knew nothing about it.[103] The king's loss of
confidence in him is therefore hardly surprising, but James could
not afford politically to inflict any public slight on Gledstanes. So
he created two courts of high commission. In 1615, after Gledstanes's death and Spottiswoode's transfer to St. Andrews, he
combined them into one.

Each commission was large and contained a number of laymen, especially that of Gledstanes, which was full of government officials. A quorum was five, of which the archbishop must be one. They had jurisdiction over laymen who were "offenders either in life or religion, whom they hold any way to be scandalous," and over ministers and teachers "whose speeches in public have been impertinent and against the established order of the kirk or against any of the conclusions of the bypast General Assemblies or in favours (*sic*) of any of these who are banished, warded, or confined for their contemptuous offences." In theory the courts were not supposed to involve themselves in matters of doctrine. They were empowered to call on the secular authorities for help in forcing people to appear and in executing their judgments. They could act as courts of appeal from other ecclesiastical jurisdictions. Whether this superseded the appellate jurisdiction over commissary courts given to the court of session by the last parliament was left unclear in 1610; the proclamation merging the courts in 1615 specifically prohibited the session from taking jurisdiction over cases in ecclesiastical courts, though whether the council had the authority to review the actions of the high commission was still in question at the end of the reign.[104]

Because of the very general language of the king's decree, the powers of the courts were theoretically very extensive and therefore extremely unwelcome to the anti-episcopal party in the kirk, which regarded them as illegal. Calderwood was particularly scandalized that the archbishop and four laymen could exercise the highest ecclesiastical jurisdiction in the land, a possibility underlined by the king's order to Gledstanes to convene his court in Edinburgh rather than St. Andrews precisely so that the councillors could attend.[105] Others were alarmed for exactly the opposite reason. The lay members of the council were very suspicious of the idea that ecclesiastics should sit in judgment on laymen.[106] The bishops could perhaps discount the opposition of the broken remnants of Andrew Melville's following, but not that of the vast majority of the council. As a result the high commission was sparingly used in James's reign. Its records have vanished, which makes for difficulties of analysis. Calderwood, whose list is incomplete, gives a total of forty-eight ministers proceeded against and twenty-one punished. The vast majority of clerical cases date from late in the reign and involve noncompliance with the five articles of Perth. Most of the charges against laymen had to do with Popery, sexual misbehavior, and disorders in churches.[107] It is clear enough that in this period the court of high commission was not an engine of royal despotism or episcopal tyranny, but the fact that it existed certainly did not diminish the growing authority of the bishops.

A month after the announcement of the creation of these courts Spottiswoode wrote to James and argued that the time was ripe for the holding of a General Assembly. The ministers were fearful that the king's next step would be the abolition of the presbyteries themselves, wrote the archbishop, and they would consent to almost anything to avoid this. "So were it good to use the opportunity to cut them short of their power, and leave them a bare name, which for the present may please, but in a little time shall vanish."[108] The king took this advice; it was an excellent opportunity to finish the job of restoring diocesan episcopacy. Gledstanes had assured him that the creation of the high commission had been quietly accepted, and the ministers of Edinburgh had reported that his recent order suspending the meetings of the court of session from Christmas day to 8 January had caused no more than a minor ruffle.[109] In December 1609 the bishops of Aberdeen and Moray urged on James one more device for neutralizing the hostility of the Protestant rank-and-file to the final restoration of diocesan episcopacy: firm action on the part of the government to stop "the open profaning of the Sabbath days, by the salmon fishing of our dioceses." At this point the chancellor, who had a pecuniary interest in the fishings and whose distaste for the bishops' tactics was growing, decided to intervene. He wrote to the king, stressing the fact that the fishings had never been stopped on Sunday before, and that such an alteration of the ancient customs of the land should be done only in parliament. But it really should not be done at all. Canon law, he said, is explicit that fishing on Sunday is perfectly proper, God having sent the commodity and the season being short. Besides, Christ's apostles were fishermen—"I read not that any of them were either fowlers or hunters"—and on

Sunday it should certainly be permitted to the good Christian to imitate the apostles.[110] James did not stop the fishing.

Gledstanes, when he heard that the king had decided to hold a General Assembly, urged that it meet in Edinburgh or Dundee and that he be moderator. James ignored him; the assembly met in Glasgow with Spottiswoode in the chair. Dunbar was sent north, for the last time as it turned out, with 10,000 merks to be spent where it would do the most good, the now customary retinue of English ecclesiastics, and a letter from the king on the abolition of presbyteries to be used to frighten the ministers. The earl acted with his customary efficiency. Four days after his arrival letters of summons went out to the presbyteries, with the names of the delegates they were to choose included; the assembly came together on 8 June, duly chose Spottiswoode as moderator, and set to work after hearing a sermon from Bishop Law on the lawfulness of episcopacy. "Passing by *jus divinum,* he stood upon these three points, Antiquity, Universality, and Perpetuity," wrote Calderwood, a line which King James would heartily have approved. James was no Laudian in either of his kingdoms; kings, not bishops, were God's vice-gerents.[111]

The Glasgow assembly completed the restoration of diocesan episcopacy in Scotland; "in one day," lamented James Melville, it overthrew "a work seventy years in building."[112] The power of the bishop over the clergy of his diocese was not exactly made absolute, but it was pretty complete. To be sure, the General Assembly could censure a bishop, and deprive him, with the king's consent—if the assembly ever met again: there was no guarantee that it would. Presbyteries continued to exist and there was no overt attack upon them, but they were not mentioned by name. It is clear enough that Spottiswoode and his allies, including the king, hoped and expected that they, and the assembly, would atrophy from disuse. Gledstanes, in fact, let the cat out of the bag at the synod of Fife in April 1611, according to Calderwood. The synod was to decide how uniformity of discipline was to be established in the diocese, "because, as the bishop affirmed, we were to have no more General Assemblies."[113] Spottiswoode and the king were too politic to say anything so provocative, but they obviously neither anticipated nor desired that the hybrid polity of 1610 would endure forever. The Scottish church and its bishops would gradually come more and more to resemble their English counterparts.[114] Commissioners of assembly were not appointed in 1610. There was no more use for the office; the king from now on would consult with his bishops in church questions, as he did in England. When the acts of this assembly received parliamentary ratification in 1612, there was no mention of the bishops' accountability to the General Assembly.[115] Presentations to benefices at once ceased to be made to presbyteries in 1610, and went to bishops instead. Excommunication became much less frequent, now that the bishop's consent had to be obtained. The withering of the presbyteries would be a slow process—their number actually increased between 1600 and 1637.[116] Spottiswoode and his master were prepared to be patient, however. Time was on their side.

The episcopal party appeared to have guessed right in deciding to push ahead with the General Assembly in 1610; there was, wrote Scot, "great murmuring" but "weak resisting" at the synods held in the fall of the year.[117] The apparent acquiescence of ministry and people in the triumph of the bishops has led some historians to conclude that King James's version of episcopacy was, if not precisely popular, at least not unsatisfactory to all classes of laymen in Scotland, including the people who counted, as well as to the ministry, most of whom went on serving.[118] This was true enough—on two conditions. There must be no change in the layman's experience of the church and religion which could give rise to an effective charge of Popery, and the bishops as individuals and as a class must pose no threat to the material interests of the powers-that-be and must integrate themselves into the governmental machinery without jarring it. Gledstanes did not understand this. He boasted to the king of having made an "honourable rent" out of "less than nothing" at St. Andrews[119]—at the cost of embroiling himself with half the high officials of the kingdom. Spottiswoode, a far more intelligent man, did see it. His ambitions tempted him into seeking high office twice in the period following Dunbar's death, but he advanced his claims cautiously and without much expectation of success. The anti-episcopal party in the church had been routed; it could revive only if it could find allies in the governing classes, the aristocracy and the lairds, and undertake once more the role of champion of the true faith endangered by the machinations of "anglopiscopapistical" prelates. For the moment such a prospect seemed most unlikely. It looked as if the central issue of Scottish politics for the past fifteen years had finally been resolved.

With the question of episcopacy on the way to solution at the beginning of 1610, Dunbar moved to facilitate its final stages, and to tighten his grip on power, by an overhaul of the privy council. The number of members had grown substantially in the past decade, from the thirty-one stipulated in the act of 1598 to somewhere over ninety, but nowhere near that many ever showed up for meetings. The *sederunts* for the first two months of 1609, a busy time for the government, show attendance ranging between seventeen and forty; a normal figure was about two dozen. As might be expected, the most regular attenders were the people who lived in Edinburgh, mostly officials and judges. It was a council in which the chancellor had more influence than anyone else, which did not commend itself to Dunbar. So the council was to be reduced to thirty-six, and the strict provisions of 1598 regarding attendance were repeated—and flouted from the beginning; for all practical purposes the council functioned as it had before. But Dunbar accomplished his main purpose, which was to minimize Dunfermline's influence by cutting down on that element in the council which would be inclined to follow his lead. This he did chiefly by eliminating the judges. Apart from officials, only one regular member of the court of session remained on the council, and that one, Sir William Livingston of Kilsyth, was not one of the chancellor's allies. About the only solace Dunfermline could take from the new slate was that it contained only three bishops, and that Spottiswoode's ally Bishop Law was not among them, an indication that Dunbar, too, was taking note of the archbishop's political ambitions.[120]

After the reorganization of the council came that of the financial administration, once more to Dunbar's advantage. The government's financial situation had been a cause for concern in both London and Edinburgh for two years. The first indication that something would be done was the replacement in February 1608 of the inefficient and sticky-fingered Scone as comptroller by Sir

James Hay of Fingask, who was honest but otherwise not much of an improvement.[121] In the following year an exchequer commission was appointed, with Spottiswoode as president, to deal with various aspects of the king's revenue, especially pensions assigned out of his rents, and a greater effort was made, by means of stricter accounting regulations, to collect the money to which the government was entitled. The results were unimpressive: in a little more than two years Fingask accumulated official debts of over £16,000.[122] Dunbar therefore decided to take advantage of Fingask's death in August 1610 to take over the comptrollership and thus combine in himself all the great financial offices. This was a permanent change, although its full significance was not immediately apparent because so much of the work had to be delegated. For example, the late comptroller's assistant, Archibald Primrose, became collector of taxation because, as the council admitted, he was the only one who knew what was going on.

Dunbar was aware that mere reorganization was not enough; there had to be changes in financial policy as well. He therefore commissioned the veteran clerk register Sir John Skene, who had done such a useful job under somewhat similar circumstances for the Octavians in 1596, to produce another set of financial proposals. Skene did so, but he admittedly had to hurry, and the result was unoriginal and not terribly helpful.[123] More than this was needed in order to come to grips with the financial problem. So, in October 1610, Dunbar and Dunfermline laid a series of proposals before the king, dealing chiefly with commerce, which led to the revision of the customs rates and the ending of free trade between England and Scotland previously discussed. James also agreed to implement a series of proposals taken from or suggested by Skene's report, among them the punishment of lawbreakers by fining them, an idea about which James felt very enthusiastic.[124]

Since Dunbar had no intention of returning to Scotland to exercise his monopolistic financial authority in person, three committees were established to do much of the necessary work. The chancellor was the key man in all three. He was the chairman of two, the committee to revise the book of customs rates and the twenty-four-man commission of the exchequer, whose function was "to call before them all the King's officers of receipt or others indebted to his Majesty, and to take order for payments by them." The third committee was a board of six assessors, all members of the other two bodies, to work with the treasurer-depute, Sir John Arnot, whenever Dunbar was absent from Scotland. Arnot could do nothing of any importance without the signatures of Dunfermline and at least one other member of the board.[125]

The three committees had hardly had a chance to begin to work before their continuation, and much more, was called in question by Dunbar's sudden death at the end of January 1611. It came at a time when the lord treasurer stood at the pinnacle of his power. His brutal but effective tactics had restored diocesan episcopacy in the Scottish church; having succeeded in this, he was moving in the last year of his life toward still tighter control of Scottish affairs. The reorganization of the council, his monopolization of financial office, his attempt to turn Dunfermline openly into his subordinate by saddling him with responsibility on various financial committees, all point in the same direction. Possibly, had he lived longer, he might have become a power in English politics as well. The failure of the Great Contract had weakened Salisbury's position, and Dunbar had persuaded James to make his candidate, George Abbot, archbishop of Canterbury and had arranged a marriage alliance with the Howards. What is not clear is what he would have done with such power, other than to employ it against any threat to its continued growth. Of all the major political figures in Jacobean Scotland, Dunbar bears the closest resemblance to Machiavelli's prince.

A definitive assessment of Dunbar's place in Scottish history must await a more detailed study of the financial record during his tenure as lord treasurer. Throughout his career his constant preoccupation was with means rather than ends, with the accumulation of authority rather than the public uses to which it might be put. It is nevertheless true that during his five years of power Scotland underwent very substantial changes. Some of those for which his responsibility was greatest, on the borders and in the church, for example, were continuations of policies inaugurated before 1603. Others were the consequence of the royal vision of union, like the courts of high commission. Still others, like highland policy, were the council in Edinburgh's work rather than Dunbar's. Wherever responsibility lay, however, change had been more rapid and far-reaching than at any other time during James's years in England, and the government's methods were both efficient and far from gentle. Dunbar got things done. If ever there was a period of time during which James's government of Scotland could properly be called despotic, Dunbar's years of power constitute that period.

NOTES

1. See, for instance, the fulsome letter of praise of Dunbar the council sent to James in Aug. 1605, Sir William Fraser, *The Elphinstone Family Book of the Lords Elphinstone, Balmerino, and Coupar* (Edinburgh, 1897) II, 152–53, and the letter of the earl of Cassillis to James in 1606, NLS, Denmilne Mss. I, no. 62. This letter makes it very clear that Dunbar was regarded as the king's spokesman.

2. See, for example, his letter of 26 Nov. 1606 to Mar, *M&K Supp.,* pp. 38–39.

3. *RPCS* VIII, 528.

4. *Calderwood* IV, 479–80. *Scot,* p. 157. *RPCS* VII, 214. See also *Spottiswoode* III, 175.

5. See, e.g., *LEA* I, 18, 455–56.

6. The quoted phrase is in Angus's letter, dated 15 June 1606, NLS, Denmilne Mss. I, no. 69. There are also letters to the same effect from Argyll, Glencairn, and Cassillis in this collection.

7. 18 Jan. 1606, Lauriston to James, 19 June, Gledstanes to James, *LEA* I, 35, 53–54. 4 July, the council to James, *Melros* I, 15–18. *Calderwood* VI, 492.

8. *Melros* I, 15–18. *Calderwood* VI, 485, 492–93. *Scot,* pp. 157–59. The act of repeal is in *APS* IV, 281–84.

9. *LEA* I, 54–55.

10. See, e.g., James's letter to Mar in Sept. 1612 justifying his refusal of Mar's request for a peerage for Ogilvie of Findlater, *M&K,* p. 68.

11. *Calderwood* VI, 493–94.

12. *APS* IV, 324–26. *RPCS* VIII, 601. 10 Feb. 1609, John Preston of Fentonbarns to James, *LEA* I, 184. See the survey of the possession of abbatial lands in 1625 by David Masson in *RPCS,* 2nd ser., I, cxliv–cxlvi. For a good example of the intricate financial and legal problems of some of the bishops, see 17 June 1607, the bishop of Ross to James, *LEA* I, 93–94.

13. W. R. Foster, *The Church before the Covenants* (Edinburgh, 1975), p. 21. In the 1560s 100 merks was thought to be an adequate stipend for a minister—a good indication of both the inflation and the debasement of the last third of the century; see W. C. Dickinson, ed., *John Knox's History of the Reformation in*

Scotland (New York, 1950) II, 30. The relative poverty of the bishoprics is indicated by the fact that the annual revenue of Dunkeld, admittedly an extreme case, was estimated in 1605 at 400 merks; see *LEA* I, 10–11.

14. *APS* IV, 299–300. *RPCS* VII, 222–23. For an example of the king's wayward generosity, see *ibid.,* pp. 594–95. This paragraph is based largely on W. R. Foster, "A Constant Platt Achieved: Provision for the Ministry, 1600–1638," in D. Shaw, ed., *Reformation and Revolution* (Edinburgh, 1967), pp. 127–30.

15. *APS* IV, 289–92. *RPCS* VII, 340, 416, 543–44, VIII, 25–26, 96. Dumbarton eventually got some money, but not as much as was estimated to be necessary. For the question of free trade see below, pp. 84ff.

16. *Spottiswoode* III, 175–76. Oct. 1606, Dunfermline to James, *LSP,* pp. 88–90.

17. *Melvill,* pp. 634–37. *Scot,* pp. 164–65. *RPCS* VII, 218–19, 494–97.

18. 26 Nov. 1606, Dunbar to Mar, *M&K Supp.,* pp. 38–39.

19. *RPCS* VII, 370, 406.

20. *Melvill,* pp. 699–700.

21. There are accounts of this meeting in *Calderwood* VI, 604–20, *Scot,* pp. 179–84, *Melvill,* pp. 683–85, and *Spottiswoode* III, 183–87. Dunbar allegedly spent 40,000 merks in bribes to needy clerics; see Foster, *Church before the Covenants,* p. 123. The quoted phrase is from *Calderwood* VI, 601.

22. 13 Dec. 1606, Montrose to James, 16 Dec., the king's commissioners to James, *LEA* I, 69–70, 72–73. 19 Dec., Balmerino to James, Fraser, *Elphinstone* II, 176–77. *Calderwood* VI, 630.

23. *Scot,* p. 184.

24. *Calderwood* VI, 624–26, 629–30, 649–53. See also *Melvill,* pp. 687–88.

25. See, e.g., 3 July 1607, James to Sir Walter Ogilvie of Findlater and John Grant, giving them their instructions as commissioners to the synod of Moray, Sir William Fraser, *The Chiefs of Grant* II (Edinburgh, 1883), 4–6, and the earl of Abercorn's account of his success in imposing Spottiswoode as constant moderator of the synod of Glasgow, 26 Aug. 1607, Abercorn to James, *LSP,* pp. 117–19. *Melvill,* p. 730. *Calderwood* VI, 688. 17 Apr. 1608, Gledstanes to James, *LEA* I, 128–31. Foster, *Church before the Covenants,* pp. 20–21, does not believe that manipulation of stipends was very effective as a tactical device, though he states that six of fourteen of the government's clerical opponents for whose incomes he has figures suffered reductions.

26. *RPCS* XIV, 597–98.

27. *Melros* I, 23–26. J. D. Marwick, *Early History of Glasgow* (Glasgow, 1911), pp. 308–9.

28. *RPCS* VII, 52, 297–302, 311–12, 357, 374–77, 380, 521–23, VIII, 47, 68, 92, XIV, 612–14. *LEA* I, 88–89. G. F. Black, "A Calendar of Cases of Witchcraft in Scotland, 1510–1727," *Bulletin of the New York Public Library* XLI (1937), 811–47.

29. *Calderwood* VI, 689–92, 699–702, VII, 19–20. *RPCS* VIII, 72–73, 270–71, 563–64, XIV, 472. *LEA* I, 122–23. *Scot,* p. 209. 10 Mar. 1608, the

council to James, 7 Mar., 28 Mar., 30 Apr., James to the council, *RPCS* VIII, 492–94, 496, 499–500. Moray stayed a year and a half in Dumfries; he eventually obtained a charge in Dunfermline, probably owing to the chancellor's influence. See Hew Scott, ed., *Fasti Ecclesiae Scoticanae*, new ed. (Edinburgh, 1925), I, 165, V, 28, 34.

30. *RPCS* VII, 297–99, 506–9, 511, 527–28, 530–31, VIII, 97, XIV, 600. *LSP*, pp. 94–96, 102.

31. 21 Jan. 1607, Balmerino to James, *LSP*, p. 97. *RPCS* VIII, 485–86. The borderers' letter is in *LSP*, pp. 179–82.

32. *RPCS* VIII, 195–96, 262–63, 343–45, 348, 450, 591–92, 621–23.

33. *RPCS* VII, 509–10, 748–49, VIII, 31, 81, 128, 253, 561–62, IX, 714–15, XIV, 603. W. R. Foster, "Episcopal Administration in Scotland 1600–1638" (Ph.D. thesis, University of Edinburgh, 1963), pp. 156–58. The problem of assessing the Selkirkshire report is complicated by the fact that in 1611 the justice of the peace was a new officer in Scotland; the novelty may explain some of the lack of cooperation the justices received.

34. *M&K Supp.*, pp. 38–39.

35. 16 Jan. 1607, Lake to Salisbury, *Salisbury* XIX, 11–12; see also *ibid.*, pp. 44, 254, 427. 15 Feb., Sir William Seton to Lawson, 23 Feb., 10 Mar., Dunbar to the bishop of Carlisle, NLS, Mss. 5275, pp. 1065–67, 1072–74, 1102–4. *RPCS* VII, 728–29, VIII, 15–16, 485–86.

36. This letter is in *LSP*, pp. 179–82, where it is tentatively, and wrongly, dated 1609.

37. *RPCS* VIII, 278–79, 846. *Melros* I, 38–39. *Calderwood* VII, 48, mentions a mass execution in Dumfries in July 1609. The saga of the pursuit of Maxwell can be followed in *RPCS* VII, 412ff., VIII, 20ff. He remained at large for five years, murdered his ancient enemy the laird of Johnstone, who had killed Maxwell's father in the battle of Dryfe Sands in 1593, and eventually was executed.

38. *LSP*, pp. 171–73. This letter is a particularly choice sample of Dunfermline's customary style of writing to the king in this period, full of excessive flattery of James and praise of Dunbar, and of classical allusions.

39. See, e.g., *RPCS* IX, 234–35, 320–21, 478–79, X, 519–20, 566–70, XI, 216, 228.

40. This paragraph is based largely on M. Perceval-Maxwell, *The Scottish Migration to Ulster in the Reign of James I* (London, 1973).

41. *RPCS* VII, 504, 524–25. 28 Feb. 1607, Argyll to James, *LSP*, p. 101.

42. *RPCS* VII, 287–88, 340–42, 360–62, 372–73, 395–96, 423, 426–27, 511–12, 516–21, 523–25, 528–29, VIII, 9, 490–91. NLS, Denmilne Mss. II, nos. 14, 16, 22, 44. *LEA* I, 321. 7 Jan. 1607, Dunfermline to James, *LSP*, pp. 94–96. *APS* IV, 379–80. D. Gregory, *The History of the Western Highlands and Isles of Scotland*, 2nd ed. (London, 1881), pp. 311–13.

43. *RMS 1593–1608*, pp. 683–84, 719–20. *RPCS* VII, 396. 29 July 1607, James to Balmerino, Fraser, *Elphinstone* II, 155. A. Cunningham, *The Loyal Clans* (Cambridge, 1932), pp. 174–77.

44. *RPCS* VIII, 59–61, 72, 73, 93–94, 502, 737, 766–67. *Melros* I, 45–47.

45. *RPCS* VIII, 113–14, 507–8, 738, 739–40.

46. *Ibid.*, pp. 100, 156, 281, 590, 738–39, 751, X, 68–70. Ochiltree's financial straits grew so serious that in 1615 he sold his peerage to his cousin Sir James Stewart of Killeith. James later granted him an Irish peerage.

47. *RPCS* VIII, 533–34. Ochiltree's expedition can be followed in the letters between him and the council in *ibid.*, pp. 521–26, and his report, *ibid.*, pp. 173–75. See also the careful narrative in Gregory, *Western Highlands,* pp. 318–24. The story of the kidnapping does not appear in Ochiltree's reports; it can be found in a contemporary account, J. W. Mackenzie, ed., *A Chronicle of the Kings of Scotland,* Maitland Club (Edinburgh, 1830), pp. 176–77.

48. *LEA* I, 152–53.

49. *RPCS* VIII, 742–46.

50. Gregory, *Western Highlands,* pp. 326–28, in his account of the trial, suggests that James MacDonald knew that his life would be spared in return for his failure to reveal that the king had formally approved of the act of fire-raising, which had occurred in Kintyre in 1598 and had resulted in the seizure of MacDonald's father, whom he hated. MacDonald had set fire to a house knowing that his parents were inside. It is hardly surprising that James thought the highlanders barbaric.

51. *RPCS* VIII, 752–56, 759–61. The statutes and accompanying regulations are in *RPCS* IX, 24–33.

52. In Feb. 1612 the government ordered that any chief who had acquired church lands after 1587 would have to renounce them as a precondition of any new feu or tack; see *RPCS* IX, 733. For the burghs see *RCRB* II, 30, 312–13, 374.

53. S. G. E. Lythe, *The Economy of Scotland in Its European Setting 1550–1625* (Edinburgh, 1960), p. 11. The quotation is from Cunningham, *Loyal Clans,* p. 205.

54. *RPCS* IX, 16–18, 30–33, 569–70. In 1612 James granted Knox a feu of the island of Barra for life and annexed the temporalities of the abbey of Iona and the priory of Ardchattan to the bishopric of the Isles; see *ibid.*, p. 733. Knox's simultaneous tenure of two bishoprics created administrative problems, and early in 1619 he demitted the bishopric of the Isles. James conferred it on Knox's son, who had been handling most of its administrative business.

55. *Ibid.*, pp. 2, 13–15. Gregory, *Western Highlands,* pp. 334–38.

56. This is the conclusion of Gordon Donaldson, *Shetland Life under Earl Patrick* (Edinburgh, 1958), p. 10. It is supported by the fact that in 1620, five years after the execution of Earl Patrick, the council was again receiving complaints about oppression from Shetland; see *RPCS* XII, 263–64, 270–71. *Spottiswoode* III, 213. When Orkney was annexed to the crown the earl's chief creditor, Sir John Arnot, had to be paid off to the tune of £300,000; see *APS* IV, 480–83.

57. *Melros* I, 54–55. *LEA* I, 167–69. *RPCS* VIII, 379, 406, 433, 541–42, 587–88, 611, 615.

58. See, e.g., *Melros* I, 27–28, *RPCS* VII, 524, VIII, 34–35, 489–90, 494–96.

59. *APS* IV, 436. PRO, SP 14/44, no. 66. The union legislation is in *APS* IV, 366–71, the covering letter in *RPCS* VII, 534–37. For the debates in the English parliament see W. Notestein, *The House of Commons 1604–1610* (New Haven, Conn., 1971), pp. 211–54.

60. *Salisbury* XIX, 363, 440–41. On the question of uniformity of law see B. P. Levack, "The Proposed Union of English Law and Scots Law in the Seventeenth Century," *Juridical Review,* n.s., XX (1975), 97–115. Scottish resentment at the royal use of *Great Britain* came to the surface in 1630. See S. T. Bindoff, "The Stuarts and Their Style," *English Historical Review* LX (1945), 213.

61. *RCRB* II, 252–55. 10 Dec. 1609, Lake to Salisbury, *CSPD 1603–1610,* p. 569.

62. *APS* IV, 368–71.

63. *Ibid.,* p. 375. 30 Jan. 1608, Hamilton to Dunbar, *Salisbury* XX, 34–35. See also *RPCS* VII, 304.

64. 15 Feb. 1606, Dunfermline and Balmerino to Salisbury, PRO, SP 14/26, no. 50. 10 Nov. 1609, James to the council, *RPCS* VIII, 606.

65. *RPCS* VII, 290, VIII, 455, IX, 508–9, 591–92, XIV, 598.

66. *RPCS* VII, 392, 529, VIII, 8, 19, 810–13. Lythe, *Economy of Scotland,* p. 202.

67. *RPCS* IX, lxv–lxxv, 93–94, 199–200, 262–71, 377–78, 584–85, 605–6, 625–26, 630, 715–24, 727–29, 741–43, X, 620–21. *APS* IV, 285. *RCRB* II, 372–73, 375–76. 15 May 1612, Spottiswoode to Sir James Semple, Sir William Fraser, *Memoirs of the Maxwells of Pollok* (Edinburgh, 1863) II, 56–61. S. G. E. Lythe, "The Union of the Crowns in 1603 and the Debate on Economic Integration," *Scottish Journal of Political Economy* V (1958), 226. *RCRB* II, 422–23. See also the memorandum of Dunfermline and Dunbar, written in Oct. 1610, in BM, Add. Mss. 24,275, ff. 9–9b.

68. *RPCS* VIII, 93–94, 503, 550. 21 May 1608, the council to James, *Melros* I, 45–47.

69. *RPCS* VIII, 517–18, 547, 568–69, 575–76. The mine owners also tried to persuade the burghs to withdraw their opposition to coal exports; see *RCRB* II, 270.

70. *RPCS* IX, 378–79. See the figures in *M&K,* pp. 70–74. Lythe, *Economy of Scotland,* pp. 83–85, 110, 112. J. U. Nef, *The Rise of the British Coal Industry* (London, 1932) II, 224–27.

71. In this connection see the memorandum of Dunfermline and Dunbar to the king in Oct. 1610, BM, Add. Mss. 24,275, ff. 9–9b.

72. *RPCS* VIII, 234, 543–44, 552–54, 775–76. Lythe, *Economy of Scotland,* pp. 142–49.

73. See, e.g., *RPCS* VIII, 261, 546–47, 555–56, 559, 567, IX, 592, 598–99, 627–29, XIV, 558–59. *RCRB* II, 334–35, 361–67, 381–83, 385–98. NLS, Denmilne Mss. IV, nos. 4, 14.

74. See, e.g., the case of the alum monopoly, *RPCS* VIII, 593, 596. 14 Sept.

1609, Dunfermline and John Preston of Fentonbarns to Dunbar, NLS, Denmilne Mss. III, no. 26.

75. See, e.g., *RPCS* IX, 351.

76. *APS* IV, 286–87. *RPCS* VII, 434, VIII, 168, IX, 333–34. R. W. Cochran-Patrick, *Early Records Relating to Mining in Scotland* (Edinburgh, 1878), pp. xlvii, lxiv. Nef, *Coal Industry* II, 158, 162–63. There was a close connection between coal mining and the making of salt, which was produced from sea water by coal-fired evaporating pans; see Lythe, *Economy of Scotland,* pp. 49–50.

77. See, e.g., *RCRB* II, 202–3. *RPCS* VII, 293–94, 321–22, 331, VIII, 366–67, 811. Lythe, *Economy of Scotland,* pp. 38–39. T. Keith, "The Influence of the Convention of the Royal Burghs of Scotland on the Economic Development of Scotland before 1707," *SHR* X (1912–13), 256–59.

78. Dunfermline ceased to be provost in 1608 in consequence of James's order that henceforth only a resident burgess was eligible for burghal office; see *APS* IV, 435–36. During his tenure the town prospered, there was a building boom, and the king granted a new and favorable charter. Dunfermline's solicitude for Edinburgh's interests made him very popular; in 1616 the authorities built a special seat in St. Giles for the man whom, twenty years earlier, the town mob had wanted to lynch. See M. Wood, ed., *Extracts from the Records of the Burgh of Edinburgh* (Edinburgh, 1927–31) V, 320, VI, 44, 47, 142.

79. *Calderwood* VI, 716–26, 732–34. *RPCS* VIII, 116–17. The parallel with the committee of the articles was specifically drawn by Spottiswoode himself at the General Assembly of 1618; see *Calderwood* VII, 320–21.

80. 17 Apr. 1608, Gledstanes to James, *LEA* I, 128–31. *Calderwood* VI, 681–82, 704–6, 777. *RCRB* II, 260–61. *RPCS* VIII, 63, 87–88, 94, 104, 505–6.

81. *Calderwood* VI, 735.

82. 20 July 1608, James to the General Assembly, *LEA* I, 143–45.

83. *Ibid.,* pp. 198–99, 429. *Calderwood* VI, 751. Law was the first bishop to serve as moderator since 1575; see Foster, *Church before the Covenants,* p. 22.

84. *LEA* I, 145–47. For this assembly see *Calderwood* VI, 751–58; T. Thomson, ed., *Acts and Proceedings of the General Assemblies of the Kirk of Scotland* III, Maitland Club (Edinburgh, 1845), 1047–59; *Spottiswoode* III, 193–97; *Melvill,* pp. 754–55.

85. *LSP,* pp. 142–44. *Spottiswoode* III, 197. 15 Aug. 1608, Anne to Dunfermline *et al.,* Fraser, *Elphinstone* II, 158.

86. NLS, Denmilne Mss. II, no. 94. See also nos. 84, 85; *RPCS* VIII, 189–90, 536.

87. *Salisbury* XXI, 172–73. The editor of the Salisbury manuscripts has tentatively dated this letter 1609. The context indicates that it was written in Oct. 1608. Balmerino had been a member of the queen's council from its inception—hence Hay's fear that she might intervene on his behalf.

88. On this point see M. Lee, Jr., *James I and Henri IV* (Urbana, Ill., 1970), pp. 127–30.

89. *Calderwood* VII, 14.

90. See their letter to James in Sept. 1607, *LEA* I, 108–9.

91. *Spottiswoode* III, 204–5.

92. *Calderwood* VI, 826–27. *LSP,* p. 131. *LEA* I, 172–76.

93. *RPCS* VIII, 235–36. 11 Feb. 1609, Dunfermline to James, NLS, Denmilne Mss. III, no. 8.

94. *RPCS* VIII, 232. The king's letter on the subject, dated 9 Jan. 1609, indicates that Dunbar prompted the move; see *ibid.,* pp. 549–50. *APS* IV, 449.

95. *RPCS* VIII, 231–32, 551–52, 554–55, XIV, 610–11. *Calderwood* VII, 3–5, misstates the convention's decision respecting heirs to landed property; he assumes that the king's wishes were followed. *Spottiswoode* III, 201, states the decision correctly. Parliament confirmed these enactments in June 1609; see *APS* IV, 428–29.

96. *RPCS* VIII, 262, 266, 581–83. *LEA* I, 192–96. *M&K,* pp. 60–63. 15 Nov. 1610, James to the council, *RPCS* IX, 585–86. See also *ibid.,* pp. 99–100, 117; *Calderwood* VII, 158–59; *Spottiswoode* III, 208. Huntly, as the price of his release, had to return to the crown lands wadset to his ancestor by James IV in return for the original fee of 800 merks. Given the intervening inflation, Huntly could hardly have been pleased. See *RPCS* IX, 588–89.

97. *Scot,* pp. 206–11. *Calderwood* VII, 5–8. *LEA* I, 185–91.

98. 24 Mar. 1609, James to Hamilton, *RPCS* VIII, 799–800.

99. *LEA* I, 191–92, 197–98. PRO, SP 14/44, no. 66. *RPCS* VIII, 562–63. 7 June 1609, James to Mar, *M&K,* pp. 63–64.

100. On this point see *Calderwood* VII, 45–46.

101. *APS* IV, 430–31, 444–45, 461–64. Foster, *Church before the Covenants,* pp. 22–23. *Laing,* pp. 114–21. The revival of the bishops' control over the commissary courts meant that quot silver would no longer go to the members of the college of justice. Parliament therefore voted the court an annual sum of £10,000, the first direct subvention from the government that the court received; see *APS* IV, 437–39; R. K. Hannay, *The College of Justice* (Edinburgh, 1933), p. 89. For the commissary courts see G. Donaldson, "The Church Courts," in *An Introduction to Scottish Legal History,* Stair Society (Edinburgh, 1958), pp. 366–70.

102. *Scot,* p. 199.

103. *LEA* I, 203–4, 215–19, 411–13. *RPCS* VIII, 378, 381, 601–2, 604–5. *APS* IV, 442–43, 453–54.

104. See *Calderwood* VII, 57–62, 204–10, for the texts of the proclamations of 1610 and 1615. 18 Nov. 1624, Spottiswoode to Lochmaben, *LEA* II, 769–70.

105. *Calderwood* VII, 62–63. *Scot,* pp. 220–21. 15 Oct. 1611, James to the council, *RPCS* IX, 634. Spottiswoode was under no such restriction.

106. On this point see *Spottiswoode* III, 212.

107. *LEA* I, 265–66, 274–76. See the analysis in G. MacMahon, "The Scottish Courts of High Commission, 1610–1638," *Records of the Scottish Church History Society* XV (1966), 193–209, esp. pp. 200–201.

108. 12 Mar. 1610, Spottiswoode to James, *LEA* I, 235–36.

109. 17 Feb. 1610, John Hall and M. P. Hewatt to James, 18 Feb., Gledstanes to James, *ibid.*, pp. 228–31. *Calderwood* VII, 52–53.

110. *LEA* I, 220–21. 17 Mar. 1610, Dunfermline to James, NLS, Mss. 33.1.15, ff. 24–26.

111. 18 Apr. 1610, Gledstanes to James, *LEA* I, 245–47. *Calderwood* VII, 90–92, 94, 97–98. James's authorization for the money is in *RPCS* VIII, 844.

112. *Melvill*, p. 792. For this assembly see *Calderwood* VII, 94–115, *Spottiswoode* III, 205–7, and *Scot*, pp. 221–32.

113. *Calderwood* VII, 157.

114. It seems likely that it was for this reason rather than on account of any belief in the doctrine of apostolic succession that James arranged for the consecration of three Scottish bishops in England in the fall of 1610. The three then did the same service for their other Scottish colleagues; see *ibid.*, p. 150; *Scot*, pp. 234–35.

115. *APS* IV, 469–70. *Calderwood* VII, 171–73. A. Ian Dunlop, "The Polity of the Scottish Church, 1600–1637," *Records of the Scottish Church History Society* XII (1958), 164.

116. W. R. Foster, "The Operation of Presbyteries in Scotland, 1600–1638," *Records of the Scottish Church History Society* XV (1966), 22, 27–28. See also his *Church before the Covenants*, pp. 24–25.

117. *Scot*, p. 234. See also *Calderwood* VII, 119–23, 125–29.

118. See, e.g., Foster, *Church before the Covenants*, p. 29; G. Donaldson, *Scotland: James V—James VII* (Edinburgh, 1965), pp. 205–8. It seems to me that in this passage Professor Donaldson lays too much stress on the presbyterian elements in the mixed polity and too little on the king's and bishops' expectation of their eventual withering. Donaldson points out elsewhere that the tradition of the Scottish church was strongly hostile to schism: "The Emergence of Schism in Seventeenth-century Scotland," in D. Baker, ed., *Schism, Heresy, and Religious Protest* (Cambridge, Eng., 1972), pp. 277–94.

119. *LEA* I, 215–17.

120. *RPCS* VIII, 617, 815–16, 422, 621–23.

121. 11 Aug. 1609, the council to James, *Melros* I, 69–70. NLS, Denmilne Mss. V, no. 111.

122. *RPCS* VIII, 743, IX, 49–50, 62. 29 Dec. 1608, Spottiswoode to James, *LEA* I, 179–80. A. L. Murray, "Sir John Skene and the Exchequer, 1594–1612," *Miscellany One* Stair Society (Edinburgh, 1971), p. 132. BM, Add. Mss. 24,275, ff. 11–12. *M&K*, p. 155.

123. Skene's "Proposals anent the order of the Checker," edited by A. L. Murray, form an appendix to his article on Skene in *Miscellany One*, pp. 147–55. The proposals are undated; Dunbar's request for haste, to which Skene refers, suggests that the lord treasurer ordered them drawn up between Fingask's death and his own return to England, a period of about a month.

124. See his exchange with the council over the fining of the earl of Lothian, *RPCS* IX, 164–65, 174, 606–7, 609, 610–11.

125. *Ibid.*, pp. 85–86, 584–85.

4

The Dunfermline Administration

In spite of his chronic bad health the death of Dunbar was altogether unexpected. Dunfermline and his colleagues hastily sent their fellow councillor, Dunbar's friend Lord Burley, to the king to urge him to make no change in the newly created administrative machinery for the time being, and to take his time in filling Dunbar's accumulated offices.[1] Everyone had been caught by surprise and wanted time to assess the impact of the great earl's death, to bargain and maneuver in the power vacuum so suddenly created.

It was soon apparent that there would be no successor to Dunbar among the Scots at court. None of them had a great office in Scotland to serve as a power base. The two great lords who were influential enough to aspire to the position with some hope of success declined to do so. Lennox flatly rejected Livingston of Kilsyth's request that he involve himself in Scottish affairs, and Mar at this stage was more interested in a ceremonial office at court, such as the mastership of the horse, than in the vacant treasury.[2] There was the additional complication of an imponderable new element in Scottish politics, in the person of the king's favorite Robert Ker (or Carr), who in the spring of 1611 got a Garter and became Viscount Rochester in the English peerage. Rochester was the brother of Sir Andrew Ker of Ferniehirst, and there already was evidence that he planned to advance his kindred, of whom he had many. The last appointment to the Scottish council before Dunbar's death was that of Rochester's uncle Sir Gideon Murray of Elibank; the man who replaced Dunbar himself was Rochester's first cousin Scott of Buccleuch. Another of Rochester's relatives was Lord Advocate Hamilton, who could clearly be expected, sooner or later, to try to turn the relationship to advantage. Hamilton was the most important politician among Rochester's kin, but Elibank was his closest confidant and became his principal agent in Scotland, a situation which posed something of a problem for the ambitious lord advocate.

Kilsyth's request to Lennox was prompted by the fact that there was an obvious successor to Dunbar in Edinburgh. Dunfermline's pre-eminence after Dunbar was widely recognized. His most serious potential rival was Archbishop Spottiswoode, who praised the deceased lord treasurer as "a man of deep wit, few words, and in his Majesty's service no less faithful than fortunate."[3] Dunbar had certainly labored mightily in the cause of episcopacy, but unfortunately for the archbishop's political ambitions he had died too soon. The restoration of episcopacy was of too recent date for the landed classes to acquiesce in a bishop's wielding great power in the state, and the embarrassing Gledstanes was still primate. Furthermore, in the one temporal field in which Spottiswoode could justly claim that he merited consideration, finance, the awkward fact was that the chancellor, not he, held the crucial committee posts. Only if his rival made a major blunder would the archbishop have a real chance.

The chancellor had every intention of wielding Dunbar's influence, but not by Dunbar's despotic and arbitrary methods. The latter's favorite device was intimidation; Dunfermline, student of Machiavelli though he was, preferred to be loved rather than feared. From the beginning he had been a committee man, and the events of 1596 had taught him the dangers inherent in a policy of confrontation. Persuasion was his technique and consensus his objective. He would make himself so necessary and useful and agreeable to so many people that his position would become unassailable.

Another difference between Dunfermline and Dunbar was that the chancellor could not make his base at Whitehall, as Dunbar had done, nor did he want to. He disliked traveling, especially in winter, and grumbled at having to go to court. This meant that he needed allies around the king. His first thought was his friend Salisbury; in his letter expressing his shock at Dunbar's death he asked Salisbury's help in bearing "a burden both above my capacity and strength." But his visit to court in the spring of 1611 convinced him that this would not do. Salisbury's influence had obviously waned, and in any case it would be far more prudent to work through Scots. So his two chief conduits became his new kinsman by marriage, Sir Thomas Erskine, now Viscount Fenton, especially after Fenton's cousin Mar became lord treasurer in 1616, and John Murray of Lochmaben, whose family interests and estate-building plans in the southwest the chancellor furthered substantially in the next decade.[4]

Because Dunfermline's system depended on consensus and correspondence, the most desirable way of dealing with substantive issues was for the chancellor and his allies to agree upon a policy and recommend it to the king, who would then issue the necessary instructions to the council. In form, therefore, the government was carried on much as before: still, apparently, government by pen, Whitehall proposing and Edinburgh disposing. But in fact the initiative now came from the north; the governing pen belonged to the chancellor, not the king. One indication that this was so was that, by contrast with Dunbar's day, the king almost never wrote a scolding letter to his council any more, save occasionally in questions of religion. There was no more lecturing by the royal schoolmaster keeping his charges in line; the letters the king now wrote were the ones the council wanted, and expected, to receive.

James himself, as he grew older, came to prefer Dunfermline's technique to having to choose between conflicting opinions. "Conditions settled by yourselves before he [Elibank] come to the King will make his Majesty the better contented," wrote Fenton to Mar in August 1616, when Mar and Elibank, then treasurer-depute, were working out the terms of their relationship in the light of Mar's impending appointment as lord treasurer. "You know how much it troubles him when matters are in question."[5] So controversy was to be avoided wherever possible; no hard choices were to be placed before the king if Dunfermline and his associates could help it.[6] One of the king's characteristics did not change with the advancing years, however. He still tended to listen to the people around him, and to be generous to those he liked; he was the more prone to indulge such impulses because the steady supply of first-hand information which Dunbar's traveling had supplied was no longer available to him, and because Dunfermline was not on the spot to kill unwelcome proposals at once. Furthermore the chancellor could not be sure that his allies at court would always place the government's interests ahead of private ones, or his ahead of those of their other friends. These considerations, among others, prompted Dunfermline and his colleagues to ask the king in May 1611 to send all private requests to them through official channels rather than via the petitioners themselves, "who ofttimes preferring their own apprehensions and opinions to modesty and reason, doth (*sic*) blame us as crossers and hinderers of them in their hopes of your Majesty's benevolence and favor."[7]

Sometimes, of course, in spite of these precautions, an unwelcome or injudicious royal order arrived. In such cases Dunfermline and his colleagues showed considerable skill in the fine art of stalling and then, in most respectful tones, inducing the king to change his instructions. They had to be careful: James could be persuaded that he had made a mistake, but only if he did not have to admit it publicly, and if his error could be ascribed to lack of information rather than stupidity. "Alas, sir," said the earl of Mar to James's obstinate son in 1626, "a hundred times your worthy father has sent down directions unto us which we have stayed, and he has given us thanks for it when we have informed him of the truth."[8]

Dunfermline was confident of his ability to manage things and to keep control of the council. He was prepared, if need be, to take advantage of the division of authority between Edinburgh and Whitehall and to use his pipeline to the king to get James to overturn a conciliar decision of which he disapproved.[9] But he did not expect to have to do this very often, nor did he. His system worked very well most of the time, but it had one potentially serious weakness. Because it fed the king ready-made solutions, because all the responsible people in the Scottish administration were now in Edinburgh rather than Whitehall, and because there was no one who, like Dunbar, traveled back and forth between Scotland and the court on a regular basis, James after 1611 was less well informed than before about the tides of opinion in his

ancient kingdom. Most of the time this made no difference, because Dunfermline and his associates were efficient and able. But
at least once it was to have very serious consequences.

If Dunfermline was to exploit fully the opportunity Dunbar's
death presented to him, the first requirement was a journey to
court. He was not alone; a number of other major political figures
also turned up there, including Hamilton and Spottiswoode. In
spite of the presence of these potential rivals Dunfermline got
what he wanted. There were two major administrative areas in
which Dunbar's authority had been well-nigh absolute by virtue of
his offices, the treasury and the borders. In neither area was he
replaced. The government's long-range purpose on the borders
was to eliminate all special administrative machinery. The king
judged that it was too soon to do that, however; so he revived the
border commission which had administered the area between the
time of his departure for England and his grant of authority to
Dunbar at the end of 1606. The decision was made early in April
1611 and was implemented in June with the issue of a commission
to Cranston, Elibank, Dunfermline's brother Sir William Seton,
and Lochmaben's brother Sir David Murray of Clonyaird, to act as
justices in the borders. They received all the powers of the justices
of the peace in more ample form; this commission represented
what the government hoped would be a major step in the direction of ordinary local administration. The commissioners' work
was made substantially easier by an increase in the size of the
police force and by the overturning of the regulation, supported
by Dunbar, which stipulated that a Scot who committed a crime in
England, and vice versa, be returned to his home country for trial;
in July the king authorized the trial at the scene of the crime.[10]
The establishment of this commission suited Dunfermline very
well; through his brother he could make his influence felt to whatever extent he thought necessary.

The decision on the treasury was more crucial. It could be argued that the sort of power Dunbar had wielded on the borders
was no longer necessary—though there was one large-scale raid in
the old style shortly after Dunbar's death, and the new commissioners hanged thirty-eight malefactors between July and October,
all of which indicated that lawlessness was not dead there.[11] But

the kingdom's financial affairs were in far from good condition, and it would have seemed logical to appoint a new lord treasurer, and thus a new rival for Dunfermline. Spottiswoode was eager for the post and pressed the king for the appointment. But James did not do this. Instead he named an eight-man treasury commission, promptly dubbed the new Octavians, headed, like the old ones, by Dunfermline.[12] At the same time two new appointments to the council signaled the end of Dunbar's reorganization scheme. One, Viscount Fenton, was bound to be a permanent absentee. The other, Sir Alexander Drummond, a member of the court of session, marked the revival of the bureaucratizing trend which Dunbar's reorganization had interrupted; by the end of James's reign every member of the court of session would be a privy councillor, a development which Dunfermline, with his long connection with the court, very much favored. These decisions, and the king's gift to him of one of the plums Dunbar had enjoyed, the keepership for life of the palace and park of Holyroodhouse, made it clear that Dunfermline was to be Dunbar's successor. He was now head of the Scottish political and administrative structure in fact as well as in name, and was to remain so until his death in 1622.

There was to be only one major challenge to Dunfermline's supremacy during his decade of power. It started in the spring of 1612, with old Sir John Skene, the clerk register, who was nearing seventy and was anxious to retire. He sent his son James, who had been associated with him in the office for some years, to court with a letter of resignation *in favorem,* with instructions not to use it unless he could be assured of succeeding his father. Exactly what went on is not altogether clear, but the outcome was that the younger Skene, to his father's vast annoyance, succeeded him only as a member of the court of session. The vacant position as clerk register went to Lord Advocate Hamilton, who after two months forced an exchange of offices with Secretary Hay. Ostensiby the change was one of mutual convenience, but Hay was not pleased. "The Secretary is gone from hence [court] the most abruptly in the world," wrote Fenton to Mar on 22 June. "As I am informed that he is wearied of his place"—the face-saving story—"your Lordship may judge what the end shall be of that excambion."[13] By the end of July the excambion had been made, and Hamilton settled into the office he was to hold for the rest of James's reign. Hay vented his spleen on those responsible for the chain of events which led to his demotion by firing old Skene's other son John from his position as deputy clerk register for the registration of hornings. The reshuffle of offices was completed with the appointment of Sir William Oliphant as lord advocate, a promotion universally well received.[14]

The chief gainer from all this was the new secretary, who judged that the time was ripe for a move against the chancellor, but a most circumspect one: Hamilton was a cautious man. His chances looked bright. He now held a major office for the first time, and his brother Patrick was deputy secretary at court. His kinsman Rochester was riding high: James had just made him master of the horse, the office Mar had coveted. Dunfermline, on the other hand, had to be weakened by the death of his friend Salisbury in May 1612. The Scottish council displeased Rochester by warding his brother Ferniehirst in a quarrel with the new earl of Angus over the office of bailie of Jedburgh forest, deciding for Angus and forcing an apology from Ferniehirst.[15] Furthermore, Dunfermline was at odds with Spottiswoode again, on matters as diverse as customs rates and the kirk of Glasgow, and he was personally embarrassed by a story that a Popish crucifix was painted on his prayer-desk in the church in Dunfermline, a charge he was at some pains to deny.[16] Another possible count against him with the king was what Fenton called his "rude refusal of some help to the library of St. Andrews," the building and supplying of which was badly needed and much interested the king, though he was not prepared to spend much money on it.[17] The bishops were Hamilton's obvious allies in any move against the chancellor. The king shored up their position in June 1612 by issuing an order that no religious book could be produced without the approval of one of the archbishops.[18] They were pleased at the demotion of the sharp-tongued Hay, whom they regarded as an enemy,[19] and at the setback to Mar, whose cousin Fenton allegedly called Spottiswoode a false knave.[20] The plan was to make use of parliament, scheduled for October 1612, chiefly in order to ratify the acts of the Glasgow General Assembly of 1610 and the new regulations respecting the extradition of fugitives from justice as between

England and Scotland, and to vote some tax money on the occasion of Princess Elizabeth's wedding. Gledstanes apparently believed that the parliament had been called against Dunfermline's
wishes, and some color was given to this by the king's nominating
Dunfermline as royal commissioner, with Spottiswoode to manage
the legislative program. The king put this plan in the form of a
suggestion to Dunfermline, who tried to avoid being appointed
commissioner. Having failed in this, he resolved to fill both positions, to act as commissioner and preside over parliament as well;
the archbishop was left with the rather empty honor of preaching
the opening sermon.[21]

Fenton sensed that some sort of move against Dunfermline was
in the wind. Gledstanes knew it was; he thought that it would
revolve around the ratification of the acts of the General Assembly. "I will assure your Majesty that the very evil will that is carried
to my Lord Chancellor by the Nobility and people is like to make
us great store of friendship," he wrote to James on 31 August, "for
they know him to be our professed enemy, and he dissembleth it
not." The archbishop was full of praise of Hamilton, who was
working closely with him and Spottiswoode; the secretary was
"the fourteenth bishop of this kingdom."[22] If Dunfermline had
been incautious enough to attempt to prevent the passage of the
ratification of the Glasgow assembly's acts, he would certainly
have been charged with unreliability where the king's religious
policy was concerned; the affair of the Aberdeen assembly would
have been raked up once again. This was the ground on which he
was most likely to lose the king's confidence. But the chancellor
had no intention of leaving himself open to such an attack. He
made no effort to block the major elements in the bishops' legislative program; all he did was to show them the rough side of his
tongue in his opening speech. The bishops by their own admission
got most of what they wanted in the way of religious legislation.

So the attack on Dunfermline had to be made over the king's
request for money for his daughter's marriage. Not only did
Dunfermline not forward it, but he also seemingly gave aid and
comfort to its enemies. In the committee of the articles Hamilton
and the bishops worked hard, and with the acquiescence of the
burgh representatives settled on a figure of 600,000 merks ac-

cording to the bishops, 400,000 according to Hamilton. Then the attack began, led by Mar, who said that the king had told him that he wanted no more than 180,000; Lord Burley, newly come from court and therefore supposed to speak with authority, backed him. They got a good deal of support from their fellow aristocrats, who complained that in the past the tax collectors had fraudulently overcharged them. Twice that amount, 360,000 was eventually agreed upon. It would have been nothing, said the bishops, if their opponents had had their way. Spottiswoode wrote later in his *History* that the opposition came from the Catholics—including, naturally, the chancellor—who opposed Elizabeth's marriage to the titular leader of the Protestant Union. In England the explanation was that the Scots wanted her to marry one of themselves, the marquis of Hamilton perhaps, "so that they might have been sure of us every way."²³

James was annoyed. The parliament had not gone smoothly. With the terrifying Dunbar gone, previously smothered resentments had come to the surface, showing themselves most obviously in the nobility's resistance to the request for money. His comment to Mar had been misconstrued, James said. He had remarked that £10,000 sterling (180,000 merks) was the least that could be expected; "it did not follow that if the subjects willingly were contented to give his Majesty any more that you should say his Majesty did desire no more." Dunfermline, Mar, and Burley were "very well peppered to his Majesty," Fenton wrote his cousin, and pointed the moral: "you have ever liked too much to dispute in public, and at such times."²⁴ The council authorized the chancellor to head a delegation which included Spottiswoode to go to court with a message of condolence on the death of Prince Henry; the king, when he heard about it, peremptorily ordered Dunfermline to turn around and go home. The archbishop, on the other hand, received orders to come to court to discuss church business. His hopes, and those of Dunfermline's other rivals, rose once more.²⁵

Spottiswoode was doomed again to disappointment. James may have been momentarily displeased with his chancellor, but his stated reasons for ordering Dunfermline home turned out to be true. He did not want to be reminded of his grief, he said, and anyway the council had acted presumptuously in authorizing the sending of a public message without finding out if he wanted to receive one. It was behaving as though Scotland was an independent country.[26] The real target of the king's wrath was Burley, who had opposed not only the tax but also the king's list of nominees to the committee of the articles, which the nobility changed as far as they could, according to Secretary Hamilton. James expelled Burley from the council and ordered an inquiry into his conduct. Burley complained that he had been judged unheard, refused to confess any fault, and, more important, on Fenton's advice buttered up Rochester.[27] Eventually the whole business blew over, and Burley got his seat on the council back. The fact that he was one of the major Scottish enterprisers in the Irish settlement which was so near to the king's heart no doubt was a help to him.

Another disappointment for Archbishop Spottiswoode was the snuffing out of whatever hope he might have had of becoming lord treasurer. In November 1612 the king replaced Dunbar's man Sir John Arnot as treasurer-depute with Rochester's man Elibank.[28] The implications of this were clear. Rochester himself would one day become treasurer—and so he did, a year later: James granted him the office, along with the earldom of Somerset, at the time of his marriage to his beloved, murderous Frances.[29] Spottiswoode did not read the signs quite right, however, and when he tried his last ploy (for the time being) early in 1613, he floated the idea that he should be chancellor and Elibank treasurer, and he tried to enlist the aid of Secretary Hamilton. Hamilton's own ambitions diminished his enthusiasm for this gambit, however. Hamilton himself hoped to make his way to court to fill Dunbar's shoes there, but this did not suit Rochester and his advisers at all. Spottiswoode also tried to work on the queen, to stir her slumbering animosity to Mar, now Dunfermline's close ally, and thus use her to drive a wedge between Mar and the chancellor. Spottiswoode's maneuvers became too widely known, however—indeed, there is evidence that his friend Bishop Law deliberately informed a lot of people, including Fenton (who had heard the stories elsewhere), because he knew that Spottiswoode would fail: he wanted the archbishop not to court a rebuff from James by asking for Dunfermline's office. So indeed it turned out. James heard the stories, expressed surprise that Spottiswoode should contemplate replacing Dunfermline as chancellor, and said to Fenton, "Why should I do any such thing to the Chancellor, he has at this time done me very good service."[30] The king had evidently had second thoughts about the recent parliament, and had concluded that Dunfermline had behaved with rather more skill than had been apparent at first glance. He had allowed a lot of smouldering resentments to be expressed, but the substance of what James wanted he had got, including a tax twice as great as the acceptable minimum.

So Dunfermline emerged from this potentially awkward situation in a stronger position than before. The king was pleased with him, and his circumspect behavior had effectively eliminated the possibility of an attack on him on account of his religious policy. The bishops had got the ratification of the Glasgow assembly's acts; the bishops' opponents in the church, the remnants of the supporters of Andrew Melville, looked on the chancellor as a friend who would do his best to prevent the bishops from tyrannizing over them. After 1612 the bishops, apart from an occasional outburst from the pulpit, made no further efforts to make an issue of Dunfermline's putative Catholicism or his alleged enmity to them. Archbishop Spottiswoode still had the king's ear, of course, and under a veneer of cooperation kept up a steady flow of criticism, explicit or implied.[31] The new secretary also had to be watched, especially as he was now courting, and soon would marry, Rochester's widowed and extravagant sister, whose nine children no doubt seemed less of an obstacle now than they might once have been. But Dunfermline was prepared to be watchful, and there were in fact no more serious challenges to his authority.

One of the major reasons for the lack of challenges lay in the sort of government Dunfermline ran. It was a conservative regime, dedicated to the politics of consensus and to honest administration, worried about money, suspicious of change, and convinced that after the alarums and excursions of the Dunbar years a period of consolidation was necessary. It was also anticlerical, in the sense that it opposed the political ambitions of the bishops, though it was prepared to look after the welfare of the parish clergy, and, of course, there would be no softness on

Popery—Dunfermline could not afford that. The people who counted in Scotland were the landed and trading classes, so their interests would be served; in case of conflict the landowners would prevail. The government would be as conciliatory and helpful to as many people as possible, but not to lawbreakers. Law and order would be preserved where they existed and secured where they did not. Here the chancellor believed in the salutary effects of severity. Rank made no difference. In these years Neil MacLeod of Lewis, Lord Maxwell, and the earl of Orkney were all executed. It was nothing new for Scottish aristocrats to go to the scaffold; what was new was that none of these executions was political. They were all put to death, like ordinary sheep-stealers and murderers, for refusal to obey the law.

One indication of the conservatism of Dunfermline's regime was his attitude to the question of hereditary sheriffs, virtually all of whom were nobles or closely connected to them. King James had always recognized that hereditary officeholding weakened the power of the crown and had said so in *Basilikon Doron*. The hostility of the nobility to Chancellor Maitland was due in part to Maitland's attempt to overcome the ill effects of such officeholding. In certain respects Dunfermline agreed with his predecessor. He was always opposed to hereditary judgeships, and, apart from a blatant piece of jobbery in behalf of the then Lord Advocate Hamilton's father and brother in 1607–8, the only such nominee to the court of session was Sir James Skene, who succeeded his father in 1612. Skene later became president of the court, which indicates that his qualifications were not merely those of blood. In the year of Skene's appointment an additional precaution was taken: new judges must henceforth take an oath that they had not bought the office, a requirement which undoubtedly had Dunfermline's approval.[32]

With respect to sheriffs, however, the chancellor felt differently. Unlike Maitland he came from a noble family, and he himself was hereditary bailie of the regality of Dunfermline. He believed in the principle of aristocracy, as his efforts to save the Sanquhar peerage after its holder was executed for murder demonstrate.[33] He also believed, in common with the rest of his class, that only a member of the landed classes could serve effectively as sheriff.[34] In theory, eliminating hereditary sheriffs had a great deal to recommend it, but its real *raison d'être* had vanished in 1603. The king now had ample power to command the obedience of the greatest and most inaccessible officeholder, as his first cousin the earl of Orkney learned to his cost. The majority of the nobility would be bitterly resentful if they had to surrender their offices; the political cost would be far greater than the anticipated gain. Furthermore, Dunfermline was getting old. His relish for a political fight had visibly diminished; his concern now was to keep the aristocracy contented. So, as long as the noble sheriff and his deputies did their job, the chancellor was willing to leave things alone.

Dunfermline's attitude surfaced in 1613, when Archbishop Spottiswoode began a campaign to get rid of the hereditary sheriffs. Spottiswoode tried to persuade Lennox and Abercorn to surrender their offices to the king and vote for abolition in parliament. This they would not do, but they agreed to lease their sheriffdoms to James for three years. If at the end of that time the king had gotten all the others into his hands, by voluntary surrenders or acts of demission, they would not ask for them back.[35] Dunfermline and Mar showed their distaste for the plan by whipping up the aristocracy's suspicions of the bishops' political ambitions. "They begin to talk in Scotland of ancient nobility and their privileges must not be broken," wrote Fenton in October. "This does much discontent his Majesty."[36] By the middle of the following year Spottiswoode found that he could make no further progress: "I have been thought by the Chancellor and others the only instigator of those matters against the heritable sheriffs."[37]

An even more compelling argument against Spottiswoode's plan was the expense involved. Those nobles who were willing to bargain with the king wanted a great deal of money to surrender their offices.[38] The government bought some up but simply could not afford to acquire them all piecemeal in this way, and there was no hope of ending them by act of parliament, in view of the attitude of the chancellor and most of the possessors. The king was himself occasionally unhelpful; in 1616, for instance, he made the laird of Cumlege sheriff-depute of the Merse for life, which made a mockery of the principle of accountability in office on which a campaign against hereditary officeholding had to rest,[39] and in 1620 he allowed the husband of the sheriff of Ayr's eldest granddaughter to inherit that office, which otherwise would have reverted to the crown.[40] So, even though the parliament of 1617 appointed a committee to negotiate with hereditary bailies and sheriffs concerning surrender of their offices, the campaign eventually came to nothing.

Another aspect of the conservatism of Dunfermline's regime, and one which clearly distinguished it from that of Dunbar, lay in its conviction that further attempts to bring Scottish institutions into line with those of England would be unwise. The chancellor and his colleagues took no initiatives in this direction and were very cautious in implementing those already begun. The justices of the peace are a good case in point. In 1609 Dunbar's last parliament adopted a statute providing for the appointment of commissioners of the peace in each shire, resident gentlemen whose functions were to "oversee, try, and prevent all such occasions as may breed trouble and violence," and to compel those who gathered together and looked as if they might cause trouble, or who violated the laws against the carrying of guns, to find caution to keep the peace and appear before the proper authorities.[41] The statute gave assurances that no existing jurisdiction would be infringed. The commissioners were to be peace officers rather than judges; their only jurisdiction was in cases which might produce a feud—and the whole thrust of the statute was the prevention of incipient feuds, now that the king had so happily ended that traditional form of internecine bloodshed.[42] The term *justices of the peace* was carefully avoided in the text of the act, and no attempt was made as yet to appoint any commissioners. In May 1610 the king and Dunbar decided that it was safe to take the next step; Dunfermline and Dunbar were instructed to draw up a list of justices for each shire and were authorized to issue the necessary commissions. They finished the job by the end of August; on 4 October the council ordered the convener of the justices in each shire to call his colleagues together to receive their instructions. The list of justices, consisting of nobles, lairds, and the provost and bailies in the burghs, was made part of the council record in November, and is interesting in many respects. For instance, it confirms what we already know by listing in the commission for Argyll only one man not named Campbell. Prominent Catholics were not on the list. There were few Gordons included, and Huntly and Errol were conspicuously absent. Some had courtesy appointments, like Lennox, Fenton, and other permanent residents at court.[43] A full analysis of the people named is badly needed; it would tell us a good deal about the social and economic pattern of the various shires.

So matters stood when Dunbar died. The first task of the new regime was to issue a series of regulations spelling out the justices' powers and duties—and now they were frankly called that; the euphemism *commissioner* employed in the parliamentary act of 1609 was abandoned. Not surprisingly, their functions corresponded very closely to those of their English counterparts, with the major exception that the quarter sessions could not try capital crimes without a special warrant from the council. Their principal job was to keep the peace, though they had little authority over landed gentlemen and almost none over nobles, prelates, councillors, and members of the college of justice. Like English justices, they were expected to administer a series of statutes having to do with beggars and vagabonds, forestallers and regraters, poachers and woodcutters, weights and measures, wages and prices, roads and bridges, alehouses and maltmen, plague and lepers, and the provision and upkeep of jails for the violators of all these many laws. The justices were also to appoint constables, at least two in every parish, for six-month tours of duty. The constable's job was compulsory and unpaid; the duties were basically those of Dogberrys everywhere. Special mention was made of nightwalkers, vagabonds, people with no visible means of support, and the gun-control law.[44]

A year later, in July 1612, in response to a series of questions put by the justices for purposes of clarification, the council issued some additions and refinements, including the definition of a landed gentleman for purposes of the act: one whose yearly rent was more than 1,000 merks or ten chalders of victual. The council also arranged for an annual audit of the justices' accounts, for both fiscal and supervisory purposes. Some of the questions the justices asked were jurisdictional, the most important of which raised the delicate issue of the right of a holder of a regality to withdraw an accused man from the justices' court and try him himself. The council attempted to compromise by declaring that this right would lapse fifteen days after the justices cited the accused. The justices rejected this on the ground that it would "make them to be but as sergeants and officers to the other judges in the country." This was the crucial issue: if the justices were truly to resemble their English counterparts, their local jurisdiction would have to be comparably great. They did not get it. A council full of holders of regalities was not apt to give way on this point; in the final series of decrees the matter was not mentioned at all.[45]

The creation of this new class of magistrates was not universally welcomed in Scotland, even, apparently, by some of the new justices themselves. In June 1611 Archbishop Gledstanes gave vent to his irritation at this newfangled jurisdiction, and asserted "that the realm had many hundred years been well governed without Justices of Peace." Lord Advocate Hamilton drily replied that he was surprised that Gledstanes would impugn the king's authority and orders in this way. The archbishop, he added, had expressed no such distaste for the equally unprecedented courts of high commission.[46] More serious was the uncooperativeness of existing authorities, especially the sheriffs and burgh magistrates, an attitude made up partly of jealousy and partly of genuine uncertainty as to the scope of the justices' powers in such matters as dealing with the poor. The magistrates of royal burghs were supposed to exercise the powers of the justices within their burghs, to which they had no objection. But at the beginning they frequently dragged their feet about such things as attending quarter sessions and appointing constables, and there was considerable argument over the burghs' obligation to jail the prisoners the justices sent them from the countryside. The council in July 1612 declared that the burghs had to accept these malefactors, with the justices being liable for the charges for their upkeep. The burgh magistrates were not entirely to blame in this matter: there was a shortage of jails in many areas, and some tolbooths got very crowded.[47]

The controversies between the justices and the towns' officials became serious enough for the council to get the king to authorize the appointment in November 1612 of a special subcommittee of the council to resolve them. A conference was called for 6 January 1613, a date carefully picked to guarantee that the justices and the magistrates would both be in a properly receptive frame of mind: two days later, on 8 January, the first general audit of their accounts was due to be held. At the conference the burgh magistrates agreed to participate in the quarter sessions and to account for the fines they collected in their capacity as justices of the peace. In return they were promised that the council would settle any jurisdictional disputes they might have with the justices of the shire, and that they would not be held to account for the fines they collected in their capacity as burgh magistrates.[48] It seems likely that this had been the fear at the root of the burghs' reluctance to cooperate; the loss of the profits of justice would be a severe blow to their budgets.

So, from the beginning of 1613, the system of justices of the peace was functioning in most parts of Scotland. Even though the justices did not achieve the position in local affairs of their English counterparts, they were not altogether ineffective. Nor were they altogether unpopular; a document of 1630 which seems to be the draft of a petition from a group of lairds asks, among other things, for the appointment of more justices. They became a check on the hereditary sheriffs, whom the government did not wish to attack directly: in 1617 they acquired the authority to amend or annul obviously bad decisions by the sheriff's court, and to report cases of sheriffs' collusion with delinquents to the council. Not many suffered the indignities complained of by that Lanarkshire justice who informed the council in 1622 that some unruly coal miners whom he was attempting to discipline "defied him and all the Justices of Peace in Scotland" and hit him with a spade. The chief obstacle, of course, was the heritable jurisdictions, which Dunfermline and his colleagues were unwilling to attack, from which many of the justices profited as individuals and which they collectively showed no great desire to supersede. So their most useful work was done in those areas in which there was no directly competing authority. Professor Donaldson's verdict is accurate: "This scheme, while not wholly abortive, did not take root."[49]

The caution which was the hallmark of Dunfermline's regime was apparent also in its approach to economic and social affairs.

King James VI and I.

Archibald Campbell, 7th Earl of Argyll.

Scottish National Portrait Gallery

Alexander Seton, Earl of Dunfermline. Lord Chancellor, 1604–22.

George Gordon, Marquis of Huntly.

Scottish National Portrait Gallery

John Erskine, Earl of Mar. Lord Treasurer, 1616–30.

Sir George Hay, later Earl of Kinnoul. Lord Chancellor, 1622–34.

Thomas Hamilton, Earl of Melrose. Secretary of State, 1612–27.

George Home, Earl of Dunbar. Lord Treasurer, 1601–11.

The king left economic policy almost entirely to the council, subject to his occasional unpredictable interference, usually in the form of a grant to a favorite or an importunate suitor, or of an attempt to extend to Scotland a policy recently adopted in England. Dunfermline's regime inclined to favor the possessing classes, but not at the expense of the other elements in Scottish society. In 1613, for instance, the council experimented with a small issue of copper coinage, which would alleviate the shortage of specie and be helpful to the poor; it seems to have done little good.[50] The council also struck down an attempt by the merchant-dominated town government of Stirling to tax foodstuffs the citizens bought outside the town for their own consumption or for processing—flour bought to make bread, for example—though food bought for direct resale was subject to tax.[51] It remained suspicious of grants of monopoly, unless a new industry or manufacturing process was in question, and declared that any grant not implemented within three years would be void.[52] In June 1614 it levied a duty on imported food because supplies were abundant. But the weather that summer was awful—"daily rains, winds, frosts, and cold," wrote Dunfermline to John Murray. So the duty was lifted and the export of bestial and eggs forbidden, in the interest of preserving everybody's food supply, even though the landlords' income might temporarily suffer.[53]

But for the most part the welfare of the landed interests remained uppermost in the council's economic decisions. In February 1613 it extended to the rest of the country the extra duty of £4 a tun on wine already collected in Edinburgh and Leith, because, it said, "there is so huge and superfluous an excess and riot in drinking of wines imported from beyond seas." Artisans and craftsmen, displaying their "unsatiable thirst and drunken disposition," were neglecting their work to spend the day in taverns, which "doth make the wife and children at home to famish for hunger." A little further along in the decree, though, we discover its real purpose: to boost the sale of native beer; the landlords whose crops went into its brewing were suffering. For the same reason the council continued its vain battle against English beer by trying to keep the retail price low enough to make it unprofitable to import.[54] In the autumn of 1614 the council, acting on the king's orders, rather suddenly issued a proclamation banning the export of raw wool—James had just inaugurated the disastrous Cockayne project and was full of enthusiasm for the benefits of native cloth production. An immediate howl went up, led by the tacksmen of the customs, and the council hastily backtracked. The prohibition, the councillors explained, applied only to English wool imported into Scotland, and since they were assured "that there comes no kind of English wool in this kingdom," the proclamation really had no application.[55]

The nonagricultural interests of the possessing classes were carefully nurtured also, in such matters as the mining of metals and the production of iron.[56] The export of coal still concerned the king; late in 1614 he ordered an inquiry into its legality and economic impact. A report emerged in August 1615 which, predictably, once again declared that foreign sales were vital to the mine owners. The council agreed so to inform his majesty. One wonders just what happened, because in December James wrote to the council asking for the report.[57] Presumably he was eventually satisfied, because the matter vanishes from the records and the export of coal continued.

The evidence suggests that there was considerable economic progress in Scotland in these years. It was great enough to produce spirited bidding at the auction of the tack of the customs in 1616, and an increase in the amount which considerably exceeded the king's expectations, great enough also to lay the groundwork for a period of industrial expansion which began in the last years of the reign, though, as the famous and often-cited table of exports of 1614 shows, the value of manufactured goods exported was comparatively small—less in total than the value of skins alone.[58] A significant indication of the pace of economic development in Scotland is the fact that in 1616 the convention of royal burghs was willing to accept the prohibition of the export of raw wool which had caused such an uproar two years before, on the ground that locally grown wool could now be processed at home, and the ban was accordingly reimposed.[59]

Whatever the council's activities may have contributed to the nation's economic well-being, they did very little to alleviate the government's chronic shortage of money. From the beginning this had been a problem for Dunfermline's government. In April 1611 the king ordered the dissolution of Scone's national police force because it was no longer necessary and "our coffers there at this present [are] . . . not so well stored as we wish."[60] In the second half of the year the government undertook a thorough review of the king's revenues and debts, some of which dated back more than a quarter-century, and declared, with James's consent, that no new grants from him would be honored till the debts were paid. Financial favors to private individuals should cease; they were not only pernicious in themselves, but also "your Majesty will be daily importuned by numbers who has (*sic*) reason for them to seek, and we will be made unable to prosecute . . . that resolution . . . which for your Majesty's benefit and profit we have intended."[61] The new book of customs rates appeared in June 1611; there followed a new lease with the customs farmers which resulted in a substantial increase in the government's revenue. After a year of discussions with the English privy council to be sure that they were not working at cross-purposes, the council beginning in November 1611 issued a series of proclamations raising the value of gold money by 10 percent, in order to try to cut back on the drain of specie, a constant worry.[62] On the king's instructions the council also began to enforce the much-neglected statute against usury, which was defined as charging more than 10 percent interest. In the first eight months of 1612 some three hundred fifty people, including eight clergymen, were summoned for breaking this law. The burghs were naturally indignant and protested to the king. James was not moved. The law would be strictly enforced in future, he said; those who in the past had charged no more than 12 percent would be leniently treated, but not those who had charged more than that. It need hardly be added that usury was not eliminated, though its practitioners became temporarily more cautious and occasionally had to pay for their past peccadillos.[63]

Still the shortage of money continued. In November 1615 the council found it necessary to issue a stern proclamation, another in a long series of clearly unenforceable decrees on this subject, forbidding the government's creditors from going to court to "vex and molest" his majesty with their "idle and impertinent" suits unless they had license to do so. This had become more of a

nuisance than usual recently, and had prompted James to appoint
the courtier-poet Sir William Alexander of Menstrie as master of
requests, to keep these idle and impertinent suitors away from
him.[64] In the previous July Elibank had written the king a very
gloomy letter on receiving a royal order to pay the earl of Abercorn £30,000. There was nothing in the treasury to pay him, said
Elibank, literally nothing. The tax money voted by parliament in
1612 was already committed. By the first of June the coffers were
empty and would stay that way, because with the Whitsun term
the next batch of pension payments, amounting to more than
£72,000, came due. It was a cheerless prospect, made no brighter
by the current troubles in the western isles. Elibank closed his
letter by asking for permission to come to court to make an
accounting.

The financial situation was not good, though not quite as bad as
Elibank made out. He was a nervous man given to fits of depres-
sion, and there were signs that his patron Rochester might be
losing favor.[65] What is apparent from his career as treasurer-
depute is that, with the exception of the increase in the tack of the
customs, the government had not been able to derive any financial
benefit from Scotland's improving economy. Like virtually every
other government in western Europe, including conspicuously
that of England, it found itself saddled with an obsolete tax structure which Dunfermline, at least, was unwilling to try to alter in
any significant way. The chancellor was always unenthusiastic
about the voting of taxes in parliament because the money was
usually wasted and the political repercussions unpleasant. The
chancellor, in this as in other matters, vastly preferred not to rock
the boat, even if chronic fiscal difficulty was the consequence.

There was one path to possible financial gain for the crown
which Dunfermline was more than willing to pursue, however:
profit from the extension of law and order in the highlands. By the
summer of 1613 it seemed possible that the government might
profit from the fines to be collected from the resetters of the
outlawed MacGregors. Since the summer of 1610 they had been
the object of sustained pursuit of an unparalleled savagery, which
authorized the branding of the clan's women on the face and the
hanging of fourteen-year-old children if they attempted to escape

from their keepers. The man in charge of the pursuit was the earl of Argyll, who, now that he had consolidated his grip on Kintyre, was prepared to devote his attention to the hapless clan. Argyll's commission, issued in April 1611, was one of the few royal acts of the critical period immediately following Dunbar's death which ran counter to Dunfermline's policy. He and his colleagues were opposed in principle to the grant of so much power to a private citizen, especially a great lord,[66] but there had been a fiasco at the beginning of 1611 when a group of lords and gentlemen commissioned against the MacGregors had allowed a group of them trapped on an island in Loch Katrine to escape; so Dunfermline and his colleagues were in no position to argue effectively against the commission to Argyll. They did not trust him, however, and they especially disliked the fact that he had obtained the right to receive the fines collected from the MacGregors' resetters. But by and large they cooperated with him, as one more illustration to their master that Dunbar's departure would not adversely affect the efficiency of the Scottish administration or its willingness to be brutal if need be. The instructions issued after Dunbar's death were no less savage than his—"Let not the decease of this man work any impression in your hearts that his Majesty will be either forgetful or careless of this service," they wrote to the commissioners in February 1611.[67]

Argyll, whose previous conduct toward the MacGregors had been so equivocal as to suggest that he was himself resetting them,[68] bestirred himself now, since he smelled profit, and in two years the job was done. In March 1613 he reported that the clan was reduced to a remnant of twenty-four armed fugitives. The king therefore ordered that when the number was down to twelve, Argyll's commission and obligations would end, and that heavier fines should be collected from the resetters of the remnants of the clan—one-fifth of the value of their property instead of one-tenth. The king did take the precaution of setting up a council committee headed by Dunfermline to supervise the fining process; this committee, and the council as a whole, now began to put pressure on Argyll and the other recipients of MacGregor estates, mostly Campbells, to share their expected gains with the treasury; Argyll finally agreed that the crown should have 22½ percent of the fines he received. The total amount levied against the clan's resetters came to over £115,000, including some very large fines; the laird of Grant was assessed the huge sum of 40,000 merks. But of course not all the fines were collected in full, and there were expenses; the government's share came to only about £10,000 all told when the final accounting was completed in 1624. So the council seems to have made no effort to block another of the king's characteristic acts of generosity. In April 1615, by which time the government had received, and spent, about £4,400, James gave the remainder of the crown's share to Campbell of Lawers for his work in pursuing the clan and coping with the problem of the MacGregor children. Since there was no money to be made out of taking responsibility for these children, no one was anxious to do so; the council finally distributed them among the possessors of the former MacGregor lands.[69]

The council also hoped that some money might be forthcoming from the earldom of Orkney, which parliament annexed to the crown in October 1612. For this result Earl Patrick had mostly himself to blame. Finding himself in Edinburgh castle at the beginning of 1610 with various capital charges hanging over him, the earl decided to be conciliatory. The king was willing to listen, but he insisted that the earl must satisfy his oppressed tenants. His trial might be postponed but the charges were not to be dropped. The council for its part made it clear that there was no intention of restoring the earl to favor, and issued strict orders that the people of Orkney and Shetland were to obey the king's commissioners only from now on. The earl could not control his agents, however. Their misbehavior protracted his imprisonment in 1610, and when he did get a little relief, in August 1611, he idiotically gave his bastard son Robert some sort of commission—the earl said, to collect his debts; his enemies said, to be sheriff-depute. James and the council alike were outraged, and the earl was promptly re-arrested and confined in Dumbarton. The council remained reluctant to move decisively against him until June 1612, when it received evidence that he had ordered his brother and son to seize and victual Kirkwall.[70] This in effect sealed the earl's doom, and the annexation of the earldom followed four months later.

Dealing with Orkney involved more than coping with an over-mighty subject and his singularly inaccessible agents; it also meant integrating into the kingdom an area which had been part of Scotland only in name. Apart from the elimination of Earl Patrick's ruffianly relatives and subordinates, the most important step was to provide for uniformity of legal administration. Beginning in May 1611 the council undertook to accomplish this by a series of enactments wiping out all remnants of "foreign"—i.e., Norwegian—law, which the earl had applied when it suited him, and some of the earl's own oppressive regulations. Bishop Law was entrusted with the oversight and execution of the process of integration. After the annexation of the earldom to the crown the council ruled that customs duties and the toll which foreign ships had paid to the earl would continue to be collected. Sir James Stewart of Killeith, the new sheriff and tacksman, who had leased the crown's property and rights for 40,000 merks a year, set about trying to collect rents and back taxes, and in 1613 negotiations began with the deposed earl, who was transferred to Edinburgh for the purpose, over the terms on which he would make a formal renunciation of his earldom. Earl Patrick dragged his feet and asked for permission to go to court to see the king. Early in 1614 an acrimonious row broke out between Bishop Law and Elibank over the revenues of the bishopric. The council held hearings, tempers eventually cooled, and by October 1614 a settlement was reached, the key to which was an exchange by which the king acquired the scattered church estates and in return granted the bishop a more compact territory, within which he had the jurisdictional authority of a sheriff.[71]

While the bishop and the treasurer-depute were arguing over the value of Law's assigned estates, his diocese erupted once more, and for the last time. In the spring of 1614 Earl Patrick's bastard son, whom his father had allegedly reviled as a "false, feeble beast" for having promised in January 1613 not to return to Orkney without royal permission, violated his pledges, returned to Orkney, rallied his father's followers, and was soon in possession of the castle of Kirkwall, the most formidable fortress in the islands. It was an insane enterprise, doomed to failure from the start; the only question was how the council would deal with it. In August the council rather reluctantly accepted the offer of Earl Patrick's personal enemy, the almost equally lawless and violent earl of Caithness, to act as lieutenant and gave him money and supplies; by the end of September the garrison of Kirkwall gave up. Bishop Law, whom the council had sent along with Caithness to keep an eye on him, wrote triumphantly to Secretary Hamilton, now Lord Binning, of the surrender of the castle and the ensuing celebration, with toasts to everybody; "we caroused after the Orkney fashion."[72] Caithness promptly hanged most of the garrison. Earl Patrick's son was not hanged there, however; he was saved for a more public fate in Edinburgh, which he met in January 1615 after a trial for treason. He attempted to exonerate himself by throwing the blame on his father, who replied in kind. The councillors were very skeptical of the earl's denials, and indeed after his son's hanging the earl confessed to having given him orders to seize the castle. He, too, was found guilty of treason and was executed in Edinburgh on 6 February 1615. "It is observed," wrote Calderwood, "that this month is fatal to the king's blood."[73] Given the king's tendency to be generous to his favorites and his kinsmen, there was some expectation that sooner or later the earl's family might be restored.[74] This did not happen; Orkney remained firmly in the hands of the crown. It never turned out to be very profitable, however. King James occasionally expressed dissatisfaction with the amount of money the crown received from it, and various schemes were mooted to raise more, but they were never tried, and the islands remained in the hands of tacksmen. The council, which was much less optimistic about the possibilities of profit than was James, was chiefly concerned to keep the tack out of the hands of the Gordons,[75] and in this it was successful. At James's death the tacksman was Dunfermline's successor as chancellor, Sir George Hay, who paid the same 40,000 merks a year for the lease as had the first tacksman, Killeith.[76]

One reason why Dunfermline's government was willing to avail itself of the services of a dangerous ruffian like Caithness[77] in Orkney, a decision which ran counter to all the chancellor's principles of orderly administration, was that a much more serious difficulty erupted in the western isles at about the same time.

Things had been going fairly well in the western highlands, although, as with Orkney, the king was dissatisfied with the amount of income derived from there.[78] In September 1613 James Primrose, the clerk of the privy council, drew up a report on the condition of the area which indicated only three trouble spots, the most serious of which was Lochaber, where Allan Cameron of Lochiel got into trouble by misreading the political signs. Lochiel accepted a claim by Argyll that he was the rightful superior of the lands of Lochiel, to the vast annoyance of the marquis of Huntly, the superior of Lochaber, who did not want the seemingly endlessly expansive Campbells encroaching on his district. Huntly tried to persuade Lochiel to violate his agreement with Argyll; Lochiel would not, though he vowed that he was still loyal to the house of Gordon. Huntly stirred up Lochiel's clan enemies against him; Lochiel ambushed them and slaughtered some twenty, "learning a lesson to the rest of his kin who are alive in what form they shall carry themselves to their chief thereafter." The council was outraged and gave a commission of fire and sword to Huntly and his eldest son, the earl of Enzie, who, like his father, was a royal favorite and was now much at court. Lochiel's troubles multiplied; his hereditary enemy Lauchlan MacIntosh of Dunnachtan, hereditary steward of Lochaber, obtained a commission against him. Huntly did not care for this; Lochiel realized it, and in 1618 was able to make peace with Huntly by acknowledging the Gordons as his feudal superiors. This enabled him to continue to defy his other enemies successfully; the death of MacIntosh late in 1622 finally permitted of another compromise by which Lothiel made his peace with the government.[79]

The apparent vacillation in the council's policy toward Lochiel—severity before he made his peace with Huntly, comparative leniency thereafter—was due to the fact that it was no more keen than Huntly to see the influence of the Campbells extended. From the vantage point of Whitehall, however, the clan Campbell looked rather different. The growth of its influence and power in the western highlands no longer seemed so important to James, who was rapidly losing his earlier distrust of Argyll, especially after the earl married an English lady as his second wife in 1610 and began to spend a good deal of time at court. The Campbells had done the king good service in recent years. They had pacified Kintyre and founded a town there, Campbelltown, in 1609, in accordance with James's favorite colonization schemes, and had finally suppressed the MacGregors. So, when trouble broke out in Islay in the summer of 1614, it was predictable that James would be disposed to assign the Campbells to cope with it.

The difficulty with Islay was that there was no way effectively to extend the Icolmkill policy to the island because there was no chief to deal with. Old Sir Angus MacDonald of Dunyveg, having allegedly sold his claims there to Sir John Campbell of Calder, was dead by the beginning of 1613; his heir, Sir James MacDonald, was a prisoner in Edinburgh castle under sentence of death. Bishop Knox, the tacksman of Islay and the holder of the castle of Dunyveg, was extremely hostile to the extension of the power of the Campbells, and attempted to prevent it by letting the tack to Sir Ranald MacDonald of Antrim, but this turned out to be a mistake. The new tacksman alienated the tenants by attempting to impose Irish customs and exactions; the council had to order him to stop.[80] The bishop made another, more serious mistake: he kept too small a garrison in Dunyveg. So there was no resistance when a bastard son of old Angus seized the castle in March 1614. It was in turn almost immediately seized from him by Angus Oig MacDonald, the younger son of old Angus, who was living on Islay and who had some claim to the leadership of the clan while his older brother Sir James was in prison.

There now began a long and curious series of events whose result was the final ruin of the MacDonalds of Islay and the further aggrandizement of the insatiable Campbells. This outcome, which both Knox and Dunfermline vainly tried to prevent, was due chiefly to the incredibly stupid behavior of Angus Oig. Angus Oig, and a number of the others involved, lied when it suited them, so the truth is very hard to get at. But some things are clear. Angus Oig claimed throughout that he was prepared to surrender the castle to Bishop Knox or anyone else who held the king's warrant, provided conditions were right, but he never did so. He claimed, both before and after his capture, that one reason for his intransigence was that Argyll had assured him that if he gave up the castle, it would mean his ruin. Why he should have trusted any Campbell is hard to see, but at this stage his brother Sir James apparently still trusted Campbell of Calder, who was his brother-in-law. The part played by Sir James is not clear either. The council naturally suspected him of collusion with Angus Oig, ordered him to be put in irons, and searched his papers. These apparently revealed that he had urged his brother to obey the king and council, and that Angus Oig had promised to do so. Shortly thereafter Sir James offered to act as the king's tacksman himself. If the whole business was a complex ploy to restore Sir James to freedom and the headship of his clan—and it is not at all clear that it was—it was a failure.

The council decided that the logical first step was to test Angus Oig's good faith; perhaps he really would turn over the castle to Bishop Knox if he received the necessary remission. As a precaution against the MacDonalds' receiving any help from their fellow highlanders, the council extracted from a number of chiefs a renewed ratification of the statutes of Icolmkill, along with a guarantee that they would appear before the council every year on 10 July, and at other times on sixty days' notice. Knox was slow about setting out for Islay; Secretary Binning scolded him for his delay and harassed him into going there in September 1614 with only a handful of men. Angus Oig could not resist what seemed to be a golden opportunity. He seized the bishop, forced him to agree to support his request to be made keeper of Dunyveg and tacksman of the island in place of MacDonald of Antrim, and to leave his son and nephew behind as hostages. The bishop wrote a crestfallen letter to Binning outlining the scope of this disaster and made his way back to Edinburgh.[81]

The council received word of the bishop's discomfiture on 1 October. It took the only course now open to it: it sent a report to the king and awaited his instructions. In the report the councillors said that they had had some preliminary discussions with Campbell of Calder about suppressing the rebellion; Calder pointed out the possible objections to his appointment but said that he would be willing to undertake the assignment if he were furnished with some cannon. Calder's reluctance was feigned. Two days previously Binning had sent south by the hand of Archibald Campbell Calder's offer to take over the feu of Islay for a figure far above

any previous offer and to put down the rebellion at his own expense.[82] Binning clearly favored the proposal. Bishop Knox did
not. When he heard about it, he wrote Lochmaben warning that it
would be very costly to the government in the long run "to root
out one pestiferous clan and plant in one little better." A week
later Knox sent Lochmaben the imprisoned Sir James Mac-
Donald's offer to take over the tack, with a cautious but unmistakable recommendation that it be accepted, a solution which would
have followed the general principle of the statutes of Icolmkill.[83]
But by then it was too late. The king had decided in favor of
Calder, who received a commission of lieutenancy on 22 October.
To make assurance doubly sure, ships and men were to be sent
from Ireland. Four days later Archibald Campbell received appointment as the man to whom all inhabitants of the highlands and
isles who were at the horn must apply in order to obtain remission
from horning.[84] The Campbells looked to become more powerful
than ever.

This was a prospect which did not appeal to the chancellor at all.
His first thought was to put forward an alternative to Calder as
tacksman in the person of his nephew Sir George Hamilton, the
younger brother of the earl of Abercorn, but he could not persuade his fellow councillors to endorse this.[85] So he decided to try
something rather more daring: to persuade Angus Oig to release
the hostages and come into the king's will before Calder could get
his expedition under way. The agent he sent to Islay was George
Graham of Eryne, a plausible, Gaelic-speaking sort who turned
out to be an accomplished liar. Graham's instructions, according to
Dunfermline, were simply to get the hostages freed. He had
nothing in writing from the chancellor and no power to promise
anything specific; he was to have 1,000 merks if he succeeded.
Succeed he did, the chancellor wrote to Lochmaben on 9 December. The hostages were freed, and Angus Oig was willing to
turn over the castle to anyone Dunfermline sent there, if he and
his fellow rebels were given the chance to appear before the council to explain their behavior. The chancellor wanted the king's
decision on this, as well as authorization, which in due course he
received, to reimburse himself from the treasury for Graham's
fee.[86]

It soon became apparent that Graham had done much more than deal in generalities with Angus Oig. He had given Angus Oig a copy of what purported to be Dunfermline's written instructions, which indicated that Graham had the authority to receive the surrender and name a captain of the castle, and that the chancellor would work for the rebels' pardon and the restoration of their possessions and "a right of the lands of Islay" to them if they complied. Graham turned the castle back to Angus Oig—who said after the event that he was reluctant to receive it—and, also according to Angus, told him to hold it in the chancellor's name and not to surrender it to the king's lieutenant or the royal herald if either should arrive before word came back from the chancellor. Angus's subsequent behavior and protestations indicate that he accepted Graham's story at its face value and put his trust in the piece of paper Graham left behind with him. Had it not been for Graham, he said, he would certainly have surrendered the castle to Calder on demand.

Graham's next moves are exceedingly obscure, and he told several stories about them when interrogated, but what does seem clear is that he was stalling for time. He did not want the herald to go to Dunyveg and demand its surrender; when the herald persisted, he said angrily, "If you go forward at this time you shall spoil the whole errand, and there will be much blood spilt."[87] He hastened to Calder and tried to persuade the latter to do nothing till he returned from court, and urged him at least not to go forward without a large force and artillery because Dunyveg was strongly held. The herald went ahead, however, and so did Sir Oliver Lambert, the English commander of the forces from Ireland which were to cooperate with Calder. Angus Oig defied them, claiming that he had the chancellor's commission to hold the castle. The weather was bad—not a day these five weeks without snow, wrote the chancellor to Lochmaben on 20 February.[88] The besiegers nevertheless went ahead, Calder himself eventually arrived, and early in February 1615 the castle surrendered. Calder hanged a good many rebels on the spot; Angus Oig was sent off to Edinburgh for examination before (predictably) he met the same fate.

What accounts for Graham's behavior? There are two aspects of it which need explaining: the story he told Angus Oig, and his actions after he left Dunyveg. On the first point Dunfermline held steadily to what he had said in his letter to Lochmaben in December: his only instructions to Graham were oral ones to get the hostages freed. Whatever else Graham may have said was on someone else's instructions or on his own initiative.[89] Graham, when interrogated by the council, agreed that Dunfermline had given him nothing in writing. So the question is, did Graham, in making his arrangements with Angus Oig, do so on Dunfermline's oral instructions and with his foreknowledge and, if so, to what end? Both Donald Gregory and Audrey Cunningham, who have written the most detailed accounts of this affair, believe that Dunfermline was responsible, that he believed that all highlanders were barbarians with whom it was neither necessary nor desirable to keep faith, and that once the hostages were freed, Angus Oig, who was showing regrettable signs of willingness to surrender, should be entrapped into defying the royal agents in order to ensure that he would be hanged and the rest of the MacDonalds ruined.[90]

This is a very improbable explanation. It runs counter to the whole of the chancellor's highland policy, his support of the statutes of Icolmkill and his hostility to the aggrandizement of the Campbells, who would be the only beneficiaries of the entrapment of Angus Oig. No contemporary believed in Dunfermline's involvement. The king never questioned his denials. Archibald Campbell, who had gone to fetch Lambert and his forces from Ireland and was present at the siege, after he had seen the "instructions" Graham left with Angus Oig, wrote, "In my opinion all that passed betwixt Graham and the rebels was devised by Graham himself for relief of the pledges."[91] This seems, on the whole, to be the most logical explanation. There is no concrete evidence for the entrapment theory. Graham, in his anxiety to do the chancellor's bidding, exceeded his instructions and gave Angus Oig something in writing. The only way he could cover up this indiscretion was to have the chancellor's emissary arrive at Dunyveg to receive Angus Oig's surrender before Calder, or the herald, or Lambert arrived there to "spoil the whole errand." He failed, but he muddied the waters so thoroughly in his interrogations that he managed to avoid trouble.[92]

Angus Oig was executed in July 1615. By that time the whole job in the western isles was to do over again, because on 24 May Sir James MacDonald contrived to escape from Edinburgh castle. He eluded pursuit, reached the west, and by the end of June had raised enough of a following to seize Dunyveg and plan an invasion of his clan's ancestral territory of Kintyre. He was, he said, a reluctant rebel; all he wanted was to be the king's tacksman on Islay, but "I will die before I see a Campbell possess it."[93]

When the councillors heard of the seizure of Islay, they wrote to the king that the best way to deal with the situation was to send Argyll himself back to take charge in person. This advice constituted no change of policy on their part but, rather, an attempt to compel the beneficiary of James's policy to take responsibility for it. The king had made it clear in the matter of Angus Oig that he intended to use the Campbells to suppress the MacDonalds. When Sir James escaped, the council got in touch with various Campbells to see what they would do. Calder promised to answer for Islay, and proved unable to hold Dunyveg. Argyll's brother Campbell of Lundy would not undertake to act in Argyll's absence, and both he and Calder were being harassed by the earl's creditors; Campbell of Auchinbreck, the bailie of the earldom, was actually in ward on account of Argyll's debts. His creditors were in fact petitioning the council for relief. The earl, they said, evidently had no intention of paying his debts and was staying in England to avoid doing so, while his cautioners were arranging clandestine conveyances of their estates in order to bilk the petitioners. It was under these circumstances that the council recommended to James that he order Argyll home and that, since the earl would profit from the transfer of the MacDonald estates, he should pay for the suppression of the rebellion.[94]

James accepted his council's advice, but Argyll was very reluctant to go home. In the middle of August he finally arrived in Edinburgh and began to negotiate with the council. It took some time to settle the questions of the amount of support the government would furnish and the terms of Argyll's commission of lieutenancy; once agreement was reached and Argyll began to move, the rebellion collapsed quickly. It had lasted as long as it did only on account of his delays, and Auchinbreck, whom the council had released from ward for the purpose, had succeeded very

skillfully in keeping it from spreading.[95] Sir James was luckier than
Angus Oig; he took refuge in Ireland and eventually made his way
to Spain. In fact, so many of the leaders got away as to cause
Binning some concern; he was afraid the rebellion might break out
again.[96] So was Clerk Register Hay, though for a different reason.
In December 1615 he wrote Lochmaben a long and thoughtful
letter, designed to be shown to the king. The rebellion had been
expensive for the government, said Hay; the rents from the isles
would not repay the costs for ten years. What the crown really
needed was a cash reserve: £10,000 sterling would do more than a
garrison to keep people quiet. The poverty of the crown was an
inducement to rebellion; it was also an inducement to the unscrupulous, who might stir up a rebellion, get well paid to suppress it,
and then ask for a reward for their services—a shaft obviously
aimed at the Campbells. "It is fitting the purchasers of the new
right [i.e., Argyll and Calder] either secure it hereafter, and dis-
burden his majesty's coffers of further charge, or . . . surrender it
to his majesty."[97]

Hay's suggestions were not adopted. Argyll and Calder remained answerable for Kintyre and Islay in the customary way,[98]
and the accumulation of a cash reserve of £120,000 was beyond
the bounds of possibility. But as it turned out, Hay's and Binning's
apprehensions were groundless. The MacDonald rebellion was
the last of the old-style highland uprisings against the crown, and
so represents a landmark in Scottish history. Twenty years before,
the flight of Huntly and Bothwell marked the final triumph of the
Stewart monarchy in its long struggle with the Scottish aristocracy
for control of the central government, and the end of the possibility that the overmighty subject, either singly or in combination,
could make a mockery of the royal authority. Now Dunfermline
and his colleagues, building on the work of Maitland and Dunbar,
had extended the king's authority to the remotest corners of the
land. The flight of MacDonald, who, like Bothwell, was never to
return, and the executions of his brother Angus Oig, of Neil
MacLeod and Lord Maxwell and Earl Patrick of Orkney, drove the
point home. The king was king indeed, in Annandale and the
Hebrides as well as in Fife and the Lothians. There was an ample
amount of lawlessness and crime in the highlands after 1615, as

there was on the borders. "We grieve in our actions, abhor the cruelty of our exactions, and are ashamed of our service, in regard of the little amendment in the country," wrote the chancellor's brother to Binning in February 1616, in sending an account of an assize at Peebles where the border commissioners had just hanged twenty-one malefactors.[99] Sir William's was the natural gloom of the policeman, whose lot is never happy. But statistics of those hanged and at the horn, and picturesque tales of ruffianly der-ring-do, must not be allowed to obscure the magnitude of the achievement of King James and his ministers.

Much of the government's success in the highlands was due to the adoption of the policy of cooperation with the chiefs epito-mized in the statutes of Icolmkill. In July 1616, when the chiefs made their stipulated annual appearance for the first time follow-ing the suppression of MacDonald's rebellion, the council pre-sented them with a new series of obligations which amounted to a spelling-out of some of the implications of the statutes, and which was the last major revision of the government's highland policy in James's reign. They were to guarantee again to keep their clans-men in order, limit their households and their consumption of wine, live in stipulated places, see to it that their lands were culti-vated, keep no more than one ship and carry weapons only in the king's service, and send all their children above age nine to school in the lowlands. No one was to be served heir to an estate or accepted as the king's tenant who could not read, write, and speak English. It was partly in order to implement this requirement that the council in December 1616 enacted that a school be established in every parish in the land and a schoolmaster employed at the parish's expense, thus realizing one of the most admirable of the visions of John Knox and the first generation of reformers.[100]

The highland chiefs were willing to accept the government's restrictive conditions, no doubt with the expectation that en-forcement would not be severe for those who gave no trouble. And so indeed it turned out. In spite of the persistence of a few trouble spots like Lochaber, Sir Rory MacLeod of Dunvegan could write persuasively in August 1622 of "this delectable time of peace" in petitioning for release from the requirement of the an-nual appearance, a request granted in the following year for him and, by implication, for the other chiefs as well. The amount of peace and order must not be exaggerated, of course. Lochiel was not the only highlander still giving trouble in 1622, and in 1624 a gathering of highland landlords proposed the establishment of two twenty-man police forces to keep order there. The council endorsed this, but lack of money seems to have prevented anything being done.[101]

There can be no doubt that the policy represented by the statutes of Icolmkill was a success, in spite of some continuing difficulties and sporadic outbreaks of lawlessness. The fact that the government was willing to cooperate with the clan chiefs created in these men, their followers, and their successors a loyalty to the crown and dynasty which had never been visible before; it was the highlanders who supplied James's unfortunate descendants with their most doggedly faithful adherents. Only in the southwest highlands and the southern isles was the policy a failure. There law and order was established by means of the aggrandizement of a family which was in many ways too powerful already, which was to supply in the marquis of Argyll the shrewdest and most important leader of the opposition to Charles I, which was to survive the execution of the marquis and of his eldest son a generation later, and which was to emerge in the early eighteenth century as the greatest political family in the country. But in King James's day the potential threat did not materialize, partly because of the unusual behavior of the earl himself. Early in 1616, having yielded to the council's insistence that he pay his creditors at least the interest owing to them on his debts, he left Scotland to go back to court and give an account of his service, in the hope of a reward.[102] He returned but once, with the king in 1617. He subsequently went to the continent, became a Roman Catholic, and entered the service of Spain, an action whose potentially serious consequences he managed to avoid, since he had taken the precaution of cultivating the now all-powerful Buckingham.[103] His departure left the Campbells leaderless, divided, and financially embarrassed. This state of affairs suited the council very well; it encouraged Argyll to remain abroad, and so arranged for the management of his estates that no member of the family would be impelled to urge him to return. But the potential ability of a united clan Campbell to make political trouble was considerable, as the next generation of royal councillors was to discover.

By the end of 1615 Dunfermline might well have felt a good deal of satisfaction at his achievements. He had completed the job of seeing to it that the government's orders were obeyed throughout Scotland, and he had provided an administration which satisfied all the important sections of Scottish society. Because of his skill and tact and conciliatory policies he had tightened his grip on power; no one was hostile enough to him to support any potential rival who might wish to overturn him. There were really only two such rivals. One, Secretary Binning, had slipped a bit through no fault of his own. His brother-in-law Rochester, now earl of Somerset, was on the way down. By October 1615 the Overbury murder case had broken and Somerset was under arrest. His fall made no real difference in Scotland. The most vulnerable official, Elibank, remained in office. In November 1615 the king specifically ordered that what he called Somerset's "inconvenience" was not to alter the conduct of financial affairs in Scotland; in December he made it perfectly clear that Elibank would not fall with his patron by knighting his eldest son and giving him the wardship of the young earl of Cassillis.[104] James's decision was wise; the gifted and hard-working Elibank was an asset to the Scottish administration. So the only real consequence of Somerset's fall was that it seriously diminished Binning's chances of replacing Dunfermline at the head of the Scottish administration. Binning understood this very well and made no further attempt to do so.

Dunfermline's other potential rival, Archbishop Spottiswoode, unlike Binning, made gains in 1615 owing to the death of Archbishop Gledstanes early in May. The king promptly translated Spottiswoode to St. Andrews, named his ally Bishop Law to Glasgow, and at the end of the year consolidated the courts of high commission under Spottiswoode's control. From the church's point of view Gledstanes had certainly outlived his usefulness. His greed and his attempts to advance his family were an embarrassment, he continued his fruitless bickering with the council generally and Elibank in particular over the legal and financial privileges of the archbishopric, and toward the end of his life, if the comments of his contemporaries are a reliable indication, he became an alcoholic and behaved very oddly indeed.[105] Spottiswoode in his *History* could find nothing favorable to say about Gledstanes save that he left behind a defense of episcopacy in order to spike the rumors which the Melvilleans liked to spread that bishops died recanting, and he was critical of Gledstanes's practice of setting long leases at low rents.[106] The chief loser from Gledstanes's death, apart from his family—shortly after taking over in St. Andrews Spottiswoode told Alexander Gledstanes, minister there, to stop being a "company bearer with common folks in drinking"— was the university. Gledstanes had worked hard for the university, especially the library; Spottiswoode neglected it, and borrowed books and failed to return them.[107]

By the end of 1615 the grip of the new archbishop of St. Andrews on the levers of power in the Scottish church was complete and unchallenged, save by the few remnants of Andrew Melville's following, who now scarcely dared raise their voices. To replace Dunfermline as James's principal adviser on Scottish affairs would be very difficult for the archbishop, in view of the chancellor's recent successes, but not impossible, given time and opportunity. But as Spottiswoode was about to discover, he would have neither time nor opportunity, thanks in some part to his own miscalculations but mostly to his royal master.

NOTES

1. 4 Feb. 1611, the council to James, *RPCS* IX, 594–95. 8 Feb., Dunfermline to Salisbury, PRO, SP 14/61, no. 70.

2. 28 Feb. 1611, Lennox to Kilsyth, *Laing,* pp. 123–24. N.d. but before 22 June 1612, and 22 June, Fenton to Mar, *M&K Supp.,* pp. 40–41, 90–92.

3. *Spottiswoode* III, 214–15. *Calderwood* VII, 153, 163, on the other hand, gleefully wrote that "the curse was executed on him that was pronounced upon the builders of Jericho," and repeated a rumor that he had committed buggery.

4. 8 Feb. 1611, Dunfermline to Salisbury, PRO, SP 14/61, no. 70. Fenton's son married Dunfermline's eldest daughter in 1610. Dunfermline's channel through Queen Anne via Lady Jean Drummond became less useful after the latter's marriage in 1614, which necessitated her frequent absence from court.

5. *M&K Supp.,* p. 65.

6. See, e.g., the council's decision on the fining of Douglas of Drumlanrig in 1614, NLS, Denmilne Mss. V, no. 56.

The Dunfermline Administration

7. *RPCS* IX, 613.

8. *M&K*, p. 146.

9. In Jan. 1620, for instance, he wrote Lochmaben about a piece of the latter's business which was before the council. If the council's verdict went against Lochmaben, Dunfermline would write a favorable opinion directly to him for transmission to the king; see NLS, Denmilne Mss. IX, no. 78.

10. 4, 7, 8 Apr. 1611, Lake to Salisbury, PRO, SP 14/63, nos. 9, 14, 15. *RPCS* IX, liv–lvi, 194–96, 289–90, 624–25. In Aug. 1611 Cranston stepped down as captain of the police force; *ibid.*, pp. 244–45. There was bad blood between Cranston's family and Elibank's, which may account for the timing of Cranston's leaving a position which he might have used to harass the favorite's kin; see *ibid.*, p. 16. His replacement was Sir Robert Ker of Ancrum, Rochester's cousin, who served for two years and was succeeded by another kinsman, Sir Andrew Ker of Oxenham.

11. *RPCS* IX, 705–14.

12. *Calderwood* VII, 158. 9 Mar. 1613, Fenton to Mar, *M&K Supp.*, pp. 48–50.

13. *M&K Supp.*, p. 41.

14. *RPCS* IX, 443–45. *Spottiswoode* III, 214–15. 23 Sept. 1612, Gledstanes to James, J. Maidment, ed., *Analecta Scotica* (Edinburgh, 1834) II, 347–48. 2 Nov. 1613, Spottiswoode to James, *LEA* I, 315–20.

15. *RPCS* IX, 372–74, 394, 398.

16. 27 Apr. 1612, Gledstanes to Sir James Sempill, 15 May, Spottiswoode to Sempill, Sir William Fraser, *Memoirs of the Maxwells of Pollok* (Edinburgh, 1863) II, 55, 56–61. A. Ian Dunlop, "The Polity of the Scottish Church, 1600–1637," *Records of the Scottish Church History Society* XII (1958), 182–83. G. Baxter, ed., *Selections from the Minutes of the Synod of Fife, 1611–1687,* Abbotsford Club (Edinburgh, 1837), pp. 43–44, 54.

17. 21 Sept. 1612, Fenton to Mar, *M&K Supp.*, p. 43. 28 May 1613, Gledstanes to James, Fraser, *Maxwells of Pollok* II, 68–71. J. B. Salmond and G. H. Bushnell, *Henderson's Benefaction* (St. Andrews, 1942), pp. 38–45. After his visit to St. Andrews in 1617 James finally authorized the expenditure of £1,000 of public money for the library's roof; see *RPCS* XI, 308.

18. *RPCS* IX, 400–401. This is a comprehensive enactment revising the act of the convention of estates in 1599 (*RPCS* VI, 17–18), which assigned all censorship duties to the secretary. Comparisons with the law prevailing in England are interesting; the church's powers were far more restricted in Scotland. See J. R. Tanner, *Tudor Constitutional Documents* (Cambridge, 1922), pp. 279–84; F. S. Siebert, *Freedom of the Press in England 1476–1776* (Urbana, Ill., 1952), p. 139; and, for later modifications of the Scottish regulations, *RPCS* X, 252, 339–40.

19. See, e.g., 11 Mar. 1611, the bishop of Moray to James, *LEA* I, 264–65.

20. 15 May 1612, Spottiswoode to Sempill, Fraser, *Maxwells of Pollok* II, 56–61. Since the story came from Gledstanes, Spottiswoode did not know whether to believe it or not.

21. 21 Sept. 1612, Fenton to Mar, *M&K Supp.*, p. 43. J. Dennistoun and A.

MacDonald, eds., *Miscellany of the Maitland Club* III (Edinburgh, 1843), 113–14
(hereafter cited as *Maitland Club Miscellany*).

22. *Scot,* pp. 236–37.

23. 25 Oct. 1612, the bishops to James, Fraser, *Maxwells of Pollok* II, 61–63. 2
Nov., Fenton to Mar, *M&K Supp.,* p. 45. *Maitland Club Miscellany* III, 116–17.
Spottiswoode III, 217–18. 31 Dec., John Chamberlain to Dudley Carleton, N. E.
McClure, ed., *The Letters of John Chamberlain* (Philadelphia, 1939) I, 399. Anti-
Scottish feeling was running high again in England in 1612 on account of James's
favor to Rochester and Lord Sanquhar's hiring two of his fellow-countrymen to
kill an English fencing master who had put out his eye some years before; see
Calderwood VII, 164–65.

24. 24 Oct., 2 Nov. 1612, Fenton to Mar, *M&K Supp.,* pp. 43, 45.

25. *RPCS* IX, 489–90. *Calderwood* VII, 174–75. *Spottiswoode* III, 218–19.

26. *RPCS* IX, 745–46.

27. *Maitland Club Miscellany* III, 115. *RPCS* IX, 504–5. 2 Nov., 27 Dec.
1612, 27 Jan. 1613, Fenton to Mar, *M&K Supp.,* pp. 45–48. *Calderwood* VII,
175.

28. *RPCS* IX, 504.

29. Before James gave Rochester his earldom, he made Lennox earl of
Richmond in the English peerage. Lennox would have preferred a dukedom, and
got it a decade later, before Buckingham got his. James was very careful about his
cousin's precedence.

30. This paragraph is based mostly on Fenton's letter to Mar of 9 Mar. 1613,
M&K Supp., pp. 48–50. By May, when it was too late, Spottiswoode saw his error
and began advocating that Rochester take the treasury; see 6 May 1613, Spottiswoode to James, Fraser, *Maxwells of Pollok* II, 64–65.

31. See, for instance, his gloomy prediction of trouble unless some people
were added to the council "that are your Majesty's own," i.e., Spottiswoode's
allies rather than Dunfermline's; see *ibid.*

32. Sir William Fraser, *Memorials of the Earls of Haddington* (Edinburgh, 1889)
I, 75.

33. See his letter of 10 Feb. 1614 to Lochmaben, *LSP,* p. 215.

34. On the appointment of Lord Lovat as sheriff of Elgin and Forres in 1622,
the council described an Edinburgh burgess who claimed the office after the
decease of the previous sheriff as "a person altogether unfit and uncapable of
such a charge and burden"; see *RPCS* XII, 624–25.

35. 27 Jan. 1613, Fenton to Mar, *M&K Supp.,* pp. 47–48.

36. *Ibid.,* p. 55.

37. 11 July 1614, Spottiswoode to Lochmaben, Sir William Fraser, *Memorials
of the Montgomeries Earls of Eglinton* (Edinburgh, 1859) I, 60–61.

38. See, e.g., 18 Mar. 1615, Hamilton (now Lord Binning) and Elibank to
James, *Melros* I, 203–5.

39. See Binning's letter of 20 Dec. 1616 to the king on this question, a letter
far more critical of the king than was usual with the secretary; *ibid.,* pp. 267–68.

On the other hand, in some minor offices, such as sheriff-clerk and postmaster, Binning thought hereditary appointments were advantageous; see his letters of 14 Mar. 1617 to James and 25 Jan. 1623 to Lochmaben, *ibid.,* pp. 281–85, II, 494.

40. *RMS 1609–1620,* pp. 352–54, 778–79.

41. *APS* IV, 434–35.

42. On this point see Dunbar's memorandum of Apr. 1609, PRO, SP 14/44, no. 66.

43. *RPCS* VIII, 624, IX, 75–80, 696–97, 2nd ser., VIII, 297–300.

44. *RPCS* IX, 220–26, 2nd ser., VIII, 303–5. The regulations were issued in July 1611.

45. *RPCS* IX, 409–11, 477, 496–97, 2nd ser., VIII, 326–29.

46. *RPCS* XIV, 621–22. For the justices' attitude see 22 Aug. 1612, James to Hamilton, *ibid.,* 2nd ser., VIII, 330–31.

47. See, e.g., *RPCS* IX, 238–39, 387, 410, 497. *LSP,* pp. 300–302. L. B. Taylor, ed., *Aberdeen Council Letters* I (London, 1942), 141–42.

48. *RPCS* IX, 496–97, 503–4, 525–26, 2nd ser., VIII, 330–31, 332. Edinburgh soon profited from this arrangement; in Apr. 1613 the council decreed that all fines levied by the justices within the sheriffdom of Edinburgh go to the town government; see *RPCS* X, 36–37.

49. G. Donaldson, *Scotland: James V — James VII* (Edinburgh, 1965), p. 224. C. A. Malcolm, "The Office of Sheriff in Scotland," *SHR* XX (1922–23), 300. SRO, GD 22/1/518. For the Lanarkshire episode see *RPCS* XIII, 47–48. For a good brief survey see C. A. Malcolm, ed., *The Minutes of the Justices of the Peace for Lanarkshire 1707–1723,* SHS (Edinburgh, 1931), intro., pp. ix–xix.

50. *RPCS* X, 57, 62–63, 213–15, 236–37, 811, 823–24.

51. *Ibid.,* pp. 8–11. Stirling was evidently a rather disorderly town in this period. The bad feeling between the merchant guild and the craftsmen was persistent; see, e.g., *ibid.,* pp. 630–33.

52. *Ibid.,* p. 86. For an example of the council's behavior on monopolies see the dispute over the herring patent, *ibid.,* pp. 436–39, 640–41; *RCRB* III, 26–27; NLS, Denmilne Mss. VII, no. 36; 9 Oct. 1616, the council to James, *Melros* I, 262–63.

53. *LSP,* p. 222. *RPCS* X, 243–44, 281–82, 312–15, 325–26.

54. *RPCS* IX, 551–53, X, 207–8, XIV, 579.

55. *Ibid.* X, 273, 287–88.

56. *Ibid.,* pp. 15–17, 22–23, 95–96, 221–23, 531–33, 626–27.

57. *Ibid.,* pp. 277–78, 291, 372, 382–83. *LSP,* pp. 269–70.

58. *M&K,* pp. 70–74. James expected an increase of £10–12,000 in the customs tack; the auction netted £20,000; see *RPCS* X, 598–602, 620–21; NLS, Denmilne Mss. VII, no. 34.

59. *RPCS* X, 572, 592–93.

60. *Ibid.* IX, 161–62. Dunfermline did not like Scone, who was inefficient and erratic. Scone's salary was continued, however, and within two months nine

of his men were rehired to pursue people at the horn for nonpayment of taxes, no doubt in the hope that those rehired would pay for themselves; see *ibid.,* pp. 189–90.

61. *Ibid.* IX, 608, 611, XIV, 624. One debt, a 2,000-merk loan from the city of Aberdeen in 1584, was so old that no one on the current council knew anything about it. They were forced to ask James for details; he ordered it repaid without interest. See NLS, Denmilne Mss. IV, no. 3; *RPCS* IX, 738.

62. *RPCS* IX, 275, 288–89, 315–16, 345–46. I. H. Stewart, *The Scottish Coinage* (London, 1955), pp. 101–3.

63. *RPCS* IX, lxiv, 283–84, 631–33. W. R. Foster, *The Church before the Covenants* (Edinburgh, 1975), p. 169. NLS, Denmilne Mss. III, no. 61. *RCRB* II, 325, 329–31. *LSP,* pp. 202–4. *APS* IV, 473–74. M. Wood, ed., *Extracts from the Records of the Burgh of Edinburgh* (Edinburgh, 1927–31) VI, xi, 74, 86–90, 134, 144–46.

64. *RPCS* X, 408. T. H. McGrail, *Sir William Alexander* (Edinburgh, 1940), p. 67.

65. 15 July 1615, Elibank to James, NLS, Denmilne Mss. VIII, no. 32. About this time Elibank wrote a rather paranoid (and almost illegible) letter to Lochmaben about his enemies' machinations; see *ibid.* VI, no. 52. James nevertheless authorized the payment to Abercorn; see *RPCS* X, 380–81.

66. On this point see, e.g., the council's reaction to James's grant to the master of Tullibardine in May 1611, *RPCS* IX, 612, 616–17, 619–20.

67. *Ibid.,* p. 595.

68. See the action brought against him by Colquhoun of Luss in 1613, *RPCS* X, 177–79.

69. For the MacGregors see A. Cunningham, *The Loyal Clans* (Cambridge, 1932), ch. 6. The campaign against them can be followed in *RPCS* IX, xxxiv–xlii and 46ff., X, xvii–xxviii and 87ff., XIV, xc–xcvii, 629–64. See also SRO, GD 112/39/324; NLS, Denmilne Mss. IV, no. 52, V, nos. 23, 33, 70, VI, no. 33; J. R. N. MacPhail, ed., *Highland Papers* III, SHS (Edinburgh, 1920), 135–38; *M&K,* p. 76; *M&K Supp.,* pp. 53–56; Fraser, *Haddington* II, 120–21.

70. *RPCS* VIII, 845, IX, 59–60, 163–64, 245, 257–58, 340, 565–66, 583–84, 631, 694–95. NLS, Denmilne Mss. IV, no. 2. 5 June 1612, Law to James, *LEA* I, 289–91.

71. *RPCS* IX, 181–82, 185–87, 297, 392, 479–81, 529, 533, X, 200–201, 215, 219–20, 224, 247–48, 809, 824, 827, XI, 20–21, 308, XIV, 567–68. *LEA* I, 323–27, 333–41, 343–46, II, 357–61, 392–93. *RMS 1609–1620,* pp. 411–12. NLS, Denmilne Mss. V, nos. 16, 17. R. S. Barclay, ed., *The Court Books of Orkney and Shetland 1614–1615,* SHS (Edinburgh, 1967), intro., pp. xx, xxii–xxiii.

72. *LEA* II, 378–80. Caithness's expedition can be followed in the correspondence in *Melros* I, 143–57. See also NLS, Denmilne Mss. V, nos. 56, 75, 104, 109, 123; *RPCS* X, 276–77, 295–96, 322–23, 701–14; *LSP,* pp. 225–26.

73. *Calderwood* VII, 194–95. 17 Nov. 1614, Dunfermline to Lochmaben, NLS, Denmilne Mss. V, no. 138. *RPCS* X, 829–30. The trials of father and son, with appendices of documents, are in R. Pitcairn, ed., *Ancient Criminal Trials in Scotland* (Edinburgh, 1833) III, 272–307, 308–27.

The Dunfermline Administration

74. See, e.g., *RPCS* X, 449–50.

75. See, e.g., 22 Nov. 1621, Kellie to Mar, *M&K Supp.*, pp. 109–10. For the respective views of king and council on the potential value of Orkney see *RPCS* XIII, 384, 400–401.

76. Hay's predecessor, Sir John Buchanan of Scotscraig, paid 45,000 merks; the king's agreement with Hay stipulated that Buchanan was to pay the 45,000 to Hay for the unexpired years of his lease. Hay thus received a net profit of 5,000 merks without any expenditure of money or effort on his part; it was a reward for service. See *RPCS* XIII, 601–2.

77. Within a year Caithness was in trouble for feuding with Lord Forbes, and within two for recusancy; see *RPCS* X, 249, 256, 308, 584–85, 587, 608–9, 611; *LEA* II, 470. He had a long and unprepossessingly lawless career, went deeply in debt, and died at seventy-eight during the civil war.

78. Fraser, *Haddington* II, 77–78.

79. The relevant documents are in *RPCS* X, 184–91, 249–50, 817–21, XI, 204–5, 207–8, 456–57, 478–80, 559, 571, XII, 240, 367, 402–4, 427–29, 454, 503, 538–43, 568, 586–87, 729, 742–45, XIII, 493, 553, 770–72. The quotation is from Primrose's report, *ibid.* X, 820. D. Gregory, *The History of the Western Highlands and Isles of Scotland* 2nd ed. (London, 1881), pp. 342–47. Cunningham, *Loyal Clans,* pp. 117–27.

80. *RPCS* X, 13–14, 818.

81. *Highland Papers* III, 149–53. *RPCS* X, 698–700, 706, 710. *Melros* I, 157–58, 164–66, II, 594–96.

82. *Highland Papers* III, 156–58.

83. 11, 17, 23 Oct. 1614, Knox to Lochmaben, *ibid.,* pp. 161–65. *Laing,* p. 132. Knox had a special grievance against Calder, who was disputing the right of the bishopric of the Isles to possession of the abbey of Iona; see *Highland Papers* III, 272–73; *APS* IV, 554.

84. *RPCS* X, 718–25. *RMS 1609–1620,* pp. 417–20.

85. *RPCS* X, 275. *Highland Papers* III, 158–59.

86. *Highland Papers* III, 170–72.

87. Deposition of Robert Winram, Islay herald, *ibid.,* pp. 207–9.

88. NLS, Denmilne Mss. VI, no. 71.

89. 16 Mar. 1615, Dunfermline to James, 30 Apr., Dunfermline to Fenton, *Melros* I, 201–3, 207–10.

90. Gregory, *Western Highlands,* pp. 359–66. Cunningham, *Loyal Clans,* pp. 213–15.

91. *Highland Papers* III, 179.

92. For the Graham affair see *ibid.,* pp. 168–272.

93. 3 June 1615, MacDonald to the council, 1 July, MacDonald to Binning, *ibid.,* pp. 222–23, 262–64.

94. 30 June 1615, the council to James, *Melros* I, 222–24. *RPCS* X, 736. *Highland Papers* III, 229–31, 244–53.

95. *RPCS* X, 744–55, 757. *Melros* I, 230–33. 4 Aug. 1615, Dunfermline to Lochmaben, NLS, Denmilne Mss. VI, no. 65.

96. *Highland Papers* III, 291–92.

97. 21 Dec. 1615, Hay to Lochmaben, *LSP,* pp. 273–75. There is a detailed account of MacDonald's rebellion in Gregory, *Western Highlands,* pp. 366–90. See also Cunningham, *Loyal Clans,* pp. 215–23.

98. *RPCS* X, 766.

99. Fraser, *Haddington* II, 131–33.

100. *RPCS* X, 671–72, 777–78. The act does not say so, but the obvious intention was to apply the educational requirement to the highlanders' male children only.

101. *RPCS* XIII, 362, 464–66, 744–45, 819.

102. *RPCS* X, 439. 6 Jan. 1616, Elibank to Lochmaben, *Highland Papers* III, 303–4.

103. 16 Apr. 1617, the countess of Argyll to Sir Duncan Campbell, SRO, GD 112/39/393.

104. SRO, E17/2, no. 12. 15 Dec. 1615, Elibank to James, NLS, Denmilne Mss. VI, no. 57.

105. 7 June 1614, the council to James, *LEA* I, 330–31. 9 June 1614, Elibank to James, 28 Jan. 1615, Dunfermline to Lochmaben, *LSP,* pp. 216–17, 256–57. See also the letters to Lochmaben from Sanquhar, *ibid.,* pp. 257–59, and from Binning, Andrew Murray, and Spottiswoode, *LEA* II, 414–16, 418–19, 420–21.

106. *Spottiswoode* III, 227.

107. 22 Dec. 1615, Spottiswoode to Lochmaben, *LEA* II, 461–62. Salmond and Bushnell, *Henderson's Benefaction,* pp. 43, 45–46.

5

The Religious Question Reopened

IN APRIL 1616, after one of his reluctantly undertaken journeys to court, Lord Chancellor Dunfermline brought back with him the positive assurance that King James was finally going to visit his native land in the following year. Preparations for the great event began at once and were extensive and varied: repairing roads and royal palaces, searching out tapestries and beds, finding lodging for the men and horses in the king's train, getting the beggars off the streets of Edinburgh, "where they ordinarily convene every night and pass the time in all kind of riot and filthy and beastly lechery and whoredom."[1] The provision of food and drink was a matter of special concern. The restrictions on the hunting of game in the vicinity of the king's palaces were renewed and enforced, cattle were fattened, and wine was bought in France—too much wine: in July 1617 the council prohibited further imports for the year so that the surplus could be sold off, in spite of the protests of the merchants in the wine trade, who argued that the ban would cost the Scots their market for the goods they usually sold in Bordeaux.[2] So, gradually and haphazardly, the job of preparing the royal welcome got done, and not too badly done.[3]

The preparations all cost money, of course, and by the end of 1616 the council had concluded that existing funds, plus good will and voluntary contributions of goods and services, would not be adequate. So the king agreed to call a convention of estates to vote a tax, which, admittedly, could not be collected in time to defray the government's expenses but could be used as security for loans. The estates met in March 1617 and agreed in principle that a tax was necessary. Then the disputes began. Some wanted to wait for

the meeting of parliament planned for the king's visit; a larger sum
would be voted then, it was argued, once it was clear that the
government's legislative program would endanger no vested interests. Some pleaded poverty; others complained of overassess-
ment. Secretary Binning rebutted these arguments as best he
could. Next day a vote was taken; those who favored 300,000
merks barely won out over those favoring a lesser figure. The
losers then raised a technical point. Councillors other than officers
of state, they argued, should not have *ex officio* the right to vote: if
they had not voted, the smaller figure would have been adopted.
They made the telling argument that if such councillors were allowed to vote, some future king might pack the meeting with
foreign—i.e., English—councillors. Binning vainly argued that
precedent favored allowing councillors to vote; the majority now
refused to proceed unless a new vote was taken with the councillors absent. The government decided to sidestep: a new vote
would be taken the next day, when the councillors would volun-
tarily absent themselves. This was done, and the larger figure was
approved, with the stipulation that the tax would be collected only
if the king actually came. The government had come very close to
defeat and had had to stoop to subterfuge to avoid an awkward
constitutional confrontation. The issue of the councillors' vote was
bound to recur at the next meeting of the convention of estates—one reason, certainly, why James never called one again.[4]

The suspicions and fears expressed at the meeting of the estates
had been gathering strength for some time. People asked themselves why James should be coming to Scotland now, after so
many years of neglect and broken promises, and gave themselves a
selves a sinister answer. The king was reportedly planning major
changes in the church, and—of more direct concern to the landed
classes—he was also going to attack the "sheriffships of inheritance" and attempt "the disannulling of the Act of Annexation."[5]
James in December 1616 tried to allay these suspicions by sending
the council a letter intended for widespread distribution, especially among the clergy, in order to put an end to what he called
"any unwelcome coldness" when he arrived. There were no ul-
terior motives to his visit, James said, nothing but a "salmonlike
instinct" to see his native land again, hear complaints in person,

and effect only those changes in civil and ecclesiastical affairs which would tend to "the glory of God and the weal of that commonwealth" and meet with general approval. He would attempt nothing controversial, however desirable it might be. Fenton, who had reported the original rumors, now wrote cautiously but with relief that James was "resolved rather to bear with inconvenients that are past than to mend them with the grief and discontentment of his subjects."[6]

The disquiet shown at the convention of estates was not due merely to overheated imagination. There was unmistakable evidence to justify the widespread assumption, current in England as well as Scotland,[7] that after some five years of relative inactivity the king was indeed planning further changes in the church, and always with the same end in view: conformity with the church of England. The king's desire for conformity was not a matter merely of preference for the Anglican service or the promotion of greater episcopal (and hence royal) control over the ministry, though these played their part. As always, the king had the wider union of England and Scotland in mind, and he judged, quite correctly, that the religious differences between the two would be the greatest obstacle in its way. He knew that he could not succeed in eliminating these differences overnight, however, and he was prepared to be very patient. As long as the erratic Gledstanes was primate it would be difficult to achieve very much; so between the final restoration of diocesan episcopacy at the General Assembly of June 1610 and Gledstanes's death in May 1615 very little had been done. Dunbar had successfully urged the appointment of the Puritan-minded George Abbot to the archbishopric of Canterbury in 1611, in part certainly to mollify the Scottish opponents of episcopacy, who detested Archbishop Bancroft.[8] Some attempt had been made to improve clerical incomes, relieve the poorer clergy from taxation, and acquire a suitable endowment for the dilapidated bishoprics and for the cathedral chapters whose property had been swallowed up in what Gledstanes and Spottiswoode called "that woeful Act of Annexation." But caution was the watchword in these years. Troublesome ministers were leniently treated. There were the usual spurts of activity against Papists, the most noteworthy of which was the decision in 1614 to insist on enforcement of the regulation that everyone take communion once a year, this year on 24 April—Easter Sunday, though the proclamation was careful not to say so. The council acted on Spottiswoode's initiative in this matter, the archbishop claiming instructions from the king. In the following year the pretense was dropped; henceforth the annual communion would be on Easter Sunday.[9]

Spottiswoode and his colleagues were genuinely nervous about the spread of Popery in these years. The capture and execution of the Jesuit John Ogilvie, the one Catholic martyr of this period, heightened their fears—Spottiswoode wrote Lochmaben that he was assured that there were twenty-seven Jesuits in Scotland, two in each diocese and the Papal legate.[10] One reason for their inability to stamp out Popery, according to the bishops, was the continual backsliding and apparent immunity of the marquis of Huntly, whom they had pursued at law for years with no visible results.[11] In 1616 they set out after him again. In June he was summoned before the high commission and warded in Edinburgh castle. Within a few days Dunfermline released him, on the ground that he had the king's license to go to court. The bishops protested angrily and subsequently attacked the chancellor from the pulpit for his sympathy to Papists. Huntly lost no time heading for court; James, who had indicated that he approved of Huntly's warding, nevertheless received him, and he was ultimately released from excommunication—by the archbishop of Canterbury! The Scottish bishops were aghast at this usurpation of their jurisdiction, which suggested that James no longer cared about the independence of the Scottish church, and protested vigorously. The king and Abbot replied rather feebly; eventually the whole business was smoothed over when Huntly made formal submission to the General Assembly in August.[12]

To most Scottish clerics Abbot's absolution of Huntly was one more piece of evidence that King James was planning the amalgamation of the Scottish church with the church of England—or rather, its absorption. An isolated action means very little, of course, but this was not an isolated action. The question of changes in doctrine had also been raised, and changes in doctrine meant changes in the English direction. As early as 1611 James had indicated that he would welcome a new confession of faith, and a draft was actually prepared—in England—in the following year and sent north for the archbishops' opinions.[13] Nothing was done as long as Gledstanes was primate, but as soon as Gledstanes died the king began to move. A memorandum in Spottiswoode's hand, written in England a month or so after Gledstanes's death, indicates what James wanted: a new form of service, one feature of which was to be the elimination of extemporary prayer, a new confession of faith "agreeing so near as can be with the Confession of the English Church," a uniform method of choosing ministers and bishops, alteration of the forms of baptism, communion, and marriage and the introduction of confirmation, and a new set of canons. All this was to be put through a General Assembly "which must be drawn to the form of the Convocation House here in England."[14] Now that the ablest and most dependable of his clerical collaborators was in the see of St. Andrews, the king was sure that this ambitious program of assimilation could go forward. James had every right to expect that Spottiswoode would be zealous in the cause; he had, after all, been highly critical of those Scottish clerics who had attacked the church of England, however obliquely.[15] The king's decision to visit Scotland, made shortly after this memorandum was drafted, evidently caused some indecision as to the timing of the implementation of his program. For the remainder of 1615 all that was done was to consolidate the courts of high commission in December. It seems likely that James was trying to decide whether or not to hold back his program until he could preside over the necessary meetings of parliament and General Assembly in person. In the summer of 1616, possibly on account of the contretemps over Huntly, he made up his mind to make a start at once—rather abruptly, if one takes the evidence at face value: on 18 July a proclamation was issued ordering the convocation of a General Assembly on 13 August. The meeting was to be held in Aberdeen, ostensibly to deal on the spot with those seduced by the ill example of Huntly's backsliding. The real reason was to facilitate the attendance of the clerical moderates of the northeast, a return to the pattern of the later 1590s which had been abandoned after 1603 to suit the convenience of Dunbar— this was the first assembly since Dunbar's death.

The assembly gave the king most of what he wanted. A new confession of faith was adopted, no less Calvinistic in its theology than its predecessors but more general in tone, and less vituperative—"they left out many points of superstition damned in the Second [Confession]," commented Calderwood.[16] A liturgy was to be drawn up, and a new catechism and set of canons, and a form of examination of children between the ages of six and fourteen was adopted which resembled the Anglican confirmation, save that ministers as well as bishops could administer it. Scholarships for divinity students were to be established, two from each diocese, in order to supply that steady stream of doctors of divinity, on the English model, which James's recent instructions to St. Andrews University had authorized; the king intended that in future this degree would be a prerequisite for appointment to a bishopric. The assembly also authorized the appointment of a committee on the dilapidation of benefices and required that parish registers be kept henceforth, to record births, marriages, and deaths. It was a substantial victory for the king, and was obtained, if Calderwood and Scot can be believed, by the use of unremitting pressure. Spottiswoode named himself moderator of the assembly without any form of election and kept a tight grip on its sessions. "The crows were not more afraid of a scarecrow," wrote Scot, "than slavish ministers were of the wagging of the Bishop's finger."[17]

James was pleased with the results of the assembly. The only act he disliked was that on confirmation, which, he said, should be administered only by bishops. In addition, he wanted inserted in the forthcoming set of canons articles asserting the lawfulness, where necessary, of private baptism and private communion, the observance of the five principal holydays of the Christian calendar, and kneeling at communion. Here for the first time was spelled out what were to become the five articles of Perth. Spottiswoode made no objection to the proposed changes as such, but he did insist that they could not simply be slipped into the canons. They would have to have specific approval from the church. So James agreed to defer action on them until his arrival in Scotland. But he did instruct the council to issue orders that children were to be brought before the bishop on his diocesan visitations, "to be tried and confirmed by him"; the council implemented this order, and much of the legislation of the General Assembly regarding Papists, in December 1616.[18]

The king's letter of December 1616, cited above, was supposed to quiet the fears which his religious policy since Gledstanes's death had aroused. That it was ineffective was demonstrated by a contretemps which boiled over early in 1617. The restoration of the chapel royal at Holyroodhouse was a project James had much at heart. Bishop Cowper of Galloway, the dean of the chapel, on James's orders began a series of legal actions to recover its rents.[19] The council issued a general commission in his support, and in August 1616 approved a contract with a London carver to provide new ornaments and decoration. New organs were also ordered; they arrived at Leith in October and aroused alarm and dislike. Among those employed on the refurbishing was the great Inigo Jones. "All manner of furniture for a Chapel" was being sent to Scotland, wrote John Chamberlain to Dudley Carleton in December 1616, "which Inigo Jones tells me he hath charge of, with pictures of the Apostles, Faith, Hope, and Charity, and other such religious representations; which how welcome they will be thither God knows."[20]

They were not welcome at all. Spottiswoode reported that people began to mutter: first the organs, next the images, soon the Mass. Bishop Cowper became alarmed, and in February 1617 asked James to cancel the order for the erection of the images. Spottiswoode and some of the other bishops, and the Edinburgh clergy, endorsed Cowper's request. James was very angry at what he called the "error in your judgment of that graven work, which is not of an idolatrous kind, like to Images and painted Pictures adored and worshipped by Papists, but merely intended for ornament and decoration of the place where We should sit." Such ornamentation was used in England, James went on, and the bishops should know better than to suppose that he would countenance anything Popish. "We hope to bring to that kingdom with Us such as, by their knowledge and doctrine, shall resolve and persuade you and all others of your coat and profession." Having made his feelings clear, the king nevertheless granted the bishops' request, because the master of the works told him the decoration could not be got ready in time. Bishop Cowper was pleased at the result of his initiative but alarmed at the king's insulting tone. "The King in his letter has boasted us with his English Doctors, who (as he says) shall instruct us in these and in other points, except we refuse instruction. God make us wise and faithful and keep us from their usurpation over us, which now is evidently perceived, and hardly taken by us all." The tendency of the king's policy was beginning to cause qualms even among his supporters in the church.[21]

Dunfermline may have shared some of these qualms; if so, he kept them pretty much to himself. Enforcement of the king's policy would keep the bishops busy, and the form that policy took, of alteration of church services, could not enhance their political power. Furthermore, a series of ministerial changes and appointments in 1616 strengthened the chancellor's position. The clerk register, Alexander Hay, died and was succeeded by the busy entrepreneur Sir George Hay of Nethercliff, already in the glass and iron business, now the possessor with a partner of a nineteen-year monopoly of whale fishing, and preparing to branch out into the export of coal.[22] Hay was the first person who might be called a businessman to become a high official in the Scottish government; he was to make his influence felt in promoting the interests of his fellow manufacturers and merchants. Secretary Binning became president of the court of session and presiding officer of the council in the chancellor's absence. These changes were of no particular benefit to Dunfermline; his great gain was the appointment in December 1616 of his close political ally the earl of Mar as lord treasurer. James had made up his mind by July to make this appointment; the delay arose from the need to make arrangements with Treasurer-depute Elibank, whose continued service was absolutely necessary. Dunfermline worked very hard to ensure Mar's appointment. He helped Mar in his dealings with Elibank, and he collaborated with Fenton, currently in very high favor, to persuade James of Mar's diligence and financial acumen. Mar's appointment also had the essential support of that rising star in the London firmament, Sir George Villiers, whom Fenton carefully cultivated.[23] In October Elibank went to London, where he received a *douceur* of £6,000 and the assurance that his continuance in office would be at the king's pleasure, not at Mar's.

Mar raised no objection to this, and in December Elibank returned with the earl's patent. Mar was to remain in the office for
almost fifteen years.[24] With these appointments, the last major
reshuffle of offices in Dunfermline's lifetime, the chancellor's grip
on the levers of power was more secure than ever.

ii

King James, as the time fixed for his salmon-like journey approached, was in a benevolent frame of mind, except perhaps
where the religious issue was concerned. He found little enough
to complain of in the secular realm. In November 1616 he ordered the council to supervise the commissioners of the middle
shires more closely: there were complaints of thefts. The king also
worried about money, and, holding as he did to his simplistic
economic theory that peace equals prosperity, held others responsible for the continuing financial pinch. In authorizing the auction
of the customs tack in August 1616 he wrote, "Whereas you wrote
to us of a decay of trade there, seeing you yourselves and all the
world can bear us witness that we have maintained peace and
justice in a greater measure than any of our predecessors . . . the
cause thereof cannot proceed from us but must be ascribed to the
misgovernment of those trusted with the rule of the estate."[25] The
substantial increase in the tack was therefore very gratifying to him.
    "I am sorry to hear," wrote Fenton to the new lord treasurer,
"that his Majesty's revenue there is in no better state, and that
there is (*sic*) so many burdens on it."[26] It nevertheless behooved
Mar and Dunfermline to make a brave show for their master, and
the first months of 1617 were filled with frantic activity and last-
minute preparations. As the king approached, the council took
thought for his mental as well as his physical comfort. No one was
to injure or insult any of the king's English subjects. Binning sent
James a draft of a proclamation designed to cut down on the
number of importunate suitors he would have to hear, by requiring that the council screen all petitions before passing them on to
the master of requests. James returned it with the addition of a
clause threatening with death anyone who pleaded for forfeited
traitors or their wives. Dunfermline regarded this as much too

extreme and held up its publication, though Binning was prepared to accept it because it was not seriously meant. James agreed to settle for threatening such pleaders with his "high and heavy displeasure."[27]

Tuesday, 13 May, was the great day, the day King James crossed the Tweed at last. His large train included courtier Scots like Lennox, Lochmaben, and Fenton, five English earls, three bishops, including Lancelot Andrewes, and one future bishop, William Laud, clerics carefully chosen, as James had promised, to "resolve and persuade" their Scottish counterparts of the desirability of James's religious policy. Queen Anne stayed at home. James made his way slowly to Edinburgh; he was greeted there, and everywhere else, with suitable orations, poems, and ceremonial.[28] On Saturday evening, wrote Calderwood, "the English service was begun in the Chapel Royal, with singing of choristers, surplices, and playing on organs." The next day the king presided over a meeting of the council in order to grace by his presence the admission of his favorite, now earl of Buckingham, to the council, the first Englishman so honored. James's stay in the capital was brief; soon he was off to Falkland for about a fortnight of the hunting and hawking he had been promising himself. When he returned to Edinburgh, the evidences of his intentions in religion became clearer yet. The Whitsun communion service on 8 June was celebrated in the English fashion; all the bishops save one, and Dunfermline, Binning, Clerk Register Hay, and the earl of Argyll, now on the verge of open admission of his Catholicism, communicated kneeling. Shortly thereafter the king ordered those who were present but did not do so, notably including the new lord treasurer, to conform in future.[29]

James returned to Edinburgh after such a brief sojourn in his old hunting grounds in order to hold the parliament, which was to be the principal piece of public business during his stay in Scotland. Everyone believed that religion would be the most controversial issue; concerned ministers were congregating in Edinburgh, expecting the worst and preparing to do what they could by way of petition to prevent any undesirable changes in polity or worship. By this time the king had had a chance to discover the extent of the fear and discontent the rumors of his intentions had caused, so he attempted to disarm his would-be critics in his opening speech by saying nothing at all about religious doctrine and stressing that he hoped that parliament would act to improve clerical stipends, strengthen the office of justice of the peace, and improve the level of civilization in the country. With respect to this last, the king said that he hoped that his Scottish subjects would now demonstrate as much enthusiasm for the good features of English life as they had hitherto shown for the bad: "to drink healths, to wear . . . gay clothes, to take tobacco, and to speak neither Scots nor English."[30] James's advocacy of English ways struck a jarring note and may have contributed to the difficulty he had in getting a suitable committee of the articles elected; the nobility especially were balky because of their fear for their estates. The memory of the recent convention of estates was still fresh; during the discussions over the makeup of the committee someone questioned the right of government officials to vote in parliament and sit with the articles. James set the clerk register to search out precedents; after he had done so, James declared that officials did indeed have such a right, and that henceforth their number would be fixed at eight.[31]

Religion was indeed to be the most controversial issue at this parliament, but some of its other actions were equally important and more permanent. Many of them were designed to carry out the royal recommendation to follow the English example, even in matters where uniformity was of no particular significance, such as the authorization to lords and bishops to vote in parliament by proxy. The most important administrative change was the revival of the register of sasines, a reform which the chancellor, with his long experience on the court of session, very much favored, and which was the one specific piece of legislation he singled out in his summary of the accomplishments of this parliament as being especially beneficial to the kingdom.[32] There was also a long statute spelling out the powers and duties of the justices of the peace, which paralleled very closely those of their English counterparts. It was accompanied—and here may be seen the hand of the conservative Dunfermline administration—by the explicit assurance that no one else's jurisdictional rights were in any way diminished by the powers so granted.[33] Possibly because of the king's concern to establish the system of justices of the peace, the opportunity to come to grips with the unsatisfactory administration of criminal law provided by the death early in 1617 of Sir William Hart, the justice-depute, went by default. Dunfermline urged James to make no new appointment until he arrived and to take advantage of the opportunity to overhaul the system, but in fact nothing was done, save parliament's authorization of a committee to revise and codify criminal procedure with an eye to reducing delays. There is no evidence that it ever accomplished anything. No serious attempt was made to implement the statute of 1587 which stipulated the holding of justice ayres twice a year, and when occasional ayres were held, the council was careful not to violate the lords of regalities' right of repledging. The council instead continued to resort to the practice, increasingly used in recent years, of appointing a special commission of reliable people to try either a specific case or specific categories of crimes in a designated area.[34]

None of this legislation caused any serious controversy. On all these matters James was prepared to be very conciliatory, and in spite of the new lord treasurer's discouragement at the state of the revenue, there was no suggestion from any quarter that parliament should vote a tax. Even James's reported plan to attack hereditary officeholders turned out to involve nothing more than the creation of a committee to negotiate with them over the terms on which they might surrender their offices. It accomplished almost nothing; by the time of James's death the crown had acquired the right to nominate the sheriff annually in only eight shires.[35] But with religion it was a different story. There is no evidence that James ever intended an attack on the erections or a total repeal of the act of annexation, and in fact in this parliament a new erection was granted, of the abbey of Holyrood in favor of Murray of Lochmaben.[36] The king and the archbishop did intend to extend the policy of improving ministerial stipends, begun in 1606 with those parishes affected by the erections, to all ministers, and this determination produced the most important piece of religious legislation of this parliament, in the form of a committee empowered to do precisely that. Since his translation to St. Andrews Spottiswoode had been actively trying to remedy individual cases of negligence or worse; the minatory tone of some of his letters may have been responsible for the landed classes' uneasy belief that James intended to try to recover the church's ancient patrimony.[37] What emerged from the committee of the articles was a bill which was a very skillful, and ultimately successful, attempt to satisfy all the interests involved. A large committee was named, eight members and four alternates from each of the four parliamentary estates, plus the lord chancellor. The membership of the committee was designed to reassure the nervous, and no action could be taken without a quorum of five of each estate. As an added bit of reassurance for the landed classes, the committee's life-span was to be short. Its powers would expire on 1 August 1618.[38]

The controversy which erupted at the parliament was brought on not by the creation of this committee or by any of the rest of the legislation having to do with the church which found its way to the statute book, but by one bill which did not. This was the proposal that parliament declare that the king, after consultation with the bishops and a "competent number" of ministers, could make binding decisions on "all matters decent for the external policy of the kirk." The first version of this bill, stipulating consultation with the bishops only, was alarming even to them; the revised version produced an uproar and a protest, signed by fifty-five ministers, including not only ex-Melvilleans but also moderates like Patrick Galloway and John Hall, the two principal Edinburgh ministers. The protest was due not only to the unprecedented grant of power to the king but also to what everybody knew he intended to do with it: to impose what became the five articles of Perth. This had become apparent at a synod held in Edinburgh in mid-June, just before the opening of parliament, where the articles were openly discussed and where Spottiswoode received from the assembled ministers the same reply he had given to James the previous year: such changes could be made only in a General Assembly.[39] The protesters at the parliament did not discuss these articles specifically, however. They stressed instead the doctrinal and disciplinary excellence of the Scottish church, the authority of the General Assembly, and their fear of being forced into uniformity with the church of England, which they said James had repeatedly promised not to attempt. Once the protestation was drawn up, Galloway apparently began to get cold feet. He refused to sign it, though he agreed to the inclusion of his name on a separate list of supporters, and he then "revealed the whole purpose"—whether to the king or to Spottiswoode is not clear. So when Peter Hewat, one of the Edinburgh ministers, came to Holyrood to deliver the protestation to James, he found Spottiswoode waiting for him. There was a sharp exchange between them, and an actual scuffle for possession of the paper, which James himself interrupted. The king looked the document over and decided on a tactical retreat. He ordered the clerk register to delete the bill from the list of the articles to be presented to parliament, saying that he could act as he chose in questions of church government anyway, by virtue of his prerogative.[40] This was a claim which James had never explicitly made before, and in the end he decided not to put it to the test: making important changes in the church by fiat would alienate the clerical moderates and jeopardize the ultimate success of his plans. But the fact that he made the claim at all is an indication of the extent to which he had accepted as universally applicable the Anglican position as to the power of the crown over the polity of the church.

James digested his rebuff with apparent good humor, though it became clear soon enough that he had no intention of letting the matter drop. Once parliament was over he left Edinburgh—forever, as it turned out. He visited Stirling, Perth, and Falkland and then arrived in St. Andrews on 11 July, where, next day, he sat with the court of high commission. Spottiswoode had convened the court to try the three ministers most closely connected with the clerical protest at the parliament: Peter Hewat, Archibald Simson, minister of Dalkeith, the sole signer of the actual text of the protestation, and David Calderwood, who now had the list of subscribers in his possession. At the outset the king expressed the opinion, according to Calderwood, that the most effective way of dealing with "puritans" was to deprive them not merely of their benefices but also of their offices, so that they could not go on preaching and living on the contributions of their lay supporters. The court acted accordingly. Calderwood's destiny, which he brought on himself, was the hardest of the three. The king, who did not know Calderwood, was inclined to be lenient, but the future historian gave him no chance. He argued with James over the scope of the General Assembly's authority. He defined obedience as "rather suffer than practice," to which James rejoined, "I will tell thee, man, what is obedience. The centurion, when he said to his servants, to this man, Go, and he goeth, to that man, Come, and he cometh, that is obedience." Calderwood went on to defy the authority of the bishops and the high commission, and, apparently through a misunderstanding, declined to obey the king himself. James, who had been very patient with the argumentative minister, now became angry and ordered him to prison and then into exile. Calderwood's subsequent attempts to get his sentence reduced or remitted were unavailing. He blamed the malice of the bishops for his troubles, repeated the rumor that Spottiswoode's wife's maid was with child by him, and implied that the archbishop suffered from venereal disease. Spottiswoode's own summary of Calderwood's difficulties and the causes for his banishment, though very brief, is far nearer the truth. Calderwood, he says, was banished for making undutiful speeches.[41]

Having dealt with the contumacious ministers, James returned to the matter of the five articles. On 13 July an informal gathering of bishops and ministers was held in St. Andrews castle. The king made a rather irritable speech about the rebuff he had received at the parliament and wanted to know what objections they had to the articles. Once again the response came: a General Assembly must approve them. "'But if it fall out otherwise,' said the King, 'and that the Articles be refused, my difficulty will be greater; and, *when* I shall use my authority in establishing them, they shall call me a tyrant and persecutor'" (italics mine). James was now for the first time personally and publicly committed to the imposition of the articles; faced with the royal determination, the ministers assured him that an assembly would give him what he wanted. Spottiswoode, by his own account, was cautious; but Patrick Galloway, perhaps wanting to make up for his slip over the protestation, guaranteed the articles' passage. So the king agreed: there would be an assembly later in the year.[42]

From St. Andrews James returned to Stirling. It was probably at this time that he paid his celebrated visit to Sir George Bruce's coal works at Culross, where, on his inspection of the mine, he suddenly found himself on a loading platform in the middle of the

Forth and imagined for a moment that treason was afoot. Whatever the truth of this story, the king took a liking to Bruce and
thereafter was much more sympathetic to the viewpoint of the
mine owners, particularly in the matter of exports, than he had
been before. At Stirling James received a deputation from Edinburgh University, listened to their learned disputations, made his
famous punning speech to them, and took them under his protec-
tion. This was a matter of great satisfaction to the university: there
had been rumors that James planned to eliminate all higher education in Scotland save in the archiepiscopal cities of St. Andrews
and Glasgow.[43] From Stirling the king continued west; in Glasgow, on 27 July, he presided for the last time over a meeting of the
Scottish privy council. He stayed about a week more in the southwest; by 4 August he was in Carlisle, and the great visit was over.
It had all gone very smoothly on the social level. There was no
serious friction between Englishmen and Scots, a matter of great
importance to the king, and some of the English visitors were
impressed in spite of themselves. "The wonders of their kingdom
are these," wrote one of them: "the Lord Chancellor, he is believed, the Master of the Rolls well spoken of, and the whole
council, who are the judges for all causes, are free from suspicion
of corruption."[44] The chancellor dithyrambically declared that
"since your Sacred Majesty attained to the Crown of England,
there has nothing been done . . . [that] could advance and further
a perfect union of the two nations, so far as this [visit] has done."
That was certainly the king's intention, and as he crossed the
Solway to make his way by slow stages back to Whitehall, he must
have believed that he had succeeded. He was even willing to
permit the tiresome Calderwood to be admitted to bail, which he
would not have done if the expectation of future success for his
policy had not assuaged his irritation.[45]

iii

James's departure from his ancient kingdom was accompanied
by a flurry of instructions, the most important of which, as far as he
was concerned, had to do with religion. Patrick Galloway had
promised that a General Assembly would accept the disputed five

articles; it would therefore come together with as little delay as possible. That meant November 1617, after the diocesan synods had met in October to choose commissioners.[46] The king ordered a number of his councillors to attend; at the same time he wrote to Galloway asking for his opinion of the five articles. Galloway replied in a long and careful letter, stressing that he had communicated his views to no one and was prepared to receive enlightenment and instruction from the king wherever he went astray. Confirmation was already settled, and private baptism and communion were permissible under certain restricted circumstances. As to the celebration of the five holydays, Galloway said, he was indifferent, but there was much objection to it: why not have those which fell on weekdays celebrated on the following Sunday? The fifth article was the difficult one. Kneeling in prayer before and after the taking of communion was acceptable, said Galloway, but the action itself should be done sitting. Kneeling was not introduced until the Lateran council of 1215, along with the doctrine of transubstantiation.[47] The implication was clear: kneeling at communion was unscriptural and Popish.

If this was the view of a moderate minister who was prepared to go as far with the king as he possibly could, it is not surprising that the assembly went badly. Attendance was very slim, so slim that the opposition had an excellent case for insisting on delay. This insistence was so strong that the bishops were compelled to acquiesce for fear of outright defeat if they forced the five articles to a vote. Spottiswoode, who had begun by haranguing the assembly on the iniquitous behavior of Andrew Melville in times past, was furious and threatened that the king would enforce the articles on his own authority. But his fellow bishops and the councillors present calmed him down. Galloway devised interim articles on communion which, it was hoped, would content the king for now. The bishops in reporting to James put the best face they could on their defeat. There were too many absentees, they said. "Though we have done little, yet a way is made to all, and the same will be more easily effectuated at another time."[48]

Softening up the opposition to assure a favorable vote at some indefinite future date was not James's view of a satisfactory outcome. He poured ridicule on the communion articles and ordered them to be suppressed, called the bishops' proceedings disgraceful, and threatened financial reprisals against all ministers who refused to accept the five articles. "Since your Scottish church hath so far contemned my clemency," he wrote to the archbishops, "they shall now find what it is to draw the anger of a King upon them."[49] Concrete action quickly followed: in January 1618 James ordered the council to issue a proclamation enjoining observance of the religious holydays. At the same time rumors began to circulate that he would prohibit the meetings of certain presbyteries and kirk sessions as mutinous.[50] The king clearly was in no mood for compromise on acceptance of the articles; he intended to have his way.

Archbishop Spottiswoode's reaction to the outcome of the assembly was just the opposite. Now, for the first time, he began to show some reluctance to enforce the king's policy respecting the five articles. A concrete financial threat made to the Edinburgh clergy at the end of January 1618 was ineffective. Attendance at the Good Friday and Easter services in the chapel royal at Holyroodhouse was very thin, and thinner still at Whitsun. "Many told me after, that they were minded to communicate," wrote the bishop of Galloway to the king after Easter, "but they stood every one upon the coming of others."[51] Even more alarming to Spottiswoode was the difficulty he had in persuading Patrick Forbes to accept the vacant bishopric of Aberdeen. Forbes, an irenic and admirable man, the brother of John Forbes, the leading figure in the Aberdeen assembly of 1605, made it very clear that his reluctance was due to the turmoil the recent innovations had caused and his fear that there might be more changes which would lead to further trouble. "Where God calleth," Spottiswoode replied, "to run away, it is not modesty, but rebellion and disobedience."[52] Forbes was finally persuaded to accept.

The chancellor, although he did not say so, must have gotten a good deal of pleasure out of Spottiswoode's discomfiture at the assembly and thereafter, but there was a point beyond which it would be unwise to allow the king's anger to go. So, on 23 December 1617, Dunfermline wrote the king a long and flowery letter recapitulating all the good things that had happened since the General Assembly of August 1616, with special stress on his majesty's gracious and highly successful visit, the settling of some major feuds, and the constructive legislation of the parliament of 1617. The recent General Assembly, said Dunfermline, "agreed among themselves on sundry points and articles, importing to the policy and good order in God's service, and for uniformity in administration of the Sacraments," a description which no one who was present at the assembly would have recognized.[53] How much of Dunfermline's ornate and fulsome verbiage James believed is impossible to say. What can be said is that the king's anger apparently abated in the new year, although his purposes did not alter.

One very probable consequence of James's anger at the untoward outcome of the General Assembly was that he would interfere with the work of the committee on clerical stipends authorized at the last parliament, by either forbidding it altogether or ordering reprisals against the opponents of the articles. He was persuaded to stay his hand, however, either by Dunfermline's flattery or by Archbishop Spottiswoode, who apparently argued that good treatment for the supporters of James's policy would be more effective than threats, though what he wrote in his *History* was that James acquiesced with the understanding that the benefited ministers would provisionally obey the five articles. There is no evidence that they did so, and it is also clear that opponents as well as supporters of the king's policy received augmented stipends. There is no reason to doubt Calderwood's assertion that the latter were favored, however—so, he might have added, were influential lay teind-holders like Murray of Lochmaben—and the timing of the General Assembly of 1618, which was held in the month following the end of the commission's labors, lends weight to Calderwood's view.[54]

The basic task of the commission was to try to raise the stipend of every minister to 500 merks or five chalders of victual a year. By contrast with the legislation of 1606, the act of 1617 stipulated that the augmentation should come out of the teinds of the parish. The commission was empowered to assign such an augmentation whenever the minister's income fell below the minimum; it could summon anyone claiming a right in the teinds to prove his claim; it could combine parishes for economic reasons, provided that the spiritual functions of the church did not suffer. The highest stipend it could assign was 1,000 merks or ten chalders; it was instructed not to meddle with kirks where the stipend was satisfactory, and it was to compensate tacksmen of teinds who lost income from its decisions by renewing leases for long terms.[55]

The commission set to work in August 1617, as soon as the king left Scotland, and worked very hard and rapidly, as it had to if it was to obey parliament's order to finish in a year. The disappearance of the records makes it impossible to know the full scope of its work. W. R. Foster's analysis of the thirty-two extant complete decrees shows that in the vast majority of cases the commission arranged for a stipend of between 500 and 600 merks, and issued very long extensions to the tacksmen in compensation.[56] The commission did some combining of parishes; it also applied pressure to municipal authorities to raise stipends themselves. Its evenhandedness is indicated by the fact that neither Spottiswoode nor Calderwood was altogether pleased with the result, though for very different reasons. Spottiswoode disliked the long leases, Calderwood the excessive combining of parishes, which he certainly exaggerated.[57]

There can be no doubt of the commission's success. It managed the difficult and politically delicate feat of raising clerical stipends substantially without provoking animosity or any sort of backlash on the part of the landholding classes. There was a considerable reduction in the number of clerical complaints about inadequate stipends after 1618, though ministers still experienced difficulty sometimes in getting what was due them, and aristocratic tacksmen still occasionally harassed them. Ministers' wills demonstrate that from the first to the third decade of the century the average value of their movables went up by more than 150 percent, and their average net assets tripled. Since the rate of inflation, so serious before 1600, had leveled off considerably, this was a very substantial gain.[58]

The commission finished its work and went out of existence on 1 August 1618; on 25 August the last General Assembly of the reign of James VI, summoned to consider once more the question of the king's five articles, began its sessions at Perth. The atmosphere was one of considerable tension and hostility. The mood of the opponents of the royal policy was not improved by the recent circulation in Scotland of copies of James's famous proclamation on the lawfulness of Sunday sports which he had issued in Lancashire on his way home from Scotland the previous year.[59] Archbishop Spottiswoode knew that he must not fail again, both for the sake of his own career and to prevent the king from imposing the articles by the use of his prerogative, an action which would certainly create real trouble. So he took all the precautions he could. Experience had shown that Perth was a good site for attracting the attendance of clerical moderates. Spottiswoode, as before, assumed the moderator's chair without any pretense of an election and shut off all attempt at protest. He packed the assembly with laymen, ruled that they "were come upon his Majesty's missives" and therefore could vote—a patent illegality in Calderwood's view[60]—and stacked the privy conference with his supporters. He also had in his possession a minatory letter from the king, stating very bluntly that James expected obedience—"a simple and direct acceptation of these articles"—and indicating that if the assembly again proved recalcitrant he would impose them anyway.[61] Spottiswoode had the letter read at least three separate times in the course of the three-day meeting.

Though he expressed his optimism to Binning, the archbishop felt uneasy. The presence of the king's agent, Dr. John Young, dean of Winchester, the English-educated son of the king's old tutor, was a visible reminder of the greatly disliked policy of assimilation of the churches. There were a large number of "the most precise and willful Puritans" among the representatives of the Fife and Lothian presbyteries, and many of the laymen James had summoned stayed away, pleading illness. "I think their minds were more sick than their bodies, and are so still," Spottiswoode commented afterward.[62] So at the opening of the assembly the archbishop preached a remarkable sermon in which he declared that he and his fellow bishops did not devise the articles, did not recommend them to the king, and did not want them. But, since the king insisted, and they were neither unlawful nor inconvenient, they should be accepted. Both Spottiswoode and the king's commissioners held to this line throughout the assembly: the question was one of obedience to the king, nothing more, nothing less.

Kneeling at communion was the great issue, of course. In the privy conference Spottiswoode insisted that the burden of proof was on his opponents, to prove kneeling unlawful; eventually he was able to shut off debate by forcing a vote, itself an innovation in the privy conference. When the issue reached the floor of the full assembly, Spottiswoode demanded that the articles be voted on as a single package, and he pushed for a vote as quickly as possible. Speeches by the opposition were strictly limited: "quickly they were cut off, and sourly rebuked, rather borne down with authority than satisfied with reason," while "the defenders of the articles were permitted to discourse as long as they pleased."[63] Spottiswoode hammered away at the necessity of obeying the king, and finally he got what he wanted. The articles were approved by a margin of two to one—eighty-six to forty-one, said Binning; Calderwood gave the number of negative votes as forty-seven. The decision to include laymen in the assembly was evidently wise; in William Scot's view, if only those who were legally entitled to do so had voted, the articles would have lost. What we know of the makeup of the assembly does not necessarily bear this out, but there is little doubt that the lay votes gave Spottiswoode his comfortable margin.[64] The archbishop was greatly relieved.

So, too, if the flashes of jocularity in his report are a reasonable indication, was Secretary Binning. At the same time, however, he uttered an oblique warning to his master. "If your continual care of the good of this country and Church move your royal mind to intend hereafter any Church matters of such consequence, I beseech your Majesty . . . to employ a more fit Commissioner in my place, who am as unskillful in these subjects as I am ungracious to the opposites."[65] Plainly the king's policy was as distasteful to Binning as it was to the archbishop.

However grudging the assembly's approval, the king had had his way. The problem now was to persuade or coerce people into obeying the articles, especially those involving kneeling and the five holydays. These were the only two which required general observance—confirmation seems to have been very rarely administered after 1618—and, indeed, the matter of the holydays soon became a question of Christmas and Easter: the other three were almost universally ignored.[66] The archbishops issued the necessary instructions to all the presbyteries, and the bishops asked the king to withhold any further approvals of alterations in ministers' stipends unless they gave evidence of conformity. Christmas 1618 would be the first crucial test, and the primate was worried, especially about what might happen in Edinburgh. He wanted the king to order the town's ministers to be sure to preach on Christmas day. James did so, but the results were not very good. The ministers, all but John Hall, agreed to preach, but attendance was very thin by Spottiswoode's own admission, though we may take leave to doubt Calderwood's gleeful assertion that "the dogs were playing in the midst of the floor of the Little Kirk for rarity of people."[67]

The archbishop now decided to try the effects of a little salutary severity. According to Calderwood, recalcitrant clergy were threatened with banishment to America. Richard Dickson, an Edinburgh minister, celebrated communion in the traditional way; in March 1619 he was haled before the high commission, deprived, and warded in Dumbarton castle. John Hall resigned to avoid choosing between disobeying the king and stultifying his conscience, but he too was eventually warded, on the ground that his actions gave aid and comfort to the recalcitrant. The king instructed his officials to attend the chapel royal if they were in Edinburgh on Sunday, and a special effort was made to have a good attendance at Easter. But it was difficult. Some councillors pleaded illness or lack of preparation or both, and stayed home.[68] The bishops themselves were timid, and sensitive to the charge that the articles were Popish: they were anxious to avoid the odium which would attach to any appearance of initiative on their part.[69] Easter was rather better than Christmas; Binning's account of the decorum and attendance in Edinburgh was more optimistic, though he admitted that there were a lot of absentees. Calderwood claimed that people flocked to the churches outside the city, and that the only people who knelt at communion were government officials and those "of the poorer sort, who lived upon the contribution."[70]

The high commission was the archbishop's chief instrument for the enforcement of clerical conformity to the articles. Recalcitrant ministers were summoned before it and subjected to an inquiry as to the extent of their compliance. Most, like William Scot, "were dismissed with threatenings to conform in time coming."[71] Those who preached against the articles drew stiffer penalties.[72] The number of ministers summoned before the commission was not very large, however, which argues either that the system of selective intimidation had some success or that the archbishop concluded that it was better to wink at violations than to court the odium of persecuting ministers for adhering to the traditional ways.[73] Owing to the loss of the records of the high commission, the evidence is scanty. It is best for Edinburgh, where, in the view of the editor of the burgh records, enforcement was ineffective, a view supported by Calderwood's accounts of the frequent controversies between the conforming ministers and various officials and citizens of the town.[74] Secretary Binning, who in March 1619 received his long-overdue promotion and became earl of Melrose,[75] was under instruction from the king to report on the celebration of the holydays, especially Easter, in the capital; he put the best possible interpretation on what was obviously a bad situation, and urged patience on his master. "We have a number of ignorant and perverse people . . . I believe that time and convenience shall prevail more to reduce them to conformity nor (than) sudden or vehement instance . . . lest the scandal and difficulty of the remedy should be more hurtful nor (than) the toleration for a short space."[76]

Archbishop Spottiswoode's conduct at a conference of the bishops and a number of important ministerial opponents of the articles in November 1619 indicates that he felt much as Melrose did; he "could be content," he said, "that the Church of Scotland could have wanted these things." James's serious illness in the spring of 1619, and Spottiswoode's equivocal behavior in his diocese until he was sure of the king's recovery, had helped to stir speculation around the supper tables in St. Andrews that Prince Charles might be more sympathetic to the old ways than his father—speculation which naturally encouraged the opposition.[77] The king was "wonderfully offended" at the resistance to his policy, wrote Fenton, now earl of Kellie, to Mar in July 1619, and threatened to come to Scotland himself "if they be not settled to his contentment."[78] Lord Scone arrived at the November conference with a peremptory royal letter ordering the deprivation of all ministers who refused to conform, and insisted that the ministers state their intentions plainly: "The king," said Scone, "appointed me to take their answers." The ministers failed to show up at a special meeting called to give the necessary assurances, however, and Scone was enraged; the bishops soothed him by promising to inform James that he had done his duty. They did so in a letter which expressed their hope that the reluctant ministers would ultimately arrive at a satisfactory resolution of their doubts.[79]

King James was not sympathetic. In March 1620 he indicated that punishment for disobedience to the articles was to be extended to laymen by ordering the warding of various Edinburgh citizens who had given aid and comfort to some of the refractory ministers during their hearings before the high commission. Three weeks later the king repeated the order; when the question came to the council, it provoked a protest from the chancellor, the first overt indication of reluctance on his part to enforce the five articles. It was unreasonable and illegal, he said, to condemn the men without a hearing. Secretary Melrose replied, as he had many times before, that the only proper question was whether or not the king was to be obeyed. Dunfermline acquiesced, and the men were ordered to ward. Archbishop Spottiswoode immediately arranged that the sentence be suspended until he could write to the king in their favor. It was no part of his policy that laymen should be punished in connection with the five articles, and he was not even very eager to punish recalcitrant clergymen, who would eventually all be eliminated by the workings of time.[80] To a group of ministers summoned in January 1620 for violation of the two controverted articles he was almost apologetic. "He affirmed that it was against his heart to urge conformity, but his Majesty blamed him for his lenity."[81] On 1 March 1620 the high commission summoned John Scrimgeour, the minister of Kinghorn, one of the most conspicuous clerical opponents of the five articles. In the course of the hearing Spottiswoode made the profoundly revealing remark, "I tell you, Mr. John, the king is Pope now, and so shall be." It is not a statement which would have commended itself to James, and it indicates very clearly the archbishop's weary distaste for the task his master had set him. Scrimgeour was duly deprived of his position at Kinghorn but continued teaching there, according to Calderwood, which suggests that officialdom, both secular and clerical, turned a blind eye.[82]

The attitude of the majority of the council was even more negative than that of the archbishop. It did issue a proclamation in June 1619 at the king's behest, ordering people to obey the articles and not to write or distribute any sort of statement critical of them, an order repeated a year later with the addition of a schedule of fines for contumaciousness, but it was most reluctant to act against individuals. Clergymen, at the archbishops' request, were left to the disciplinary authority of the high commission.[83] Dunfermline was therefore openly irritated when the council received a letter from James ordering it to ward his veteran clerical antagonist Robert Bruce if it found that he had not been obedient to the articles: that was the job of the high commission. Melrose again raised the question of obedience: "'Will ye reason, whether his Majesty must be obeyed or not?' Chancellor Seton answered, 'We may reason, whether we shall be the bishops' hangmen or not.'"[84] Spottiswoode ultimately secured a postponement of any action against Bruce on the ground that he was in mourning for the death of his wife.

James failed to react to this postponement; there were more important matters now to occupy his mind. The great European crisis which was to dominate the last years of his reign had now erupted; irreversible disaster overtook the Winter King of Bohemia in December 1620. One consequence of the crisis was the decision to call parliament, which accordingly was done in April 1621. This was the first parliament since the Perth assembly, and it was clear that the government would ask for legislative sanction for the five articles. Spottiswoode carefully timed a new campaign against Catholics for the spring in order to defuse the charge that the articles were Popish, but to little effect. Early in May there was discussion in Edinburgh among the ministers, elders, and town officials about the possibility of petitioning parliament against the articles on the ground that "they are come from the Papists";

Patrick Galloway was able to block this gesture, which, he said, would be futile and simply increase the king's indignation against the town. As the time for the parliament drew near, clerical opponents of the articles descended on Edinburgh and began canvassing, as did the king's agents. The lobbying became intense enough, especially among the burgh representatives, for the council to send two clergymen to ward in Dumbarton, and to issue a proclamation on 23 July ordering all ministers who had no legitimate business in the capital to go home. They obeyed, but not without a Parthian shot against the five articles in the form of various "informations and admonitions" to the parliament. "Here," they said, is "the sound of the feet of Popery at the doors."[85]

Clearly the government had cause to be nervous about what might occur at the parliament. The principal purpose of the session was to get a tax voted to further James's objectives in foreign policy rather than to ratify the articles, and there was a real possibility that concessions would have to be made in one direction to achieve success in the other. Parliament opened on 25 July, a week after the king's commissioner, the marquis of Hamilton, arrived in Edinburgh. Hamilton's appointment marked a new and rather disquieting departure in Scottish politics. The marquis was a courtier who spent most of his time at Whitehall and was neither active in nor knowledgeable about affairs north of the Tweed; his qualification for the job was that he was Buckingham's friend and, arguably, now the Scot who stood highest in the king's favor.[86] This was the first time that a strictly courtier Scot had been employed to conduct an important political operation in Scotland. There were no ill effects, thanks to the old king's knowledge of Scottish affairs and the skill of his councillors in Edinburgh, but it was an ominous precedent for the future.

An indication that Hamilton's appointment would not cause trouble came at once. The government got the committee of the articles it wanted, and the opening speeches rang the changes on the arguments for swift and uncomplaining acceptance of the five articles. Hamilton denied that James had any notion of introducing English ceremonies, or Popery, or liberty of conscience; he also promised in the king's name that if parliament would consent to these articles there would be no more ceremonial changes.[87] There was little difficulty in the committee of the articles, most of whose time was taken up with the tax bill. This question caused a good deal of controversy and was one reason why the parliament lasted as long as it did, though Calderwood declared that the delay was intentional, to give Melrose, Hamilton, and the bishops a chance to lobby in favor of the five articles.[88] To sweeten the pill a bit for the clergy, the government included an enactment reviving the committee on clerical stipends which had functioned so well in 1617–18, and a second one to see to it that ministers on erected church lands got the minimum stipend of 500 merks or five chalders of victual.[89] On the day before the vote the secretary was nevertheless still very apprehensive; one of the controversial elements in the tax package might have to be dropped, he thought, to get the religious legislation through.[90]

As it turned out, Melrose's fears were groundless. The five articles were voted on first, and passed by a margin of twenty-seven votes, "albeit we were exceedingly disappointed by the treachery of some small boroughs who violated their promises" and who lost various "acts and ratifications" drawn up in their favor in consequence.[91] The tax bill, including the controversial provisions, subsequently passed with only ten dissenting votes. The defection of these burghs may have resulted in a vote rather closer than was planned—because the voting lists as given by Calderwood suggest that Dunfermline arranged for some of the negative votes that were cast. His speech on the final day, to be sure, "proved as he could the articles to be lawful, and alleged, they required not much reasoning, being already concluded by learned bishops, fathers, doctors, and pastors, convened at Perth for that effect. But," adds Calderwood, "in very deed he was mocking!" James was told that he publicly remarked, "Why should ye not adore the Sacrament and follow the Church of England?" a comment not calculated to please the king.[92] The articles' margin of victory came from the bishops and the aristocracy; the lairds were evenly divided and the burghs narrowly opposed. Of the fifteen aristocrats voting no, five were close connections of the chancellor, though he himself voted for the articles and cast a proxy in their favor. This demonstration looks much too extensive to be accidental, and was designed to warn the king, and the archbishop too: go no further. It was not the only warning James received, according to the embittered Calderwood. Just as the king's commissioner was about to touch the acts with the scepter, a frightful thunderstorm broke which kept the members huddled in the parliament house for an hour and a half. This was obviously an indication of God's displeasure, and the day, said Calderwood, "was called by the people, 'Black Saturday.'"[93]

The king's reaction was to take advantage of his victory rather than to heed any warnings. On 12 August he wrote to the bishops encouraging them to go forward, and in September he issued a comprehensive order to the council. Every public official, including themselves, and every advocate and clerk as well, was to be on record as conforming to the five articles, on pain of dismissal and/or suspension from the practice of law. The council greeted these instructions with notable lack of enthusiasm and carried them out in a very perfunctory manner. On 22 November, almost two months after James issued his instructions, Dunfermline asked the twenty-four councillors present if they were prepared to obey the articles; they said they were. The next day the members of the court of session and the legal profession were summoned and told that they must show obedience by Christmas. "So," wrote Calderwood, "they were dismissed with this gentle and general admonition, without particular inquiry." Local officials, the council decided, would be summoned only if a bishop or minister made a specific complaint.[94]

With respect to recalcitrant ministers there was rather more purposeful activity on the part of the high commission for a short time, and there were a few deprivations. Within a year, however, this also began to wane, though the archbishop could still be provoked to anger if a minister were imprudent enough to deny the high commission's jurisdiction over him.[95] In April 1622, at a diocesan synod in St. Andrews, Spottiswoode "rebuked some ministers that urged kneeling too much upon the people"—an astonishing and highly significant reversal. "It was reported," Calderwood went on, "that the Bishop of Canterbury had written to him, and desired him not to urge the ceremonies now, when weightier affairs were in hand."[96] We do not know whether Spottiswoode received such advice from Archbishop Abbot or not. We do know that he was convinced that the articles were unenforceable. The reason why Easter was not properly celebrated in Edinburgh, he wrote Lochmaben in 1623, was "an obstinate purpose and resolution in that people to hearken to no persuasion that can be given them, nor to obey any direction that way."[97] There is no doubt that by mid-1622, in spite of occasional flare-ups, the sustained effort to enforce the five articles of Perth had come to an end, and many ministers who had conformed under pressure resumed their traditional practices.[98]

King James was not given to public admission of error, and he never gave any formal indication that he felt that the five articles had been a mistake. His pledge to the parliament of 1621 to innovate no further can be read as a consequence of the exigencies of foreign policy rather than a confession that he had blundered. If he indeed retained his belief in the rightness of the articles, he may well have consoled himself with Melrose's soothing assurance that time and convenience would ultimately prevail. His anger could still be spasmodically aroused—he blocked the appointment of Robert Boyd, who had been ousted from the University of Glasgow for nonconformity, as principal at Edinburgh, and in 1624 he insisted on severe punishment for a group of Edinburgh dissidents who, just before Easter, publicly accused one of their ministers of softness on Popery and urged that communion be celebrated in the old manner. This episode temporarily revived James's enthusiasm for enforcement of the stipulation on kneeling at communion; he also insisted that the council issue a stern proclamation against privately held nonconformist religious gatherings, which, he suspected, were numerous in Edinburgh. Yet he made no objection when Lord Chancellor Hay defined these conventicles so narrowly that most people could truthfully deny attending them.[99] The exigencies of those "weightier affairs" to which Abbot allegedly referred also had much to do with the slackening of the effort at enforcement. Most of whatever attention the ailing and aging king gave to public affairs in these years went to foreign policy. Scotland had contributed generously to the financing of that policy, proportionately far more generously than had England. Furthermore, James's marriage diplomacy in both Spain and France, requiring, as it did, unpopular concessions, official and unofficial, to the Catholic minority, suggested that it would be wise not to create further disaffection in his ancient kingdom by too vehement an insistence on acceptance of articles which so many Scots regarded as Popish.

There is no doubt that the king suffered a serious defeat over the five articles of Perth, in spite of the mathematics of the votes in 1618 and 1621. Historians have universally condemned the articles as a very bad blunder, and they are certainly right, though not, perhaps, for the reasons usually assigned. What they have not stopped to ask themselves, however, is why James, whose touch in Scottish politics was normally so sure, made this error. The answer is almost always given by implication: James was obstinate, he was getting old and more and more impatient of opposition, fourteen years of association with the likes of Richard Bancroft and Lancelot Andrewes had brainwashed him—all of which may be in some measure true but nevertheless still begs the question.

In the first place, these five practices represented only a very small part of the program of change in the church which James outlined to Spottiswoode in 1615 and set in train at the General Assembly in 1616: a new liturgy, a new catechism, and a new set of canons. They were a beginning, and a fairly minimal beginning at that. There is evidence, indeed, that these five changes were chosen precisely because they were apt to cause less backlash than any others which might be made. The king made no effort to extend the aborted decorative scheme of the chapel royal to other churches, for instance, or to impose the wearing of surplices—he took note, perhaps, of the adverse comment which the wearing of them by the English divines in his train to conduct services during his visit had caused. It has been recently argued that compromises of various sorts were possible on four of the five, and that only the requirement of kneeling at communion produced widespread and deep-seated opposition.[100] This analysis for the most part follows that of Patrick Galloway in his letter to the king in November 1617, a cautious and hedging statement which minimized the potential difficulties in James's policy. The essential point, however, and one which has been consistently overlooked, is that prior to his public commitment to their imposition at the conference in St. Andrews in July 1617, and for a while thereafter, James had no reason to suspect opposition to the substance of the articles at all. All the objections he had heard, from the time he had first proposed inserting them into the contemplated revised list of canons, had been procedural: the articles must be approved by a General Assembly. Spottiswoode said so, the protesters at the parliament said so, Calderwood at his trial said so. The minister's protestation at parliament had made no mention of any of the five articles; the nearest it came to the substance of the dispute was to assert that the kirk was pure in doctrine and discipline and that other churches might profitably be changed to conform to it, rather than vice versa, and to allude to their fears of anglicanization. So when in June the king withdrew the parliamentary bill which would have acknowledged his right to act by prerogative, and in the following month consented to the holding of an assembly, he had, he thought, eliminated the possibility of trouble by yielding to the objections he had heard from both his supporters and his opponents.

Yet trouble came, and when it did, in the form of the assembly's rejection of the five articles in November 1617, the king was both surprised and enraged. James's surprise was perfectly genuine — so, indeed, was his rage. His intelligence system had failed him. Spottiswoode and his episcopal colleagues had given him no reason to anticipate this rebuff, had made no attempt to dissuade him from his forward policy. Spottiswoode's opposition to the articles developed after 1617, and was based entirely on pragmatic considerations. The stance of the clerical opposition had also encouraged the king. Calderwood was no Andrew Melville, and his opposition to James, while courageous, was expressed much more circumspectly. He kept his argument as narrow and legalistic as possible in an attempt to avoid punishment. Melville, who always concerned himself with the broader aspect of things, would have left James in no doubt that he regarded the articles as Popish. James, who had experienced precious little backtalk of any kind from a clergyman since he banished the formidable Andrew a decade ago, undoubtedly took Calderwood's procedural concerns at face value. This was the thrust of the ministers' objections: very well, he would meet them.

Dunfermline's administration must bear a share of the responsibility for James's misinformation too. This was not merely a matter of the chancellor's unwillingness to involve himself in most church questions; the difficulty lay in a combination of the people and the system which he had evolved for dealing with the king since the death of Dunbar. In the first place, there was no important lay official in the Edinburgh administration both fully conversant with the state of Scottish opinion and with access to James who was a good Protestant, or even much of a Protestant at all, save Elibank, and Elibank dealt with the king only on financial questions. Mar was a good Protestant, to be sure, but during the past decade Mar had spent a great deal of time at court. Those peripatetic aristocrats whom the king occasionally saw, like Huntly and Argyll, were obviously worse than useless in this respect. Second, Dunfermline's system, based as it was on correspondence rather than travel, had the utterly unintended consequence of causing the king to be badly misled as to the state of Scottish opinion. Dunbar, with his annual journeys, was able to give James advice based on his soundings of all elements of that opinion. It is most unlikely that Dunfermline, with his connections in Edinburgh and among the ministers, was unaware of the possible difficulties the articles would cause. But his comments on religious matters in his letters to James and to his friends at court were few and generalized. So the king got his information on religious questions, and on the state of opinion on such questions, both within the church and without, from Spottiswoode and his bishops. There is no evidence that any of them advised the king to adopt the policy of the five articles. But they uttered no warnings, and by the time they realized how much trouble was in store for them, it was too late.

Most historians, in discussing the impact of the king's blunder, have confined themselves to the realm of religious policy, but it had a far broader significance than that. For the future of James's episcopal kirk it was, of course, very important. In those areas, mostly in the south, where there was substantial resistance to the articles, Spottiswoode and his colleagues on the bench were faced with an impossible choice. They could bring on themselves the odium of attempting to enforce an extremely unpopular policy and run the risk of having its unpopularity transferred from the policy itself to the system by which it was enforced, or they could do nothing in the face of the popular hostility, allow their newly acquired authority to be flouted with impunity the first time they tried to use it in a matter about which laymen felt deeply, and watch the inevitable erosion of their prestige among laymen and their clerical subordinates alike. The archbishop much preferred the latter course. He did not wish to promote further schism in the church; he knew that there were a good many ministers otherwise acquiescent in episcopacy who balked at kneeling at communion. He knew his master well enough to realize that while James lived there was no hope of a reversal of policy. But the king was getting on in years, and, as Spottiswoode reminded the opening session of parliament in 1621, the articles governing the church had been changed before and could be changed again.[101] Until such time as change became a feasible option, the wisest course was to do as little as possible.

Dunfermline no doubt derived a certain amount of enjoyment from the archbishop's dilemma, and was not above making it marginally more annoying by his manipulation of the votes at the parliament and his grumbling about being called upon to serve as the bishops' hangman. On this last point his instinct was certainly right, although the evidence is too scanty to indicate how clearly Dunfermline saw into the problem. For the general refusal to accept the five articles had profound implications for the civil government as well. The consequence, in the words of W. R. Foster, was "the creation of a permanent nonconforming party" made up of clerics and laymen alike.[102] For Dunfermline, his colleagues, and successors, this meant that the habit of obedience to royal authority, so carefully nurtured by Maitland, Dunbar, and himself, always in collaboration with the king, was now being undermined. If the habit of obedience is ingrained in a society, general refusal to obey a particular law need not have any particularly serious implications beyond that law itself. But in the Scotland of the early seventeenth century general obedience to royal authority was far from second nature; the habit was too new to survive this sort of strain. Scotland was not plunged into anarchy, of course; the bad old days of an enfeebled crown and aristocratic gangsterism and feuds did not return. But the controversy over the five articles of Perth had shown that the power of the Scottish government, vastly enhanced though it was by the union of the crowns, nevertheless had its limits and could successfully be rendered nugatory. Ever since he had succeeded to the English throne King James had gone from strength to strength, from victory to victory in his government of Scotland, until at the time of his visit in 1617 the power of the crown had reached its apogee. Now the king had suffered a major defeat. God's vice-gerent was not all-powerful; successful defiance was still possible; in the matter of obedience there was still a choice. These were the lessons of the five articles of Perth. They would not be forgotten.

NOTES

1. *RPCS* X, 470–72.

2. *Ibid.* XI, 15–16, 170, 215, 240–41.

3. The preparations for the royal visit can be followed in *ibid.* X, cv–cxv, 458ff., XI, viii–xix, 5–136 *passim.* See also NLS, Denmilne Mss. VIII, nos. 5, 6, 11.

4. *Melros* I, 265–67. *M&K,* p. 78. *APS* IV, 581–85. Much of the detail in this paragraph comes from Binning's extremely interesting report to the king, dated 7 Mar. 1617, *Melros* I, 270–78. There was no question of calling a parliament at this juncture, since one was planned for James's visit. In June 1617 a loan of 100,000 merks was authorized and quickly arranged, with the proceeds of this tax as security; it was repaid a year later; see *RPCS* XI, 159, 167–69, 374.

5. Dec. 1616, Fenton to Mar, *M&K Supp.,* p. 72.

6. PRO, SP 14/89, no. 83. *RPCS* X, 685–86. 20 Dec. 1616, Fenton to Mar, *M&K Supp.,* pp. 71–72. 25 Dec., Binning to James, NLS, Mss. 3134, f. 94.

7. See, e.g., 14 Jan. 1617, Nathaniel Brent to Carleton, *CSPD 1611–1618,* p. 424; 20/30 Mar., Lionello to the doge and senate of Venice, *CSP Venetian 1615–1617,* pp. 476–78.

8. In noting Abbot's death in 1633 the presbyterian historian John Row described him as "not violent against honest ministers and professors in his time, and . . . a great friend to Scotland"; see John Row, *The History of the Kirk of Scotland,* ed. D. Laing, Wodrow Society (Edinburgh, 1842), p. 368.

9. *RPCS* X, 215–17, 316–17. NLS, Denmilne Mss. VI, no. 15. *Calderwood* VII, 191. The archbishops' phrase occurs in a letter to James in July 1613, *LEA* I, 311–13.

10. *LEA* II, 399–401. Ogilvie was executed early in 1615.

11. See, for instance, the bishops' letter to James on 23 June 1614 and Spottiswoode's to Lochmaben on 11 July, *LEA* I, 341–43, II, 351–54.

12. For this business see *Calderwood* VII, 212–14, 218–19; *Spottiswoode* III, 230–35; *LEA* II, 474–78. In Dec. 1616 James reinstated Huntly on the council; see *RPCS* XI, 48.

13. 2 Mar. 1611, James to the bishops, Sir William Fraser, *Memoirs of the Maxwells of Pollok* (Edinburgh, 1863) II, 13–14. 4 July 1612, Alexander Hay to James, *LEA* I, 293–94.

14. *LEA* II, 445–46.

15. See, for instance, the comments in Spottiswoode's letter of 11 July 1614 to Lochmaben on a recent sermon of Patrick Galloway's, *ibid.*, pp. 351–54.

16. *Calderwood* VII, 223, 225–26. Calderwood gives the text of the confession, pp. 233–42.

17. *Ibid.*, pp. 222, 227–33. *Scot*, p. 244. *LEA* II, 807–9. W. R. Foster, *The Church before the Covenants* (Edinburgh, 1975), pp. 126–32. For the proposed liturgical revisions, which in the end proved abortive, see G. Donaldson, *The Making of the Scottish Prayer Book of 1637* (Edinburgh, 1954), pp. 27–40, and his edition of "A Scottish Liturgy of the Reign of James VI," *Miscellany of the Scottish History Society* X (Edinburgh, 1965), pp. 89–117.

18. *Spottiswoode* III, 237–38. *RPCS* X, 669–73, 846–47.

19. Jan. 1616, Cowper to James, *LEA* II, 466–67.

20. N. E. McClure, ed., *The Letters of John Chamberlain* (Philadelphia, 1939) II, 42. *RPCS* X, 492–94, 593–94, XI, 65. *Calderwood* VII, 242. 14 Jan. 1617, Nathaniel Brent to Carleton, *CSPD 1611–1618*, p. 424.

21. 13 Mar. 1617, James to the bishops and ministers of Edinburgh, 26 Mar., Cowper to Patrick Sampson, *LEA* II, 496–500. *Spottiswoode* III, 238–39.

22. *RMS 1609–1620*, p. 524. *RPCS* X, 330, XI, 138–39. NLS, Denmilne Mss. VII, no. 35.

23. See, e.g., Fenton's letters of 2 and 17 July and 12 Aug. 1616, *M&K Supp.*, pp. 63–65.

24. The negotiations over Mar's appointment can be followed in Fenton's letters between July and Dec. 1616, *ibid.*, pp. 63–73. Mar and Elibank in fact worked well together; see 21 Feb. 1617, Fenton to Mar, *ibid.*, p. 74.

25. *RPCS* X, 602, 847.

26. 10 Feb. 1617, Fenton to Mar, *M&K Supp.*, pp. 73–74.

27. 1, 6 May 1617, Binning to James, *Melros* I, 287–88, 293–94. *RPCS* XI, 121–23.

28. A collection of these poems and speeches, called *The Muses' Welcome*, was subsequently printed after receiving the royal approval and distributed in both England and Scotland; see *RPCS* XI, xlii–xliii, 418–19.

29. *Calderwood* VII, 246–47. *RPCS* XI, 137–38. In the course of James's visit five other Englishmen became councillors; see *ibid.*, pp. 163–66, 169.

30. 28 June 1617, an English courtier to Bacon, PRO, SP 14/92, no. 75.

31. *Calderwood* VII, 250. *APS* IV, 526–27.

32. *APS* IV, 535, 545–47. 23 Dec. 1617, Dunfermline to James, *LEA* II, 538.

See also H. M. Conacher, "Land Tenure in Scotland in the 17th Century," *Juridical Review* L (1938), 23–24.

33. *APS* IV, 535–41.

34. 14 Mar. 1617, Binning to James, *Melros* I, 281–85. *APS* IV, 550. For repledging see 6 May 1624, the council to Lennox, *RPCS* XIII, 505–6.

35. *APS* IV, 549–50. *RPCS*, 2nd ser., I, 658–60.

36. *APS* IV, 575–76.

37. See, for instance, Spottiswoode's threatening letter to the laird of Grant on 16 June 1616 charging Grant with improperly withholding the rents of the kirks of Strathspey, Sir William Fraser, *The Chiefs of Grant* II (Edinburgh, 1883), 41.

38. *APS* IV, 531–34.

39. *Calderwood* VII, 249.

40. For this episode see *ibid.*, pp. 250–56, and *Spottiswoode* III, 241–45.

41. *Spottiswoode* III, 247. See also *Calderwood* VII, 260–83.

42. For this meeting see *Spottiswoode* III, 245–47. The quoted remark of the king comes from this passage.

43. R. Chambers, *Domestic Annals of Scotland from the Reformation to the Revolution*, 2nd ed. (Edinburgh, 1859), I, 485. *Calderwood* VII, 246. The editor of *RPCS* was so bemused by James's elephantine wit that he quoted the speech twice, XI, xxxv–xxxviii and 196–98.

44. Sir Anthony Weldon, "A Perfect Description of the People and Country of Scotland," in P. Hume Brown, ed., *Early Travellers in Scotland* (Edinburgh, 1891), p. 102. There was no Scottish master of the rolls; Weldon probably meant Clerk Register Hay.

45. 23 Dec. 1617, Dunfermline to James, *LEA* II, 537. *RPCS* XI, 203. *Calderwood* VII, 273–74.

46. *RPCS* XI, 253–54. *Calderwood* VII, 284, alleges that the assembly was delayed so that the bishops could be sure that the "right" commissioners were chosen. In view of the outcome of the assembly this seems unlikely.

47. 5 Nov. 1617, Galloway to James, *LEA* II, 511–15. 7, 20 Nov., Binning to James, *Melros* II, 621–23.

48. 20, 28 Nov. 1617, Binning to James, 28 Nov., the bishops to James, *LEA* II, 519–23. *Scot*, pp. 251–52. *Calderwood* VII, 284–86.

49. See his letters of 6 and 11 Dec. 1617, *LEA* II, 524–26.

50. *RPCS* XI, 296–97. *Calderwood* VII, 289.

51. *LEA* II, 558–59, 562–63. *Calderwood* VII, 289–90, 297–98.

52. The correspondence is in *LEA* II, 542–56; the quotation is from Spottiswoode's letter of 16 Feb. 1618, p. 551. *Calderwood* VII, 296, nastily remarked that Forbes accepted the bishopric "to repair his broken lairdship." From 1617 on Calderwood's comments about the bishops in general and Spottiswoode in particular became more and more venomous. He alleged, for example, that Spottiswoode arrived too late at the deathbed of Forbes's predecessor because he was unwilling to interrupt his Sunday card game; see *ibid.*, pp. 287–88.

53. *LEA* II, 534–40.

54. *Spottiswoode* III, 248–51. *Calderwood* VII, 303–4. For Lochmaben see Bishop Cowper's letter to him of 10 Aug. 1618, *Laing,* pp. 149–50.

55. *APS* IV, 531–34.

56. Nineteen of the thirty-two ended up between 500 and 600 merks, eight between 600 and 700, four between 850 and 1,000, and one, where there was no evidence of any stipend to begin with, below 500. The minimum extension of a tack was for 57 years, the maximum, 203 years. See W. R. Foster, "Episcopal Administration in Scotland 1600–1638" (Ph.D. thesis, University of Edinburgh, 1963), pp. 405–6. See also Foster's "A Constant Platt Achieved," in D. Shaw, ed., *Reformation and Revolution* (Edinburgh, 1967), pp. 130–31.

57. *Spottiswoode* III, 252. *Calderwood* VII, 302–5.

58. 30 Dec. 1621, Law to James, *LEA* II, 675–76. Foster, "Constant Platt," pp. 136–37. The testamentary figures there cited show some falling off in the 1630s. See also Foster, "Episcopal Administration," pp. 309–13, 317. Foster also points to the considerable amount of new church building in this period as evidence of the church's increased wealth; see *ibid.,* p. 327.

59. *Calderwood* VII, 298.

60. *Ibid.,* p. 308.

61. The letter, dated 10 July 1618, is in *ibid.,* pp. 308–11.

62. 27 Aug. 1618, Binning to James, *LEA* II, 573–77. 2 Sept., Spottiswoode to Lochmaben, *Laing,* pp. 150–51. The "willful Puritans" phrase is Binning's.

63. *Calderwood* VII, 323.

64. *Scot,* p. 264. The fullest account of this assembly, which ran from 25 to 27 August, is in *Calderwood* VII, 303–35. See also Calderwood's letter of 13 Dec. 1618, PRO, SP 14/104, no. 26, and I. B. Cowan, "The Five Articles of Perth," in Shaw, ed., *Reformation and Revolution,* pp. 171–73. The archbishop's sermon is in *The Spottiswoode Miscellany* I, Spottiswoode Society (Edinburgh, 1844), 65–87.

65. 27 Aug. 1618, Binning to James, *LEA* II, 573–77.

66. Foster, *Church before the Covenants,* pp. 183–86.

67. *Calderwood* VII, 339–41. *Spottiswoode* III, 257. 28 Nov., 6 Dec. 1618, 30 Jan. 1619, Binning to James, *LEA* II, 585–86, 588–89, 592–93.

68. *Calderwood* VII, 352–55, 357, 364. *RPCS* XI, 506, 596, 635–37. 4 Feb. 1619, Binning to James, *Melros* II, 625–26.

69. See, e.g., *LEA* II, 601–2. On the charge of Popery see, e.g., 4 July 1620, the bishop of Aberdeen to James, *ibid.,* pp. 633–35.

70. *Calderwood* VII, 359–60. 29 Mar. 1619, Binning to James, *LEA* II, 598–600.

71. *Calderwood* VII, 392.

72. See, e.g., the case of Thomas Hogge of Dysart, *ibid.,* pp. 365–77.

73. G. MacMahon, "The Scottish Courts of High Commission, 1610–1638," *Records of the Scottish Church History Society* XV (1966), 200–201. W. R. Foster, who is on the whole sympathetic to James's policy, argues somewhat inconsistently on this point. He states that from 1619 to 1620 the number of ministers in the synod of Fife who rejected kneeling at communion fell from one-half to

one-tenth; on the other hand, he attributes the decline in the number of cases in the records of summons for noncompliance to laxity of enforcement. See Foster, *Church before the Covenants,* pp. 186–90.

74. M. Wood, ed., *Extracts from the Records of the Burgh of Edinburgh* (Edinburgh, 1927–31) VI, intro., pp. xxii–xxiv. *Calderwood* VII, 361–64, 390–91, 596–621.

75. This was one of several advancements in early 1619, the first such batch since 1606. Buccleuch and Fenton got earldoms also, and Lennox's brother and the marquis of Hamilton got English earldoms.

76. 16 Apr. 1623, Melrose to James, *LEA* II, 711–12. For some of the secretary's other reports see *ibid.,* pp. 592 (Christmas 1618), 598–600 (Easter 1619), 678–79 (Easter 1622).

77. *Calderwood* VII, 364, 401.

78. *M&K Supp.,* p. 93.

79. BM, Add. Mss. 19,402, f. 135. For this conference see *Calderwood* VII, 397–409.

80. *Calderwood* VII, 394, 434, 439–41. NLS, Denmilne Mss. IX, no. 43. *RPCS* XII, 249–50, 264. *LEA* II, 624–25, 629–31.

81. *Calderwood* VII, 412.

82. For Scrimgeour's trial see *ibid.,* pp. 414–24.

83. *RPCS* XI, 579–81, XII, 279–81. *LEA* II, 626–27.

84. *Calderwood* VII, 450.

85. *Ibid.,* pp. 460–61, 464–69, 475–87. *RPCS* XII, 395, 475, 546–47. 26 July 1621, Melrose to James, *Melros* II, 411–16.

86. John Chamberlain, in his account of James's "deathbed" speech to his son during his serious illness in the spring of 1619, reports that the king commended to Charles the earls of Arundel and Pembroke, Lennox, Kellie, and John Ramsay, and especially Buckingham and Hamilton; see McClure, *Letters of John Chamberlain* II, 227.

87. 26 July 1621, Melrose to James, *Melros* II, 411–16. *Calderwood* VII, 488–90.

88. *Calderwood* VII, 489–93. 27 July, 2 Aug. 1621, Melrose to James, *Melros* II, 421–24. For the tax bill see below, pp. 204–7.

89. *APS* IV, 605–9, 631–32. Little is known about what, if anything, was accomplished; see Foster, *Church before the Covenants,* p. 164.

90. 3 Aug. 1621, Melrose to James, *Melros* II, 425–26.

91. 4 Aug. 1621, Melrose to James, *ibid.,* pp. 426–27. The only recorded acts of this parliament in favor of burghs benefited Edinburgh and Elgin, both of which voted right. George Hay, *LEA* II, 661, gave the vote as 78–51, *Calderwood* VII, 498–501, as 77–50.

92. *Calderwood* VII, 496–98. For the allegation to the king see *M&K,* p. 102.

93. *Calderwood* VII, 498–501, 505. Calderwood gives the vote thus: bishops, 11–0 in favor; nobility, including officers of state, 35–15; lairds, 11–11; burghs, 20–24.

94. *Ibid.,* pp. 507–9, 515. *RPCS* XII, 597–98.

95. See, e.g., the account in *Calderwood* VII, 536–41, of the deprivation of David Dickson, minister of Irvine, in Jan. 1622. A year or so later Dickson was able to return to his parish; see *ibid.,* pp. 567–68.

96. *Ibid.,* pp. 547–48.

97. *LEA* II, 713–14.

98. There is no evidence of the high commission's hearing any case of a minister accused of failure to conform to the Perth articles after 1622; see Foster, *Church before the Covenants,* p. 190. For the ministerial backsliding see the memorandum written early in the next reign in J. F. S. Gordon, *Ecclesiastical Chronicle for Scotland* I (London, 1875), 488–90. P. H. R. Mackay, "The Reception Given to the Five Articles of Perth," *Records of the Scottish Church History Society* XIX (1977), is a convenient summary of the efforts at enforcement.

99. For the episode in Edinburgh see *Calderwood* VII, 596–621; *LEA* II, 752–58; *M&K Supp.,* pp. 210–11; *RPCS* XIII, 490, 503–4, 519–22, 577–78, 582–83, 611–12, 660–62, 694. For Robert Boyd see *Calderwood* VII, 566, 569. Before James's anger was known, Spottiswoode told Boyd he wanted him for St. Andrews; see *LEA* II, 697–98.

100. Cowan, "Five Articles of Perth," pp. 160–77.

101. 26 July 1621, Melrose to James, *Melros* II, 411–16.

102. Foster, *Church before the Covenants,* p. 192.

6

Last Years: ·
The War and the Economy

AS WAS THE CASE in England, the last phase of King James's
reign in Scotland was dominated by the problems arising from the
opening phases of the Thirty Years War. The overriding issues in
the two countries were very different, however. Until the military
expeditions of 1625 and thereafter, the impact of the war in Scotland was much less immediate and severe than in England, since
the Scottish government had no independent foreign policy and
virtually no influence on the decision-making process in London.
So in Scotland there were no constitutional confrontations, no
impeachments, no divisive political clashes, no disputes over the
policy the government ought to adopt toward the war, though
there was some suspicion that King James's marriage diplomacy
might entail concessions to Catholics, and the rejoicing when
Prince Charles returned from Spain a bachelor and a Protestant
was as heartfelt in Edinburgh as in London.[1] Apart from the continuing problem of the five articles of Perth, the privy council in
these years devoted most of its attention to the economic condition of the country and the financial condition of the crown, both
of which the war affected adversely.

Scotland's direct involvement with the war began in October
1620, when the king requested a voluntary contribution for the
defense of the Palatinate. The government's preoccupation with
economic questions began well before then, however, thanks
chiefly to the clerk register, Sir George Hay. Hay was busy and
ambitious, more energetic than his aging senior colleagues, and

through his connection with the marquis of Hamilton he stood well with the all-powerful Buckingham; he was, therefore, far more influential than his comparatively minor office would seem to have warranted.

Hay's influence on the economy was most apparent in the government's more sympathetic attitude toward industrial monopolies; Hay was himself an industrial monopolist and promoter on a considerable scale. Ironically enough, one of his own monopolies, glassmaking, was having considerable trouble. There was the usual problem of defending it against interlopers, but the real difficulty, as the council explained in a letter to the king in July 1619, was that the English market was closed to Hay's glass, which had been recently classified there as "foreign" and prohibited, while Scottish coal, which was used in English glassmaking, was heavily imported there. The council asked that James either allow Scottish glass to be sold freely in England or cut off the supply of Scottish coal to English glassmakers. This ploy was effective, since Scottish coal was regarded in England as far more suitable for glassmaking than English coal, owing to its relative freedom from noxious gases; the king agreed in February 1620 to open the English market to Scottish glass. The council then took steps to protect the monopolists' home market. A committee was appointed to inspect the quantity and quality of the glass produced in Scotland, as compared with English drinking glasses and sheet glass usually bought in Danzig, to see if it would be possible to ban the importation of foreign glass. The committee reported favorably, with some reservations—no great surprise, since Hay was on the committee. In March 1621, therefore, the importation of foreign glass was prohibited for the duration of the patent of monopoly, which expired in 1641, always provided that the manufacturers could match foreign glass in quantity, quality, and price. With these advantages the trade flourished; by the end of the reign Scottish drinking glasses were being exported to London in fairly substantial quantities.[2]

A much more controversial economic decision, because it impinged on a considerable existing economic interest, had to do with the tanning of leather. As a result of complaints on the part of the cordiners about the poor quality of Scottish leather, parliament in 1617 had authorized the council to do whatever was necessary to remedy the situation. Late in 1619, after a prodding letter from the king, the council appointed a subcommittee to hold hearings and make a recommendation. It concluded that the remedy was to import some English tanners—twelve was the suggested number—to teach their incompetent Scottish colleagues their business. The council accepted this report, after brushing aside the argument of the Edinburgh city fathers that only parliament could authorize such a major reform, and instructed the subcommittee to calculate the costs of its proposal. These costs—salaries for the Englishmen, and so on—would be borne in the first instance by the as-yet-unnamed "keeper of the seal," the person who would have the power to certify that each piece of leather, both domestic and foreign, met the new, improved standards of quality, and who would recoup by collecting a fee for each hide stamped. The keeper, who, if the subcommittee's calculations proved to be accurate, stood to collect a gross sum of over £280,000 over the life of the patent, turned out to be none other than the lord treasurer's son and heir, Lord Erskine. He found it necessary to make a special trip to court to get the king's approval, obtained it in March 1620, and set to work. By June he had recruited seventeen English tanners instead of only twelve, and on 1 July the council issued a long recapitulatory order in which their Scottish pupils were instructed to use the Englishmen well and setting 1 November 1621 as the date after which all Scottish-produced hides must meet the new standards and have seals to attest their quality.

Trouble was not long in coming. As early as January 1621 Erskine was complaining that many Scots tanners were not taking instruction and were persisting in the old methods of production; within two months some 150 tanners had been summoned before the council for disobedience. Worse still, the cordiners themselves, whose complaints had led to the reform, were attempting to sabotage Erskine's plans, according to the council, by raising the price of boots and shoes and implying that the council was responsible, on account of the charges owing under Erskine's patent. The council was rightly indignant, since the charges had not yet gone into effect; it ordered that the prices be reduced to the level of

November 1619. The charge of sabotage was probably unfair. The cordiners seem to have been up to nothing more sinister than a certain amount of overcharging at public expense, and they evidently obeyed the council's order—at least the council did not find it necessary to repeat it. The tanners remained obstinate, however, in spite of the council's cheerful assertion in July 1621 that "the work undertaken for reforming the abuses of tanning and barking of leather within this kingdom is now brought to a reasonable good perfection," a necessary precondition to allowing Erskine to start collecting his fees. After the collection began, Erskine required the cooperation of sheriffs and burgh officials with his deputies, and often did not get it, prompting the council to order such cooperation in February 1622. The resistance continued, as did citations to the recalcitrant; the controversy lasted well beyond the end of the reign.[3]

There were a good many other grants of industrial monopoly made in these last peacetime years, covering all sorts of manufacturing processes, from sugar refining to the making of pottery out of a certain kind of clay, but only one caused any real controversy. This was the grant in November 1619 of a twenty-one-year monopoly of soap-making to the busy entrepreneur Nathaniel Udward. The purpose of the monopoly, according to Udward, was to put an end to Scotland's dependence on "filthy and pestiferous" soap imported from abroad by greedy merchants who bought the miserable stuff very cheaply and sold it at exorbitant prices. The result, said Udward, was to give Scotland a very bad reputation abroad: "Strangers ... frequenting this kingdom ... may not abide the stinking smell of the napery and linen clothes washed with this filthy soap." Udward was to have his process fully operative within eight years, at which time the council, if satisfied, was to ban the importation of foreign soap, on Udward's undertaking to compensate the government out of his profits for the resultant loss of customs revenue.

Within less than two years Udward asked the council to impose the ban; he claimed that he was now prepared to supply Scotland's needs. A mixed committee of councillors and Edinburgh burgesses, appointed to investigate, agreed that Udward was able to do so. Udward accepted the council's conditions respecting the prices of the various sorts of soap and the quantity to be kept on hand, and got his desired prohibition as of 10 August 1621. Complaints began very quickly, from importers who lost trade and from western burghs who grumbled about the cost of transporting Udward's soap overland from his works at Leith. In 1623 Udward saw the handwriting on the wall; the king thought the monopoly unwise, and Kellie, among others, thought him dishonest. He pliantly agreed to the cancellation of the ban on imported soap. He then demonstrated that he knew more than one way to skin a cat by getting James to grant him a reversion of the office of conservator of the Scottish staple at Veere, where, according to the outraged complaint of the convention of royal burghs, he set about arranging for a monopoly of the soap-importing business for himself. The burghs added that the soap he made in Leith was worse than the imported stuff. Udward's various grants from the king were nevertheless valid, and the burghs had to buy them up at considerable cost to themselves.[4]

In established industries the issues were how best to promote manufacture and provide for the needs of the consumer rather than the creation of a monopoly. In 1620 another attempt got under way in Edinburgh, supported by the town magistrates, to launch a manufacture of fine woolens by importing foreign workers, chiefly English and Dutch. The council worked on the matter through 1620 and finally approved the patent in April 1621, but once again nothing came of it. In its traditional lines of production, however, the industry continued to expand; by the 1620s large amounts of woolen hose, for example, were being exported from the manufactory at Leith.[5] Coal created much more controversy, because the desire to keep coal cheap and plentiful for the domestic consumer clashed with the desire of the mine owners to expand the foreign market. The Dutch, in particular, were welcome customers because they sent their ships to the loading platforms in the Forth and paid cash. The council paid heed to the complaints it received, but the interests of the aristocratic mine owners, several of whom were councillors themselves, usually prevailed. In December 1620, for instance, the council heard a complaint that a group of these owners had gotten together at a dinner party and conspired to fix the price of a load of coal at four shillings instead of the customary three. The council ordered that the price be reduced to the old level and for good measure repeated its formal prohibition of export. Two months later the plaintiffs were back again, complaining that not only had the owners not complied but they had also cut the size of the load and restricted service by refusing on any given day to sell to someone who had bought coal elsewhere on that day. The council decided to sentence three of the owners to a fine and imprisonment, immediately suspend the sentence, and look further into the whole problem of pricing and exports. In March 1621 it agreed to a modest price rise, to 3 sh. 4 d. per load; on the vexed question of permitting exports it passed the buck to parliament, which in August appointed a committee to look into the question. In November, alleging the bad weather and the prospect of a severe winter, the council once again banned the export of coal, a position which the convention of royal burghs supported at its meeting the following summer. The evidence indicates that there was in fact no shortage of coal; the burghs' attitude stemmed from a desire to keep the price low and from the fact that their citizens did not greatly profit from the export trade, which was carried on mostly in foreign ships. The prohibition remained, but it was ineffective and could be legally violated; the chancellor's nephew, the earl of Winton, got a license from the king to export half his coal in June 1622.[6]

The council's economic activity in these years extended beyond individual industries and entrepreneurs, of course. In 1619 it completed a long series of regulations designed to standardize weights and measures. It took steps against overcharging, especially on the part of middlemen[7] and marketers of raw material, though it was careful about investigations where the great were concerned. One, involving an accusation against Lord Forbes, among others, for overcharging for raw wool at certain fairs, took almost three years to complete.[8] The council protested to James about discrimination against Scottish merchants in Ireland, and kept him from yielding to importunate suitors who asked for positions as inspectors or assayers of this or that with the hope of making money by harassment of the people involved in the business in question.[9] It did its best to compel the repair of damaged or washed-out bridges. In the parliament of 1621 it sponsored legislation on bankruptcies and fraudulent business practices; it also attempted to protect the employers of agricultural labor by providing that anyone hired from Martinmas to Whitsun (November to June) could not leave his employer at Whitsun, with the busy season coming up, unless he could prove that he had another job. It even looked into the methods of wool gathering in Orkney. It was the custom there to pull the wool off the sheep instead of clipping them; James thought the practice cruel and prohibited it. The inhabitants of Orkney defended the practice; the council was somewhat taken aback, but on inquiry it learned that the wool which was pulled was that which came off easily in the spring, and that a clipped sheep was apt to die of exposure in the long winter. The ancient custom was allowed.[10]

One rather more controversial matter was James's order, issued just prior to his departure from Scotland in 1617, that the Scots follow the English example and prohibit the use of foreign ships for the export of Scottish goods when Scottish (or English) ships were available. The merchant-dominated convention of royal burghs was very hostile to this proposal; the shipowners naturally favored it. The economic interest of the councillors as individuals lay with the exporters rather than the shippers; they also believed that such a prohibition, while appropriate enough for England, would be harmful to Scotland, where native shipping was in much shorter supply—it was one more example of James's belief that what was good for England must be good for Scotland as well. The burghs attempted to satisfy the king by agreeing to use Scottish ships where possible, but a formal prohibition of the use of foreign ships would kill the export trade in herring with the "east countries," which went in Dutch flyboats at about one-third what Scottish shippers would charge. The king's proposal, they said, would in fact hurt the shippers themselves. Foreign countries would take retaliatory measures, and the Scottish ships employed in the French carrying trade would suffer. The king dismissed the latter argument: the French had to export their wine any way they could, or be "extreme losers"; he insisted on the principle being applied, though he said he was always prepared to make exceptions in particular cases. The council and the burghs continued to delay; by the summer of 1619 the king's patience was beginning to wear thin. The council applied some pressure and at last persuaded the burghs to accept the king's plan for everything except the "easterling trade," for which Dutch shipping was essential. The council, over the vehement protests of the shipowners, accepted this in November 1619. The delaying tactics of the burghs and the council, and their justificatory arguments, evidently impressed James. He accepted the council's decision, and we hear no more about the matter.[11]

Food supply and money supply also concerned the council in these years; there was too much of the former and, as usual, too little of the latter. The harvests of 1617 and 1618 were excellent; the council, composed as it was of landlords with rent rolls and profits to consider, placed a high tariff on imported grain, so high that the convention of royal burghs protested it, and began to prosecute violators. Melrose, in a memorandum drafted early in 1619 and obviously intended for the king's eye, defended this policy by pointing out that a few years previously, in a year of good harvest, the merchants trading to the Baltic bought grain cheaply there, undersold the Scots producers, and then took advantage of the resulting glut to buy cheaply for resale abroad. The merchants' protests got nowhere, the harvests continued good, and the duty continued to climb until in October 1619 it was set at the very high rate of £1 on every boll of imported wheat and one merk on all other victual. Export was encouraged by a nominal export duty of a half-merk a chalder. Then, with the bad harvest of 1621, came a dramatic reversal. In November 1621 the export of victual was prohibited; in 1622 the duty on all imported grain was dropped to a shilling a boll and importation positively encouraged, and in the following year, as the dearth continued, the council legislated ineffectively against the inevitable forestalling and regrating. The abrupt shifts in the government's policy were disconcerting to the merchants, who argued vigorously against the import duties, which, they claimed, had resulted from an unusual glut in 1618 caused by a combination of good harvests and reduced exports on account of the royal visit. High import duties, they said, meant that there was no way of providing against crop failure by laying in reserves; they were prepared to promise to re-export foreign victual in good years so as not to drive down domestic prices, and to accept a prohibition of exports when those prices reached a certain level. The council was not at all anxious to come to a decision on these questions during the abnormal conditions of the early 1620s. Eventually, early in the next reign, after the scarcity ended with the good harvest of 1624, a more or less permanent compromise between the merchants and the landed interests was worked out, whereby imports of grain were prohibited if the price level fell below a certain point, and exports if it became too high.[12]

The council's hostility to the export of specie was due not only to orthodox economics but also to a genuine shortage of currency in circulation. James's authorization of a new English coinage in 1619, and his permission to the English to refuse substandard gold and silver, angered the council; it was a violation of the agreement of 1605 by which all such changes were to be made with mutual consent, and it would have the effect of draining all the good, heavy coins out of Scotland. The council pointed this out to James in a letter whose tone came as near to disrespect as that body ever got. It issued a vehement proclamation against the exporters of gold and silver, attempted to alleviate the currency shortage by twice authorizing the coinage of a limited amount of copper—though it did prescribe that no one need accept payment in copper of more than 6 d. in each pound—and finally, in June 1620, it asked the king to legalize the circulation of foreign coin. James was uneasy about this, but he finally agreed to it, after Elibank assured him that it was absolutely necessary, and a list of those coins which could legally circulate was prepared. All others were supposed to be surrendered for recoinage. These measures did not solve the problem. In July 1621 the master of the cunziehouse issued a gloomy report deploring the continuing shortage of small coin, the illegal export of specie, and the circulation of bad foreign money. The crop failures of the 1620s made matters worse, since food had to be purchased abroad. Merchants continued to export money, protest against the council's methods of trying to prevent it, and argue that certain trades, notably that in the Baltic whence most of the imported victual came, could not be carried on without such export.[13]

By and large the last peacetime years were good ones for the

Scottish economy. Harvests were bountiful and exports increased, as did the importation of industrial raw materials such as iron, flax, and hemp, a good indication of industrial expansion, which was in fact to continue, though not interruptedly, until the civil war.[14] Prior to October 1620, when the king made his request for aid for the Palatinate, the war had had little direct impact on Scotland. True, the herring fishermen had complained of the aggressive and illegal behavior of the huge Dutch fishing fleet. In this and other matters, however, the London government was unwilling to complicate its foreign policy too far by exerting itself on behalf of Scottish economic interests. But the fishermen seem not to have suffered very much; the expansion of the export market continued, particularly in the Baltic, where by the 1620s the Scots were sending some six to seven million fish a year.[15] There were rumors of Spanish designs on Scotland in 1619, and in the spring of 1620 some levies were recruited for the service of the Winter King.[16] Then James's request arrived, and the Scottish involvement began.

In asking for a voluntary contribution for the Palatinate James clearly hoped to avoid a meeting of parliament, which would entail dealing with financial and religious problems at the same time. His hope may have been based in part on the fact that at this point the condition of the Scottish treasury was unusually good. Customs duties, which the government had been collecting without benefit of tacksmen since 1617, when it received a bid which it suspected of being collusively low, were rolling in at an annual rate better than that for which it had been willing to continue the tack.[17] The proceeds of the taxation of 1617 were great enough to permit of a gift of £10,000 to Lord Treasurer Mar and to buy up the hereditary sheriffdoms of Selkirk and Roxburgh from their holders for 20,000 merks and £20,000 respectively, as well as to make repairs to the palace at Linlithgow and to project them for the royal castles at Dumbarton and Inverness.[18] The king's request made the council very uneasy, however. The nobility, summoned to discuss the matter, overwhelmingly recommended that parliament be called and a tax voted there. Bishop Forbes said that there were too few in attendance to bind everyone: he and Spottiswoode were the only bishops present. The archbishop argued that some lesser men, notably some of the holders of annualrents (interest payments) and wadsets (mortgages) on noblemen's lands, were richer than many nobles, and Melrose himself, though he supported James's request, remarked that a parliamentary tax would produce the money more quickly. So the meeting firmly recommended to James that he summon parliament.[19]

James was annoyed. He wrote again, repeating his request for a voluntary contribution, on the ground that the money was urgently needed and that it would take too long to collect a tax. Melrose replied, pointing out that once the tax was voted, loans could be raised on it from the burghs, which were the only sources of ready cash anyway, and Spottiswoode followed with a letter to Lochmaben speculating that James might get £100,000 sterling from a parliament and nowhere near as much from voluntary contributions.[20] The nobility convened again in January 1621 and came to the same conclusion as before. This time they decided not to trust to the effect of letters alone; Spottiswoode was designated to go to court and try to persuade James to accept the council's recommendation. The archbishop was the obvious choice. He had strongly advocated that a parliament be called, and he could discuss with James better than anyone else the problems inherent in getting a parliament to accept both a huge tax and the five articles of Perth, which required parliamentary ratification in the interest of greater compliance. Spottiswoode's appearance at court forced the king's hand. James really had very little choice, since by the time the archbishop arrived in London, in mid-February, the English parliament which James had had to call for the same purpose was already in session. On 25 February he wrote to the council, agreeing to the summons. But he was still querulous, and was irritated that the meeting could not be held before the summer. The council must get the maximum amount voted, by taxing annualrents and eliminating the exempt, such as the members of the court in session. "There have not wanted complaints of all and every one of you," he wrote to the councillors, intimating that the deaf ear he had hitherto turned to such complaints might begin to hear.[21] One councillor in particular felt himself to be the target of the royal wrath: Treasurer-depute Elibank, who went to London in April 1621 to discuss with James the sudden loss of revenue caused by the recent decline in trade—the war was taking its toll. While there Elibank learned that James had ordered an inquiry into his conduct touched off by accusations made by Stewart of Killeith, now Lord Ochiltree, with whom Elibank had been at odds over Ochiltree's accounts as tacksman of Orkney. The charges proved groundless, but they had the effect of triggering an apparent attack of melancholia, and Elibank died at the end of June.[22] His death was a serious loss at a time when the government, confronted by the king's demands for large amounts of money and a declining income owing to a combination of bad weather and falling trade, stood in greater need than ever of all the financial expertise it could muster.

When parliament met, late in July 1621, James sent a letter which dealt only with the foreign crisis and the need for money. The five articles of Perth were never mentioned. He would have liked to have come to the parliament in person, James said, but the "combustions of Christendom" kept him at home. The money for which he was asking was destined for the preservation of the true religion and of his daughter and son-in-law, and was designed to avert war by the timely provision of aid—James dwelt once more, rather incongruously, on the advantages of peace.[23] At the opening session the government's orators divided their efforts between the necessity of subjects' giving and the propriety of accepting the five articles; Hamilton, the king's commissioner, laid stress on the fact that the money was to be used to recover the Palatinate by diplomacy rather than war. In the committee of the articles the principle of voting a tax was quickly accepted; the points at issue were the amount and the question of the taxation of annualrents. It was finally agreed to raise £400,000 by levying 30 shillings in the pound on land of old extent for each of the next three years. The regular members of the court of session retained their exemptions, but they in fact agreed to pay this particular tax "as if not exempt." The question of annualrents was much stickier; neither the burghs nor the small barons wanted this tax, but it too was finally accepted, at the rate of 5 percent on the net take. Getting parliament to accept this sizable tax, the largest ever voted by a Scottish parliament, as well as the five articles of Perth, was a considerable achievement for the king's ministers. James was duly grateful, and wrote letters of thanks to his supporters.[24]

The tax on annualrents was the brainchild of Clerk Register Hay and was aimed primarily at the middle class, as the council's expository regulations of 1622 make clear. It was an unprecedented levy, and one of major significance; it represented the first broadening of the direct-tax base in James's reign. Parliament was persuaded to adopt it on account of the emergency, but it turned out to be permanent; it was included in the taxes voted in the reign of Charles I, even after the coming of peace in 1629, after which it became increasingly unpopular. Among the reasons for the burgesses' hostility to this tax was that it would reveal the size of their estates. So the citizenry of Edinburgh very quickly made an offer to the government, to compound for their share of the taxation, both ordinary and extraordinary, for the sum of £40,000, spread over four years instead of three. This offer was one the council simply could not refuse; it was more than twice what Edinburgh would have paid as its share of the regular national tax of £400,000. James authorized Mar to deal first with Edinburgh and then with the other royal burghs, which he did, and on the whole with very favorable results. The council records indicate that some half-dozen burghs compounded for the tax. The government evidently did as well elsewhere; the total ultimately realized from the tax approximated Archbishop Spottiswoode's estimate of £100,000 sterling.[25]

James was pleased with the generosity of his Scottish subjects, but he realized that, given the worsening economic situation, reductions in governmental expenditure were necessary. One of his economies turned out very badly: the order to abolish the border police force as of 1 November 1621. This proposal had surfaced once before, early in 1618, as part of an English plan for the reorganization of the administration of the "middle shires," which James had decided was necessary during his visit to Scotland. The Scottish government had objected to this and certain other features of the plan, and in the upshot the set of regulations promulgated in September 1618 changed things very little. Dunfermline and his colleagues did not in fact believe that anything much needed changing. They particularly disliked the king's requirement that a list of notorious malefactors be drawn up who, when caught, would be transported to the wars or to Virginia; they argued that there were very few such persons in the area, and that anyone who thought himself liable to transportation would be much more likely "to become fugitive than to abide the hazard of that article." In their view, whatever difficulties existed on the borders stemmed from administrative breakdown on the English side, where the English privy council's inquiry in 1618 turned up a list of sixty wanted men in Cumberland alone.[26]

James apparently was convinced by his councillors' arguments; the reason he gave in 1621 for his order to abolish the border guard was that Scotland was so quiet that its services were no longer necessary.[27] Lawlessness on the border had indeed diminished greatly, but not greatly enough to justify this. Within three months the council was deluged with complaints of the recrudescence of thievery, mostly of sheep and cattle. Ministers were afraid to visit their parishioners, and parishioners to go to church, because the thieves would strike at their empty houses. The council summoned the border landlords to a meeting in March 1622, when it was concluded that some equivalent to the police force should be provided if the troubles were not to increase. It seems likely that officialdom suggested this conclusion, since by happy coincidence James had already made such arrangements, not without expressing his surprise that "after so long time of severe punishment these shires should be troubled in that kind." Three local magnates, Murray of Lochmaben and the earls of Buccleuch and Nithsdale,[28] were to be given responsibility for keeping order; each was empowered to appoint ten men as agents with powers of fire and sword to pursue malefactors. This was a decidedly regressive step whose only virtue, that it cost the government nothing in wages, was also its principal defect, since it meant far less control by the council of its agents. In practice it worked out less badly than might have been expected because Lochmaben and Nithsdale were almost never in Scotland, which meant that major responsibility fell upon Buccleuch, who was conscientious and reasonably efficient—efficient enough to hang some fifty malefactors in his first fourteen months in office. By the end of the reign Buccleuch had managed to get the situation pretty well in hand, overcoming a good many obstacles en route: the uncooperativeness of officials in England and Ireland respecting fugitives and of local magistrates respecting the jailing of malefactors, and one appearance by Nithsdale, whose arrogance and attempts to ignore customary procedures led to a good deal of confusion and bad feeling.[29]

James had a good many other ideas about ways to increase his Scottish revenues. The customs were to be set in tack again, so as to anticipate revenue. The king was uneasy about the impact of the sumptuary law parliament adopted in 1621; he thought it might reduce customs revenues. The council reassured him: the forbidden goods were mostly smuggled, and if the law were suspended, the money spent on ostentation would hamper people's ability to pay the new taxes. As he had so many times before, James declared that pensions must be cut, and that none should be paid at all on the next two installment days, save to old servants. The number of salaried officials was to be reduced. No new building would be undertaken. The king approved the ban on the export of victual; when export resumed, he would turn it into a royal monopoly and pocket the profits himself. And, of course, James declared that he would grant no new pensions, save two already promised.[30]

Dunfermline and his colleagues can be excused if they felt cynical about the royal promises; they had been hearing the same litany for well over thirty years. "I think," wrote Kellie to Mar in January 1622 with more hope than conviction, "he will not do any thing that may hinder you in going on in that course that was settled at your being here."[31] James's actions had already belied Kellie's hopes. In December he had made a gift of the fines collected from those convicted of exporting specie and granted a pension, both of which the council courageously refused to honor, the former on the ground that it would open the door to a swarm of applicants who would quickly empty the treasury. The prospect of a large take from the tax rapidly quelled James's temporary fit of caution; among other things he began to convert pensions previously paid in Scots money into sterling, an utterly irresponsible act at this juncture. By April 1622 the situation was so bad that Mar resolved to write to Prince Charles and Buckingham about the king's disastrous generosity, and to send Archibald Primrose, who was as knowledgeable on financial questions as anyone in Scotland, to London to explain the situation in detail. Melrose lent encouragement, suggesting the language Mar should use in his letters to Charles and the favorite, and attempting to buoy up his colleague's spirits by pointing out that all of James's treasurers sooner or later came to grief on account of their master's irresponsibility—a most unusual display of despondency and criticism on the part of the veteran bureaucrat. The chief occasion of all this was a gift to Hamilton of £10,000 sterling—£120,000 Scots. Primrose's trip was in vain. Hamilton was Buckingham's friend and wanted his money, and Mar had neglected the favorite by failing to provide fir seed and some four or five *thousand* young trees which James had asked him to send south the previous October to beautify Buckingham's house at Burleigh-on-the-Hill. On 15 May 1622 the council was forced to record the king's order to pay Hamilton "howsoon so much money of the taxation can conveniently be had."[32]

That date, 15 May 1622, was of considerable significance in the history of Scotland, although no one knew it at the time. It marked Dunfermline's last appearance in the *sederunt* of the privy council. At the beginning of June he took to his bed; on the 16th death ended his remarkable career at the age of sixty-six.

That the happiest nations are those which have no history is one of those meaningless aphorisms whose meaning is perfectly clear. Dunfermline would certainly have subscribed to it. Tranquillity was his goal during his decade of power, and, for the most part, tranquillity he achieved. The contrast with what went before and after is striking: the repressive violence of Dunbar's despotic regime, and the blunders of Charles I which led to the revival of the alliance between kirk and aristocracy which was to ruin Charles as it ruined his grandmother. Equally striking is the contrast between Dunfermline's orderly, smoothly run, scandal-free administration and the rudderless and corrupt condition of that of England during his years of power. By whatever yardstick Dunfermline's performance is measured, it was a remarkably successful one.

Dunfermline was not cut out to be a mover and shaker. He was skeptical by nature and had no faith in grandiose schemes. His job, as he saw it, was not to innovate but to consolidate Maitland's and Dunbar's work, a task which suited his temperament, since, like so many skeptical men, he was a conservative. This involved maintaining the system as he found it and, more important, bringing all the important elements in Scottish society, especially the nobility, to acquiesce in it. His methods were conciliation and compromise; his success was remarkable, until in his final years his consensus was disrupted by the five articles of Perth and the coming of war. Curiously enough, what appeared to be his principal handicap as a statesman, his religion, actually became something of an asset. He was what was called in England a "church Papist," a man who conformed to the church established by law, though secretly believing, and almost certainly practicing, otherwise. The two near-disasters of 1596 and 1605–6 led him to adopt the stance which proved in the end to be most beneficial to his career: avoidance of personal involvement in religious issues, a continuous effort to keep these issues, and churchmen too, out of politics, and a minimum of legal discrimination against the losers in the internecine struggle in the church. He managed so well that during his decade of power he succeeded not only in overcoming the handicap of his putative Catholicism but also in acquiring a reputation for fairness to all shades of opinion which reconciled many otherwise disgruntled ministers to his regime, and in the end caused both his political rival Archbishop Spottiswoode and the embittered presbyterian Calderwood to praise him in their histories. "He exercised his place with great moderation," wrote Spottiswoode, "and above all things, studied to maintain peace and quietness."[33] Dunfermline would have been content with that judgment.

Dunfermline's passing caused far less change in the conduct of the Scottish government than had his accession to power in 1611. For the last year of his life his influence had been waning; his health had been giving way, and there were signs of mental slippage.[34] Furthermore his behavior at the parliament of 1621 as reported at Whitehall had seriously annoyed the king; he had evinced his distaste for both the religious articles and the unprecedented taxation, innovations which went against his conservative grain.[35] But there had been no thought of displacing him. His death naturally precipitated a scramble for his vacant offices. The logical candidate for the chancellorship was Melrose, the unswerving advocate of obedience to the king's wishes, whose influence waxed as Dunfermline's waned, but it was widely believed in both Edinburgh and London that he would refuse it if it were offered to him. Whatever the truth of this opinion, he did not get it; James's choice was Clerk Register Hay, the author of the tax on annualrents which had so pleased the king, and the marquis of Hamilton's (and therefore Buckingham's) candidate. When Dunfermline died, Hay happened to be at court. He campaigned vigorously for the office, allegedly even promising Buckingham's friend the Catholic Nithsdale that as chancellor he would be friendly to Catholics. What might be called the Hamilton connection got more from the reshuffle than any other group. The marquis himself got the keepership of Holyroodhouse, and Sir John Hamilton, Melrose's brother but described by both Calderwood and Kellie as the marquis's servant, became clerk register. Spottiswoode, if he had any ambitions—his denial of interest in the chancellorship has a *pro forma* sound—was disappointed. Mar also came up empty, and in fact worse than empty: he was forced to accept an unwelcome treasurer-depute in the person of Sir Archibald Napier, another of Hamilton's protégés. Mar was not in good odor with the favorite on account of his attitude toward Hamilton's warrant; James, who was not unfriendly to his old schoolmate, was evidently persuaded to foist Napier on him by the analogy of the English administration: Napier would be the Scottish equivalent of the chancellor of the exchequer. There were also reports that a number of people with royal warrants for money out of the proceeds of the tax of 1621, of which Mar was the official collector, were not being paid, but that some of Mar's collection agents, who were also government creditors, were repaying themselves. About the only silver lining the disgusted Kellie could find was that the bishops had gotten nothing.[36]

Yet the dominance of the Hamilton connection turned out to be more apparent than real. Melrose and Mar were much too solidly entrenched, both in Edinburgh and with the king—they were still Tam o'the Cowgate and Jock o'the Slates to James—and their political alliance was cemented by a marriage between Melrose's son and Mar's daughter. The new chancellor, in the unsettled conditions of war and famine that prevailed in 1622, was not prepared to challenge them as long as they shared power with him. So things seemingly went on much as before, a triumvirate sharing power, with Melrose, who now attended to the day-to-day administrative chores which had been Dunfermline's responsibility, as the most important figure. Kellie, who at one point had thought of selling his post as captain of the guard and leaving court, reconsidered and stayed on. Mar made his peace with Hamilton, although Kellie always remained suspicious of him. Napier, by his own account, got along well enough with Mar as long as James lived.[37] Yet in fact things were not the same. There was no one to provide Dunfermline's kind of steadying leadership, his ability to conciliate and compromise. Mar was argumentative, and Melrose and Hay, not being aristocrats themselves, did not have Dunfermline's influence with the nobility. It was a government of elderly men, grown old in the service of their elderly master—Hay, the youngest, was fifty in 1622—and uneasily aware that they lacked Dunfermline's latter-day invulnerability to the eddies of faction at James's court. The marquis of Hamilton had to be cultivated. He was a young, charming womanizer, inexperienced in Scottish politics but the favorite of the king and of the king's favorite, especially after he accepted one of Buckingham's parvenue cousins as a wife for his son and heir. Hay, who owed his position to Hamilton, was especially aware of the need of standing well with him and made frequent journeys to court to that end. All these things taken together—the relatively advanced age and political uncertainty of the triumvirate, and the difficult conditions of wartime economic dislocation and dearth they faced—naturally inclined them to follow Dunfermline's cautious and conservative example.

The one major potential innovation of this period stemmed from a distasteful economic proposal with which the triumvirate was confronted in its first months of power. In August 1622, at the prompting of the English cloth manufacturers, James proposed that the export of raw wool be henceforth limited to England and ordered that commissioners be sent to London to discuss the plan. The Scottish reaction was unanimously hostile. In some places, such as Aberdeen, there was opposition to any export at all, on the ground that it drove up the cost of locally made plaiding which was the staple of the town's trade with the Netherlands. The landowners naturally supported export, but they immediately pointed out that if it were limited to England, they would receive the lowest conceivable price for their wool—which, of course, was precisely what the English clothmakers had in mind. The council in reporting to the king added that even if the plan were less objectionable than it was, the present period of dearth would be the wrong time to launch it. The mere rumor of the plan had caused some tenants to leave their holdings or demand reduced rents. The council concluded by asking the king to explain why the plan would not cause economic loss to Scotland and be an outright subordination of Scottish to English interests.[38]

Faced with this vehement reaction, James abandoned the scheme and, to save his face, adopted the suggestion in the report made by Sir William Seton, the late chancellor's brother, in the name of the East Lothian landowners, that the way to deal with what was now a surplus of raw wool was to develop Scottish cloth manufacture. This was no new idea, but the way the council went about dealing with it was. In July 1623 a sixty-nine-man commission was set up under the presidency of the chancellor, charged with the development of the manufacture not merely of woolen cloth but of whatever commodity it believed Scotland needed. This was an independent commission, not a committee of the privy council. It was deemed to consist of the three "persons" of nobles, lairds, and burgesses; whatever any two of them agreed upon was to be considered adopted, a machinery which guaranteed control by the landed interest. "This," writes Professor Lythe, "might have been one of the outstanding politico-economic innovations in European history . . . and might have become a prototype for industrial parliaments elsewhere."[39] Nothing like it existed in James's other kingdoms. Unfortunately there is no indication that it ever achieved any results.

Another group organized at about the same time was much more active. This was the conciliar committee on grievances, which James created in May 1623 in order to redress "the just grievances of his subjects arising upon certain projects made by particular persons for their private gain, which, carrying show of general benefit to the whole kingdom, proved in effect to be heavy oppression and general grievance to all his subjects": i.e., patents and monopolies, which had caused a great deal of agitation in the English parliament of 1621–22 and, as has been shown, in Scotland as well. The committee found plenty of work, by no means all of it confined to monopolies. The convention of royal burghs submitted a long list of complaints, beginning with a request for an end to all monopolies and restraints of trade, so that their trading privileges would not be impaired. The committee naturally asked for particulars. The burghs' chief grievances turned out to be Erskine's tanning patent, the tobacco and soap monopolies, the licensing of coal export, and the council's policy on the import and export of food. The committee did its best to meet the burghs' objections. The soap and tobacco monopolies, referred by the committee to the full council, were eliminated. The restrictions on food export were lifted after the good harvest of 1624, and the negotiations set in train which led to the compromise on imports and exports of food mentioned earlier. On the matter of coal export the committee agreed with the mineowners that domestic sales were not great enough to permit them to operate at a profit; until they were, export, under license, would go on. Lord Erskine vigorously defended himself against his critics; the committee arranged for a test to be made of his methods as opposed to the traditional ones, set for June 1625. In only one instance were the burghs flatly rebuffed: the committee would not consider suspending the recently enacted sumptuary law. The committee worked hard and conscientiously, and did its best to be fair. There can be no doubt that its existence and authority helped to alleviate that sense of grievance which always exists in times of dearth and economic dislocation.[40]

One major problem which neither the committee on grievances nor the parent council could solve, however, was the impact on the poor of three successive years of crop failure, coupled with floods and a cattle murrain, which by 1623 led to very large numbers of deaths; this was "the most serious demographic crisis of seventeenth-century Scotland."[41] The existing poor law was not much help. The kirk sessions in each parish were theoretically responsible for the poor, but they treated the responsibility not as a legal obligation but as part of their duty as Christians. A statute of 1617 gave the justices of the peace the power to deal with vagrants, but the attempt to make each parish formally accountable for its own poor, as in England, foundered for lack of accurate records—the keeping of parish registers was required only in

1616—and on the peripatetic habits of vagabonds, who traveled about in swarms and did a good deal of successful begging at such events as weddings and funerals. Now, suddenly, the council was confronted with a serious crisis. The dearth meant evictions of tenants and unemployment—the poor had multiplied sixfold, the council reported to James in July 1623—and they were dying like flies "in the fields and the highways."[42] So in June 1623 the council issued instructions to the sheriffs, JPs, bailies of regalities, and burgh authorities to levy local taxes to raise money to buy food, the obligation to run until 1 September, when, it was hoped, the new harvest would begin and the poor find work. In the following month the council spelled out its intentions toward vagabonds more precisely. The justices at their quarter sessions were to appoint leviers and collectors of a poor rate in each parish, the rate to vary between one and five shillings a week; the money was to be used for constables' salaries and to support vagrants in prison and awaiting trial. The poor were ordered to be back in their parishes by the last Sunday in August and apply there for relief or risk the punishment reserved for sturdy beggars. The JPs were ordered to meet and report to the council on how they proposed to implement these instructions.[43]

If the responses which have survived are an accurate index, the JPs were unwilling to do anything much. In most shires they simply passed the burden on to the parishes. In Selkirkshire the justices pointed out that the town of Selkirk would neither cooperate nor acknowledge their authority, which set a bad example to the rest of the shire; they suggested that the council authorize "some common work" in each parish and imprison those who refused to do it. In Edinburgh the justices argued that the poor were too sick and weak to go home, and that there were not enough jails in the sheriffdom to hold 10 percent of the town's beggars. In East Lothian the response was even more hostile: the law was vague, the one-to-five shilling spread was unfair, and "every contribution is odious and smells of a taxation"—which this one certainly did, since the need for constables' salaries and maintenance for those awaiting trial would not cease with the end of the dearth. About the most the council could obtain in the way of cooperation came from Perthshire, where Chancellor Hay was personally present.

There the justices placed responsibility on the parish, whose kirk session could levy a tax; any landlord who took responsibility for his own poor was exempted, and anyone who felt that he had been unfairly assessed because of an excess of poor in his parish by contrast with others in the shire could appeal to the justices for relief. Compulsory assessment, even in this dire emergency and for a limited time, had failed; poor relief would remain a matter of voluntary charity on the part of individual kirk sessions.[44]

Among the reasons for the council's sudden concern for the condition of the poor was the falling-off in tax collections. James was informed that Annandale was so hit by dearth that no money could be collected there,[45] a condition by no means limited to Annandale and which helps to explain the negative attitude of the East Lothian JPs. The economic troubles of these years meant that the collection of taxes was considerably in arrears, and the treasury was operating in its usual hand-to-mouth way. But by the end of 1624 things began to improve. In October the king congratulated Mar on the condition of the treasury, which was better than James had expected; in January 1625 the council lifted the ban on the export of victual.[46] There was a troublesome small outbreak of plague, but conditions appeared to be returning to normal when, at the end of March, the news arrived in Edinburgh that King James was dead. One of the longest and most constructive reigns in Scottish history had come to an end.

It was a reign full of remarkable achievement, for which the king himself deserves much of the credit. In the generation and more which followed the publication of S. R. Gardiner's magisterial history of England, most historians found little good to say of King James. "James I slobbered at the mouth and had favourites; he was thus a Bad King," epitomized the usual verdict.[47] Many of the scholars who have been at work since World War II, however, have come to somewhat different conclusions. While not minimizing James's sins of omission and commission as king of England, they have rightly emphasized that he inherited a difficult situation and that the policies and blunders of Charles I were far more crucial than his. This is not the place to argue James's role in the history of England. It is worth remembering, however, that the crisis which led to the civil war began in Scotland, and that James left behind him there a kingdom in which the authority and prestige of the crown were far greater both administratively and geographically than ever before.

Much of James's work had been accomplished, and the foundation laid for most of the rest, before 1603. When the king went south to claim his inheritance, there were three major tasks still to do: to complete the process of securing royal control over the church by restoring the powers of the bishops, to extend law and order throughout the kingdom by getting a tighter grip on the highlands and borders, and to bring about the much-desired union. The last never materialized, and James had to remain, as he put it, a husband to two wives all his days. But he never ceased to work toward the union, not always usefully, as in the case of the five articles of Perth. His other two goals he substantially achieved, the first in collaboration with Archbishop Spottiswoode, the second by adopting policies worked out for the most part by the council in Edinburgh.

There was a fourth task, to be sure, one which James never set himself seriously to grapple with, and which might well have defeated him if he had: bringing solvency to the Scottish crown. The king's policies resulted in considerable economic prosperity, which was in some jeopardy on account of the war when he died, but that prosperity was never successfully tapped for the royal coffers. But in this respect James was not much different from his predecessors and contemporaries, most of whom died, as he did, heavily in debt.

The king's achievement was considerable; what made it even more remarkable was the fact that he was an absentee. It was not easy to govern successfully at long distance in seventeenth-century Europe, especially when significant changes were being made. James succeeded because of his intimate knowledge of the Scottish scene and the people who counted there, and also because, in the years before 1603, he had built up a loyal and efficient group of servants in both church and state whom he could, and did, trust. Very few men lost the king's confidence and "fell"; Balmerino's case was exceptional. Very few "new" men, unknown to James before 1603, were of any consequence in the Scottish government, except for the sons of old friends and associates, such as

Lord Erskine and the earl of Lauderdale, Chancellor Maitland's son. There was a danger here, of course. By 1625 the administration was controlled by elderly, rather tired, and by now rather inflexible men who could not easily be replaced and who might well find it difficult to work with a new master—as Kellie wrote to his cousin the lord treasurer in November 1623, in commenting on the king's poor health, "It may come that young folks shall have their world. I know not if that will be fit for your Lordship and me."[48] But it is difficult to criticize James for his failure to minimize his successor's problems by altering a regime which had worked so effectively for him.

The major political dividing line in these years was the death of Dunbar in January 1611. By that time almost all the major changes had been made. The bishops were restored, unremitting pressure had quieted the border and the statutes of Icolmkill were operative in the highlands, and the treaty of union was dead, though a number of institutions patterned after those of England had been introduced, notably the justices of the peace and the courts of high commission. Dunbar operated rapidly and brutally, and rode roughshod over opposition. His successor was very different, both in purpose and in method. Dunfermline's objectives were to consolidate and conciliate, and he was as successful in his aims as Dunbar had been in his. There were discontented groups in Scottish society when Dunfermline died, such as the tanners who objected to Lord Erskine's patent, but the only widespread grievances were the result of two initiatives of which Dunfermline disapproved: the Perth articles and the unusually heavy tax of 1621. His death made little immediate difference, since the triumvirate which succeeded him followed in his footsteps; in the long run, however, it might have, since the balance of political influences was potentially unstable and became still more so with the sudden death of the marquis of Hamilton early in March 1625, a few weeks before that of James.

"As he lived in peace, so did he die in peace," wrote the sorrowful Kellie the day after the king's passing, "and I pray God our King may follow him in all his good, which for my part I think was no small portion."[49] James, though he might have wished for a more extended account of his princely attributes, would certainly have approved of listing his devotion to peace as the first of his many good qualities. For the government and people of Scotland the king in the years after 1603 was something of an offstage voice, the unseen director of the actors on the boards in Edinburgh. But those actors never for a moment forgot that he was there. He and his three great ministers gave Scotland peace— more peace, more order, more general prosperity, more widespread acceptance of the authority of the crown than she had ever known before. The fact that his successor was to ruin his work should not be allowed to obscure the magnitude of James's accomplishment. The quasi-medieval kingdom which he began to govern in 1585 forty years later had become a recognizably modern state. Scotland was indeed governed by the pen, as all states with any pretension to civilization must be. For James's epitaph let his archbishop, whom he commissioned to write the history of the Scottish church, have the final word:

He was the Solomon of this age, admired for his wise government, and for his knowledge in all manner of learning. For his wisdom, moderation, love of justice, for his patience and piety (which shined above all his other virtues, and is witnessed in the learned works he left to posterity), his name shall never be forgotten, but remain in honour so long as the world endureth. We that have had the honour and happiness many times to hear him discourse of the most weighty matters, as well of policy as divinity, now that he is gone, must comfort ourselves with the remembrance of these excellencies, and reckon it not the least part of our happiness to have lived in his days.[50]

NOTES

1. *Calderwood* VII, 580. RPCS XIII, 374–75.
2. *RPCS* XI, 138–39, XII, xv–xvii, 374, 428, 439–41, 451–52, 771–72. *Melros* I, 337–38, 342–43. S. G. E. Lythe, *The Economy of Scotland in Its European Setting 1550–1625* (Edinburgh, 1960), pp. 41–42. J. U. Nef, *The Rise of the British Coal Industry* (London, 1932) I, 120, 181–82, 219. Interestingly enough, wood rather than coal seems to have been used in the making of Scottish glass.
3. *RPCS* XI, 613–15, XII, 159–71, 177–79, 181–82, 184, 189–93, 296–98, 304–7, 398–400, 424, 427, 429, 432, 450–51, 472, 519–20, 642, 685–86. *Melros* II, 352–53. 22, 31 Jan., 24 Feb. 1620, Kellie to Mar, *M&K Supp.*, pp. 95–98. See also L. B. Taylor, ed., *Aberdeen Council Letters* (London, 1942) I,

175–76, 194–95. There is a good summary of this business in the editor's introduction to *RPCS* XII, v–xiii.

4. Lythe, *Economy of Scotland,* pp. 36–37, 40–41. J. Donaldson and A. Gray, *The Scottish Staple at Veere* (London, 1909), p. 196. *RPCS* XII, 106–7, 505–6, 508, 516–19, XIII, xx–xxiii, 236, 249–53, 294–95, 388, 408–9, 487, 795–801. M. Wood, ed., *Extracts from the Records of the Burgh of Edinburgh* (Edinburgh, 1927–31) VI, x. *RCRB* III, 153–55, 162–64, 175–76. 27 Apr., 13 May 1623, Kellie to Mar, *M&K Supp.,* pp. 164–66, 168–69. An interesting sidelight of the investigation of 1621 was the estimate that only two-thirds of the soap imported each year actually paid customs duty. This would argue for a fairly inefficient customs service.

5. Lythe, *Economy of Scotland,* pp. 36, 39. Wood, *Extracts* VI, xviii. SRO, E17/2, no. 21. *Melros* II, 366–68, 386–87. *RPCS* XII, 292, 337–39, 472. *Calderwood* VII, 457–58, pointed out one of the less desirable (to him) results of the Edinburgh initiative: English and Dutch cloth workers at St. Paul's Work in Edinburgh set up a maypole on May Day, 1621.

6. *RPCS* XII, 387–88, 418–19, 433–35, 467, 474, 605–6, 752–53, XIII, 47–48, 207–9, 570–71. *APS* IV, 630–31. *RCRB* III, 132–33. Lythe, *Economy of Scotland,* pp. 48–49.

7. See, e.g., in *RPCS* XII, 203ff., the series of prosecutions of maltsters for charging illegally high fees for converting barley into malt.

8. The royal burghs' complaint was made in July 1618; the council's decree upholding it appeared in Mar. 1621. See *RCRB* III, 55, 113; *RPCS* XII, 437–38.

9. See, e.g., *RPCS* XII, 84–85, 211–12; *Melros* I, 309–11, 350–51.

10. *APS* IV, 613–16, 623–24. *RPCS* XI, 67, 510, XII, 6, 111–12.

11. For this question see *RPCS* XI, 202–3, 255, 409, 465, 518–19, 571–72, XII, 27, 67–69, 79–81, 87–88, 108–9; 7 Nov. 1617, Binning to James, 10 June, 4 Nov. 1619, the council to James, *Melros* I, 327–29, II, 346–48, 621–22; *RCRB* III, 66–67, 87–88; *LSP,* pp. 243–45, 316–17.

12. *RPCS* XI, 431–32, 473–74, XII, 94–95, 159, 455–56, 598–99, 702–4, XIII, 203–4, 240–41, 647–48, 674–75, 732–36, 832. *RCRB* III, 72–75, 147–50, 169–71. *Melros* I, 318–21. M. Perceval-Maxwell, *The Scottish Migration to Ulster in the Reign of James I* (London, 1973), pp. 303–8, attributes the decline in trade between Ulster and Scotland after 1619 to the Scottish tariff on imported victual.

13. *RPCS* XI, 533–35, XII, 110, 115–16, 124–28, 139–40, 223–25, 767, 771, 785–89, XIII, 120–21, 248–49, 329–31, 489. *Melros* I, 340–41, II, 361–62, 372–73. *LSP,* pp. 328–29. *M&K,* pp. 97–98. *APS* IV, 629.

14. T. M. Devine and S. G. E. Lythe, "The Economy of Scotland under James VI," *SHR* L (1971), 102. The figures cited in W. R. Foster, *The Church before the Covenants* (Edinburgh, 1975), pp. 81–82, on the increase in the amount of alms given to the poor at the parish level in the two decades prior to the civil war are a further indication of increasing prosperity.

15. Lythe, *Economy of Scotland,* p. 58. For a survey of the problem of the

fishery in Anglo-Dutch relations in this period see Charles Wilson, *Profit and Power* (London, 1957), pp. 32–40.

16. 8 Mar. 1619, Binning to James, *Melros* I, 324–26. *RPCS* XII, 88, 108–9, 255, 257–61, 272–73.

17. *RPCS* XI, 214–15, 249, 306–8, 339–40, 343, XII, 595. NLS, Denmilne Mss. VIII, nos. 34, 36. 11 Sept., 7 Nov. 1617, Binning to James, *Melros* I, 295–96, II, 621–22. 17 Oct., James to (Mar?), *M&K,* pp. 81–82. A. Murray, "Customs Revenues and Ports, 1621," in P. McNeill and R. Nicholson, eds., *An Historical Atlas of Scotland c. 400 — c. 1600* (St. Andrews, 1975), p. 94.

18. *RPCS* XI, 522, 586–87, XII, 289–90, 335. 31 May 1619, James to Mar, *M&K,* p. 86.

19. *RPCS* XII, 366, 379–80. *Spottiswoode* III, 259–60. 25 Oct. 1620, the council to James, 23, 27 Nov., Melrose to James, *Melros* II, 373–82.

20. 21 Dec. 1620, the council to James, 22 Dec. 1620, 29 Jan. 1621, Melrose to James, *Melros* II, 387–92. 9 Jan. 1621, Spottiswoode to Lochmaben, *LEA* II, 643–45.

21. 8 Mar. 1621, the council to James, *Melros* II, 392–93. 21 Apr., James to the council, 16 May, James to Mar, *M&K,* p. 94. See also 11 Apr., Kellie to Mar, *M&K Supp.,* p. 107.

22. 29 Mar. 1621, the council to James, *Melros* II, 396–97. *Calderwood* VII, 462. *Spottiswoode* III, 260–61. 2 Aug. 1621, James to Hamilton, *LSP,* pp. 340–41.

23. NLS, Denmilne Mss. X, nos. 17, 19. The council shortened the king's text before it was read.

24. *APS* IV, 597–600. The extraordinary lords of session made a declaration, which was accepted and entered on the record, that their payment of this tax should not be regarded as a precedent; see *ibid.,* pp. 693–94; R. K. Hannay, *The College of Justice* (Edinburgh, 1933), p. 133. The exempted groups eventually compounded for a lump sum of 10,000 merks; see *RPCS* XIII, 409–10. Melrose's letters to James from 26 July to 4 Aug. 1621 constitute the best account of this parliament; see *Melros* II, 411–27.

25. Sir James Balfour thought so; see J. Haig, ed., *The Historical Works of Sir James Balfour* II (Edinburgh, 1824), 84. *M&K,* pp. 103–6. Wood, *Extracts* VI, xlii, 224. *RPCS* XII, 591–93, 633, 655–56, 689–90, 704–5, 747–48. *Melros* II, 438. 3 Aug. 1621, Spottiswoode to James, *LEA* II, 655–56. 17 Dec., Kellie to Mar, *M&K Supp.,* p. 111. For Hay's responsibility for the tax on annualrents see *Memoirs of Archibald, First Lord Napier, Written by Himself* (Edinburgh, 1793), p. 13.

26. For the new border commission see *RPCS* XI, lxxvi–lxxix and the documents there cited, and XII, 92–93, 105–6, 145–51, 219–22, 765. 13 Jan. 1619, James to the council, Sir William Fraser, *Memorials of the Earls of Haddington* (Edinburgh, 1889) II, 87. 13 May 1618, 25 Aug. 1619, the council to James, *Melros* I, 311–12, 339–40. NLS, Denmilne Mss. IX, no. 43. For the English side see P. Williams, "The Northern Borderland under the Early Stuarts," in H. E. Bell and R. L. Ollard, eds., *Historical Essays 1600–1750 presented to David Ogg* (New

York, 1963), pp. 1–17. Williams argues that after Dunbar's death there was a gradual relaxation of control and a good deal more disorder in the border administration. As regards the English side he seems correct. With respect to Scotland, about which he says much less, his argument seems very doubtful. Cumberland was an area in which after 1603 the landlords, including the crown, increasingly squeezed their tenants, which may well account for the lawlessness there. See A. B. Appleby, "Agrarian Capitalism or Seigneurial Reaction? The Northwest of England, 1500–1700," *American Historical Review* LXXX (1975), 574–94.

27. *RPCS* XII, 582–83.

28. Robert Maxwell, first earl of Nithsdale, was the younger brother of the executed Lord Maxwell. He had the good sense to marry Buckingham's cousin, which led to his restoration to the family estates and an earldom.

29. For the dismissal of the guard and its consequences see *RPCS* XII, ciii, 582–84, 650, 657–60, 672–79, 694–96, 775–79, XIII, 160–61, 356–57, 367–68, 428–31, 470–73, 475–76, 509–11, 525–26, 539–40, 542, 625–26, XIV, 587–88; *CSPD 1623–25*, p. 82.

30. 29 Nov. 1621, the council to James, *Melros* II, 434–37. *RPCS* XII, 626. *M&K*, pp. 98–102. A survey ordered by Charles I in 1625 revealed a total of forty-eight pensioners receiving slightly over £66,000 a year; see *RPCS*, 2nd ser., I, 201–5.

31. *M&K Supp.*, pp. 112–13.

32. *Melros* II, 441–44. 30 Oct. 1621, 1, 22 Mar., 29, 30 Apr. 1622, Kellie to Mar, *M&K*, p. 103, *M&K Supp.*, pp. 113–16, 118–20. 10 Apr., Melrose to Mar, NLS, Mss. 3134, ii, no. 98. See also *M&K*, pp. 109–11; *RPCS* XII, 721.

33. *Spottiswoode* III, 263. *Calderwood* VII, 548–49.

34. See his rambling and repetitious letter to Kellie's secretary in Nov. 1621, PRO, SP 14/123, no. 108.

35. *M&K*, p. 102.

36. The best source for the political maneuvering following Dunfermline's death is Kellie's correspondence with Mar, *M&K Supp.*, pp. 122ff. See also 19 June 1622, Spottiswoode to Lochmaben, *LEA* II, 689–91; 19 June, Melrose to Lochmaben, *Melros* II, 461–63; 21 Oct., James to Mar, *M&K*, p. 116; *Calderwood* VII, 557; *M&K*, pp. 142–43.

37. *Memoirs of Archibald, First Lord Napier*, pp. 8–9. *M&K Supp.*, pp. 127–28, 130–31, 144, 159, 161–62.

38. 23 Jan. 1623, the council to James, *Melros* II, 490–93. See also Taylor, *Aberdeen Council Letters* I, 201–4, 206–12; *RPCS* XIII, 70, 106, 141–42, 172, 773–77; *CSPD 1619–1623*, p. 439.

39. *RPCS* XIII, 233–35, 290–91, 299–302. Lythe, *Economy of Scotland*, p. 95.

40. The work of this committee can be followed in *RPCS* XIII, 219ff. See also *RCRB* III, 141–42, 147–52, 169–71, 177–79, and the assessment in Lythe, *Economy of Scotland*, pp. 93–94.

41. R. Mitchison, "The Making of the Old Scottish Poor Law," *Past and Present* 63 (1974), p. 65. The deaths were probably due more to diseases such as typhus, which people weakened by hunger could not resist, than to actual

starvation. For statistical evidence see M. Flinn, ed., *Scottish Population History from the 17th Century to the 1930s* (Cambridge, 1977), pp. 116–26.

42. *Calderwood* VII, 594. *Melros* II, 526–28.

43. *RPCS* XIII, 257–60, 287–90.

44. The shires' responses are in *ibid.*, pp. 805ff. For good brief summaries of the state of poor relief in James's reign see Mitchison, "Poor Law," pp. 59–67, and T. C. Smout, *A History of the Scottish People 1560–1830* (London, 1972), pp. 84–87.

45. 4 Mar. 1624, Kellie to Mar, *M&K Supp.*, p. 194.

46. *M&K*, p. 127. *RPCS* XIII, 674–75.

47. W. C. Sellar and R. J. Yeatman, *1066 and All That* (New York, 1931), p. 62.

48. *M&K Supp.*, p. 183.

49. 28 Mar. 1625, Kellie to Mar, *ibid.*, p. 226.

50. *Spottiswoode* III, 270.

Index